IMAGES
of America

SLOVAKS OF THE GREATER MAHONING VALLEY

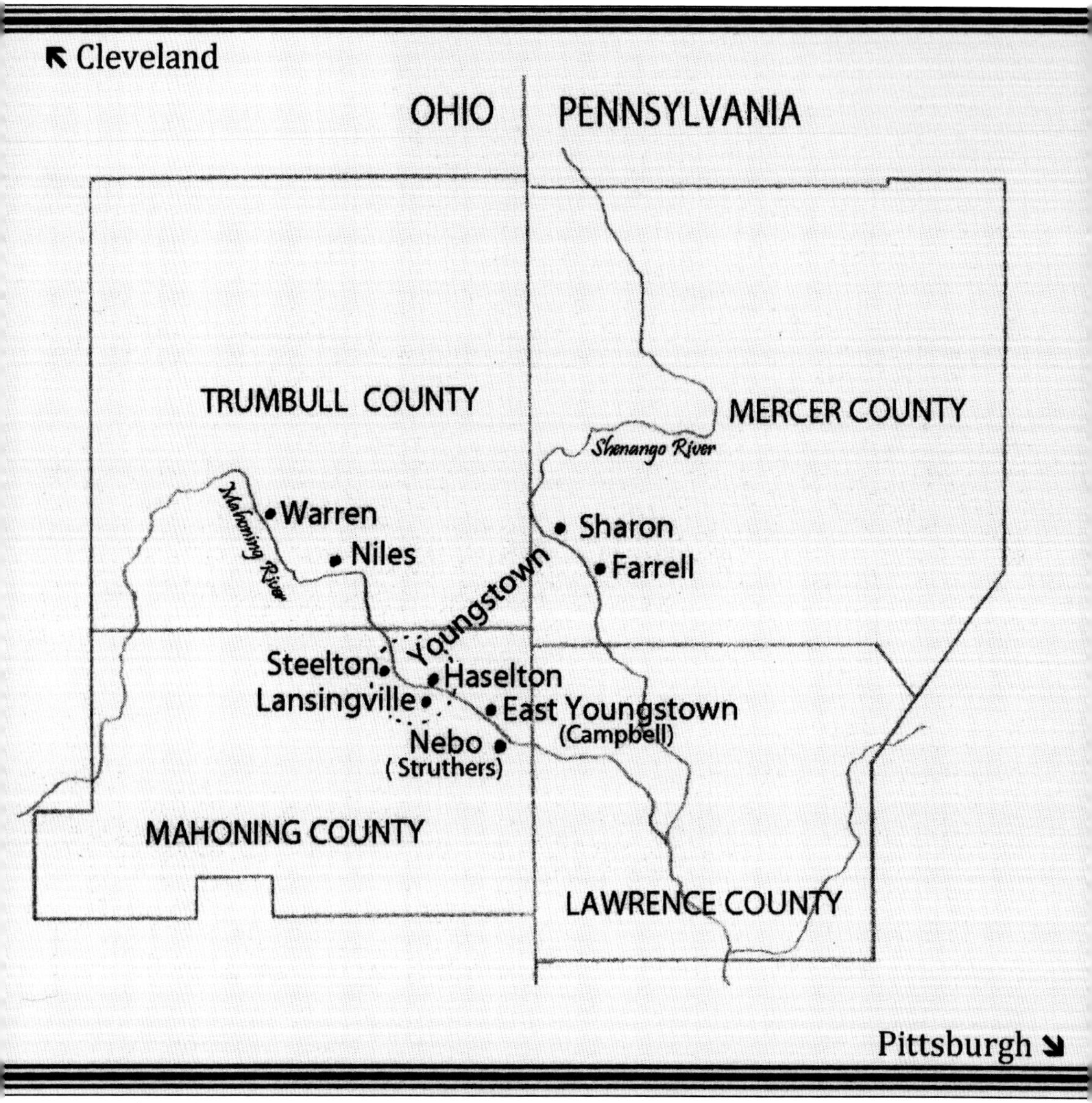

By the early 1900s, Slovak immigrants had formed communities in the four-county area that comprised the Greater Mahoning Valley. Mahoning and Trumbull Counties along the Mahoning River in Ohio and Mercer and Lawrence Counties along the Shenango River in western Pennsylvania saw the greatest influx, as new immigrants sought out earlier immigrants who were already there. (Map drawn by Len Summers.)

On the Cover: Michael Baker (Pekar), on the far right, and members of the fire brigade pose outside at the Youngstown Sheet and Tube's Campbell Works in about 1925. At that time, the Youngstown Sheet and Tube Company was the third largest producer of steel in the United States. The heavy white woolen trousers the men had on were worn for protection from the heat in the mills. (Courtesy of Loretta Ekoniak.)

IMAGES
of America

SLOVAKS OF THE GREATER MAHONING VALLEY

Susan J. Summers and Loretta A. Ekoniak

ARCADIA
PUBLISHING

ISBN 978-0-7385-8259-7

Published by Arcadia Publishing
Charleston, South Carolina

Printed in the United States of America

Library of Congress Control Number: 2011926095

For all general information, please contact Arcadia Publishing:
Telephone 843-853-2070
Fax 843-853-0044
E-mail sales@arcadiapublishing.com
For customer service and orders:
Toll-Free 1-888-313-2665

Visit us on the Internet at www.arcadiapublishing.com

This book is dedicated to our mothers, Helen Gurella Gubany and Margaret Baker Hanuschak, who brought us up to love America but always to remember our Slovak roots

CONTENTS

Acknowledgments

This project would have been impossible without the help of many people. We would especially like to thank Florence Katula Galida from the Campbell Historical Society; Marian Kutlesa from the Struthers Historical Society; Toni Sheehan from the Genealogy Society at the Sharon Community Library; Lucille Kramer, our Lansingville source; Joseph Hornack, from the Slovak Institute of the Benedictine Abbey in Cleveland; Ralph Pfingsten, author of *The History of the Ravenna Arsenal*; and various church historians, official and unofficial, for looking through their collections for photographs that might be useful in our book. We also want to acknowledge authors of the 1976 *History of the Slovak People of the Mahoning Valley* published for the US bicentennial and the 1950 *March of the Eucharist* about the churches of the Youngstown Diocese. These books contained much valuable information and many leads for our project. Thank you to John Gingery and Michael Kupec, who gave us copies of the 1935 *Slovak Baseball League* by Mike Kornick. We want to thank Patricia Felger and Colleen Mastrovaselis, who kept urging Sue to pursue the idea of putting this book together instead of just thinking about how nice it would be! Most of all, we want to thank the many individuals who read our notices and put time and effort into hunting through boxes in closets, basements, and attics for photographs that they had not thought of in years. They helped us get a true representation of the many unique individuals who came to this valley from the old country, as well as the children and grandchildren who contributed so much to this area. It was only through the efforts of all these contributors, who entrusted their precious family photographs to us, that we were able to put together such a wonderful collection and preserve these memories for future generations! Of course, Sue and I especially need to thank our great editors, Melissa Basilone and Sandy Shalton, as well as our wonderful husbands, Leonard Summers and Michael Ekoniak Jr., for putting up with the piles of papers and photographs that have taken over our homes for the last year and for supporting us in so many different ways!

Introduction

At the turn of the last century, steel mills formed an almost continuous band in the Greater Mahoning Valley from Warren, Ohio, to Lowellville, Ohio, and then on into the nearby western Pennsylvania towns of Sharon and Farrell. These belching, hot, dirty giants of industry—built to take advantage of the valley's rich iron ore and coal deposits and to provide for the growing demand for steel in construction and manufacturing across the nation—needed workers, and it needed a lot of them. This area was a leader in the production of that valuable commodity, and, therefore, at the end of the 1800s and into the new century of the 1900s, the sight of skies aglow with flames and the smell of sulfur in the air, rather than bringing thoughts of brimstone and eternal damnation, brought the promise of a future bright with the vision of prosperity. Such was the Mahoning Valley, as seen by the Slovak emigrants fleeing poverty in the old country, where the future held no hope of improving their lot in life. In return for their labor, the mills held out to these workers the promise of a better life and the opportunity to provide for a family, a home, and goods they could not have dreamt of in their native homeland. So, starting in the 1870s, Slovaks responded to the promise of work and good wages by leaving their homes and coming to this valley.

According to Genevieve Novicky and Steve Hruska in their introduction to the *History of Slovak People of the Mahoning Valley* (written and published by the Slovak Bicentennial Committee of Youngstown and the Mahoning Valley in 1976 for the American bicentennial celebration), the first Slovaks arrived in the Mahoning Valley from the eastern parts of what is now Slovakia but was then part of Austria-Hungary. These first immigrants included Jozef Almasy, Ján Borovsky, Martin Farkas, Ján Hamrak, Štefan Korčnak, Michal Mazur, and Ján Zabrinsky. Many of them came alone and had to wait years to save up enough money for their families to join them. By 1890, there were 30 Slovak families and about 50 single men in the Youngstown area. These first Slovaks sent money home to their families, and after saving enough money, they brought their families to the towns of our valley—Niles, McDonald, Warren, Youngstown, Campbell, Struthers, Lowellville, Sharon, and Farrell all saw an influx of Slovaks. One man wrote to his brother, his cousin, or his neighbor in his home village in Spišská zupa (the word *zupa* means "county"), Šariš zupa, or Zemplin zupa, and the stream of Slovak immigrants grew. The 1922 Census of Slovak People Living in Mahoning County, Ohio, published by the District Assembly of the Slovak League of America listed 2,069 different Slovak family surnames living in nine different areas from Haseltine to Struthers and from Steelton to Lansingville. By the 2000 US census, over 65,000 people in the Mahoning Valley area listed Slovak as their ancestry.

New Slovak immigrants tended to settle in the same areas where there were already established Slovak families who would help them in this new country far from their native land. They built churches and schools to help maintain their Slovak identity and to help them adjust to a new way of life in America. The first Slovak church, established in 1896, was SS Cyril and Methodius Roman Catholic Church, followed by St. Mary's Greek Catholic Church in 1900 and

Ján Hus Evangelical Lutheran Church in 1903. By the early 1920s, congregations established in the Mahoning Valley in Ohio included six Roman Catholic, three Byzantine Catholic, two Evangelical Lutheran, one Presbyterian, and one Baptist Slovak church, as well as several more in the western Pennsylvania towns of Sharon and Farrell. They formed fraternal assemblies and organizations—such as the National Slovak Society, the First Catholic Slovak Union, the Slovak Evangelical Union, and the First Catholic Slovak Ladies Union—to provide help for each other during an era when there were no unemployment benefits or disability programs. They published their own newspapers, beginning with the *Youngstownské Slovenské Noviny* started by the Reverend Oldrich Zlámal in 1900, to keep informed about both local and world events. They started their own businesses—at first to serve their fellow Slovaks but eventually serving their entire community. They got together to play music and perform in dramatic skits, compete in organized sports, have picnics in the countryside, establish social and political clubs, celebrate successes, and mourn losses.

Some may wonder why the Ruthenian, or Rusyn, congregations are included in our book about Slovaks. While the Rusyns are a distinct ethnic group, those who settled in this area came from the eastern Carpathian highland area of present-day Slovakia. They settled in the same areas as the Slovak immigrants and socialized and intermarried with them. They share many of the same traditions and are so intermingled in northeastern Ohio and western Pennsylvania (just as they were in Slovakia) that it would have been difficult to talk about many of our families without acknowledging both sides. So, with no intention to offend anyone, we have included the Rusyns; they are part of our story.

Though many of our grandparents or great-grandparents came here with little formal education, they sent their children to school, and their grandchildren went to college. They became proud US citizens and defended their new country during wartime. Slovak Americans in these towns and cities became engineers, musicians, business owners, teachers, doctors, nurses, policemen, lawyers, clergymen, nuns, sports figures, scientists, judges, and politicians. Slovak Americans in our valley have entered and thrived in all parts of American life. And through all the years they have been here, while they have prospered as Americans in the fullest sense, they have continued to cherish their roots. Our parents, grandparents, or great-grandparents left their homes and came to the United States of America to find a better life for themselves and their children, but they never forgot their native country. They worked hard to make a good life here, but they also kept many of the customs they had in the old country. The Slovaks of the Greater Mahoning Valley have made a life here built on the values of the old country and strengthened by the vigor of the new country. Those young immigrants, who started their journey with only their faith and the dream of a better life, fulfilled that dream through their hard work and sacrifice and died secure in the knowledge that their journey was worth the cost. This book is our tribute to our parents, grandparents, and great-grandparents, who, through their courage and hard work, made it possible for all of us to enjoy the American dream.

One

From the Old to the New

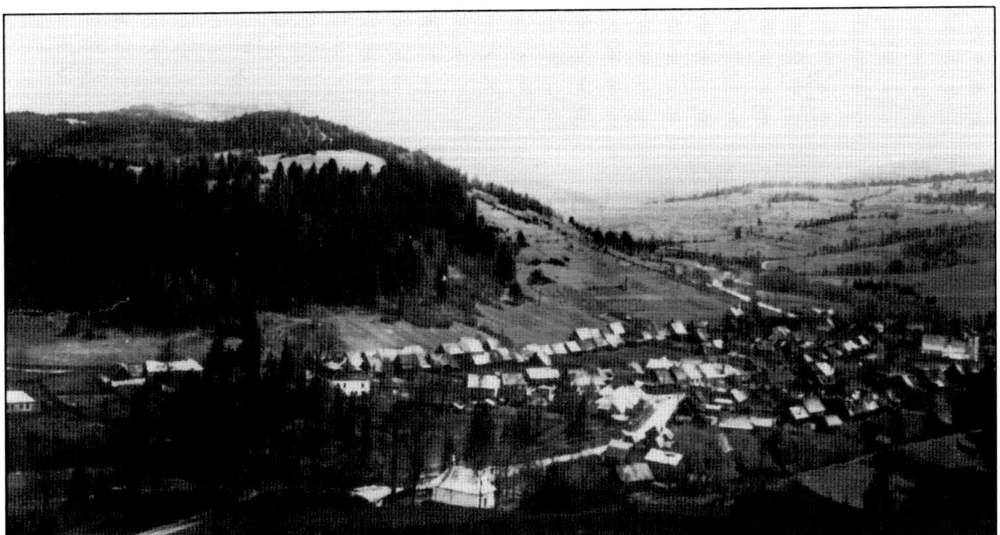

Looking back at what might be last sight of their birthplace around the turn of the 20th century, Slovaks immigrated to the Greater Mahoning Valley from villages and towns like Hanušovce, Spišská Nová Ves, Levoča, Bratislava, Stráže, Prešov, Košice, Kelča, and Poráč. In this photograph, the Slanské Mountains serve as the background for Hanušovce. (Courtesy of Ann Matvey.)

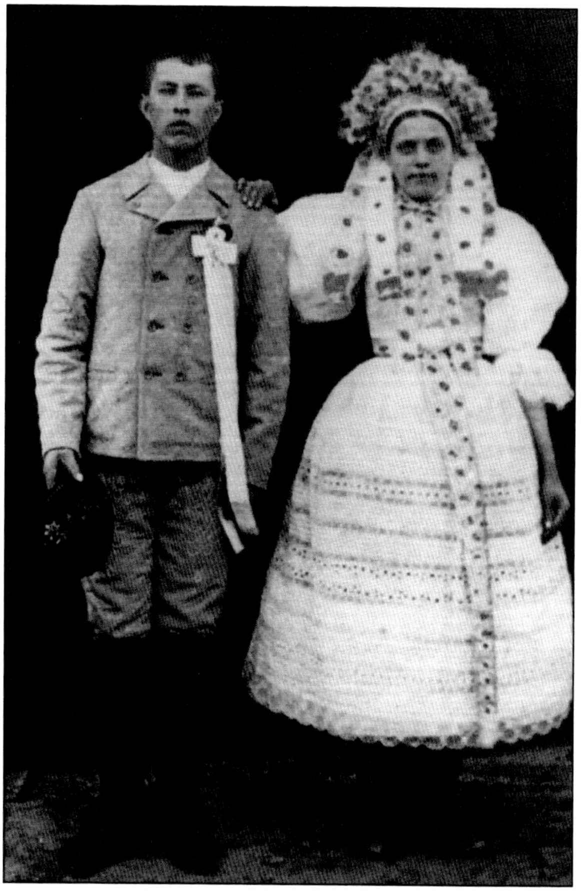

Joseph Radovich and his wife, Anna, are shown here in the traditional wedding attire of Stupava, Slovakia, from where he immigrated to America in 1908. It took him four years to earn enough money to return to Stupava for his wife and young daughter, Mary. They had three other children in the United States: John, Ann, and Joseph. He worked at Republic Steel for 44 years and died in Lansingville at the age of 104. (Courtesy of Darlene Radovich Gaal.)

A photograph might be the only remembrance of family that immigrants took to America. Shown here shortly before Andrew Hirt left for America with his wife, Mary, and their young son, Andy, is the Hirt family of Pohorela, Slovakia. From left to right in the first row are Mary Syč Hirt and Andrew Hirt Sr. with his sister Rosalia; his mother, Mary, holding Andy Jr.; and his brother Joseph with his wife. In the second row are Andrew's sister Ann and his brother, Carl. (Courtesy of Florence Tessari Hirt.)

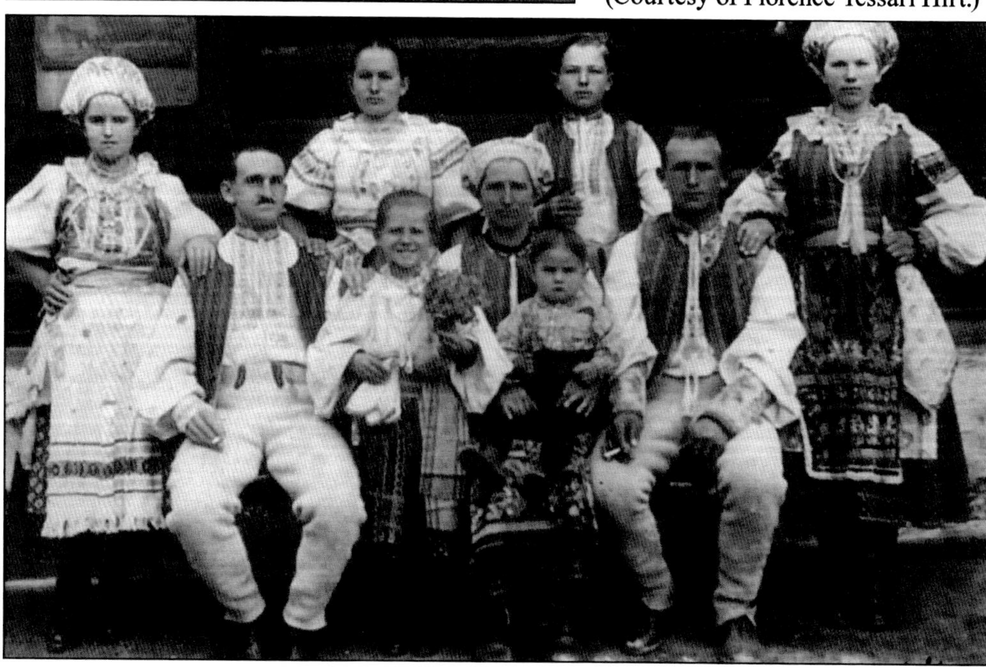

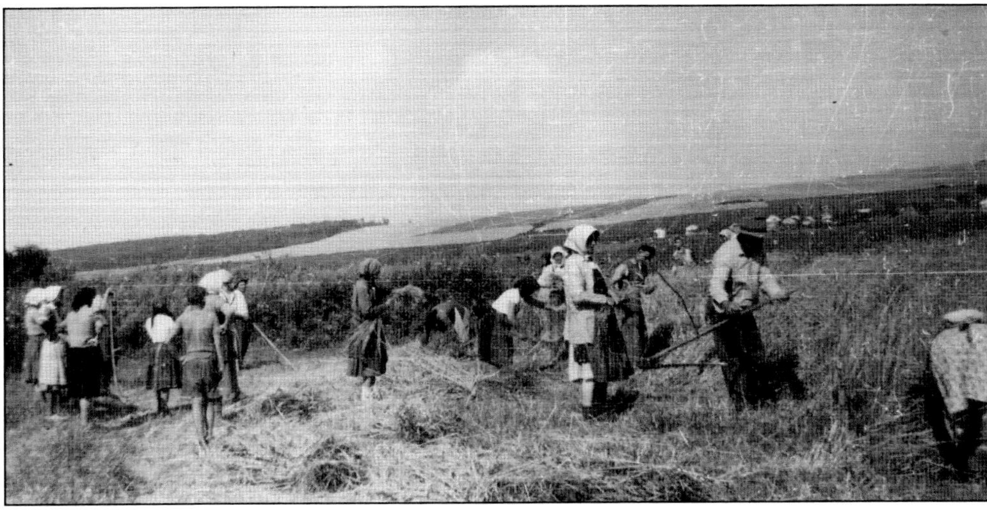

Most people in Slovakia were dependent on agriculture for their livelihood. It was a life of hard physical labor for not only the men but also the women and children, who all put in long, tiring days. Often, the results of their efforts went to the owners of the land they worked, and they received very little for their labor. (Courtesy of Elizabeth Semyan Williams.)

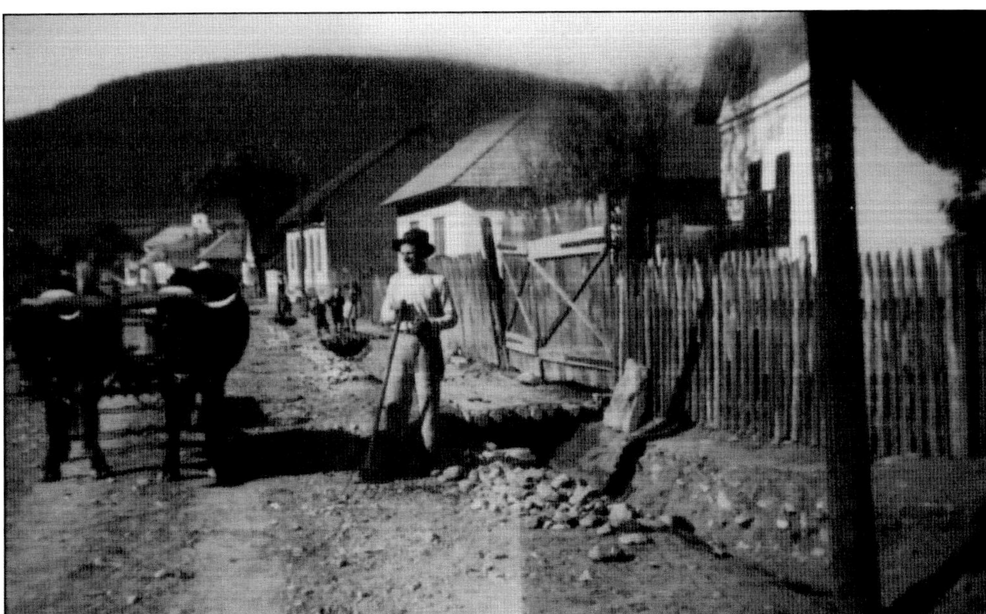

Even in the mid-1940s, farm labor was carried on by man or animal power, as seen in this photograph taken near the Kollar family village of Kluknava in Slovakia. This life was not easy, as there was little chance of improvement, and many came to America looking for better opportunities for themselves and their children. (Courtesy of Mary Ellen Kurta Wilcox.)

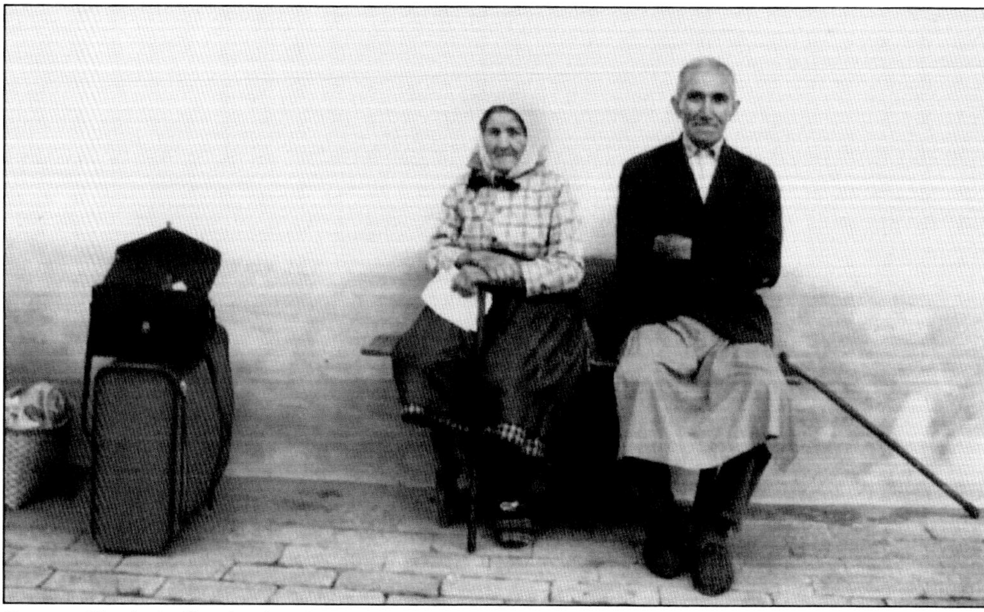

Zuzana Skadra's first husband, Joseph, was killed at the age of 30 in a farming accident, leaving her with three young children: Joseph (just six months old), Laddie, and Marie. Joseph's brother Paul married Zuzana, and together they had two daughters. This photograph shows Zuzana with her second husband, Paul, near Bratislava, in what was then Czechoslovakia, at the start of their travels. (Courtesy of Lillian Bigley Johnson.)

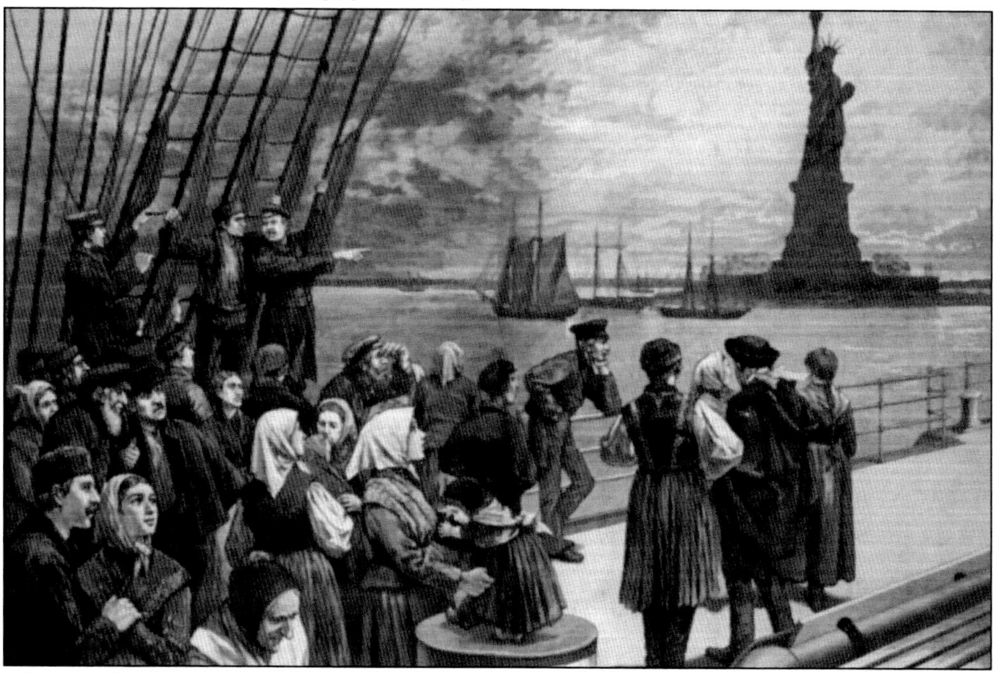

After an often uncomfortable voyage in steerage where they had to cope with seasickness, lack of privacy, poor food, and other discomforts, the passengers eagerly looked forward to their first glimpse of the beacon that drew them to this new land, the Statue of Liberty in New York Harbor. (Courtesy of the Library of Congress, LC-USZ62-38214.)

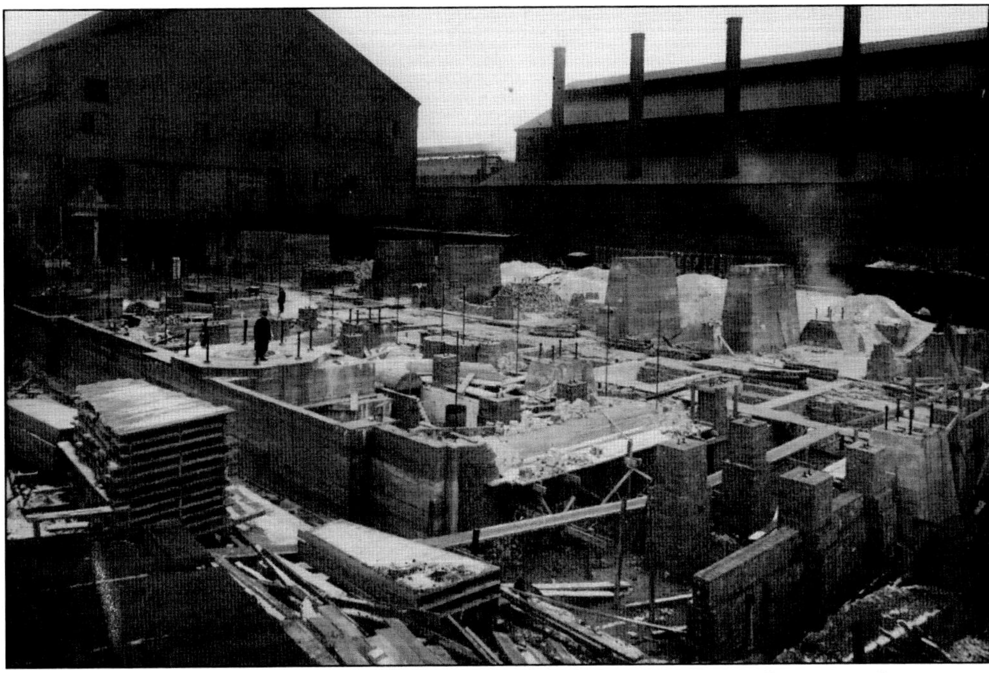

In the late 19th and early 20th centuries, the Mahoning and Shenango Valleys were the center of industrialization. The birth of the steel industry put Youngstown, Ohio, on the map. This photograph showing the mills still under construction was taken along the Mahoning River between 1905 and 1910. (Courtesy of the Campbell Historical Society, Florence Katula Galida.)

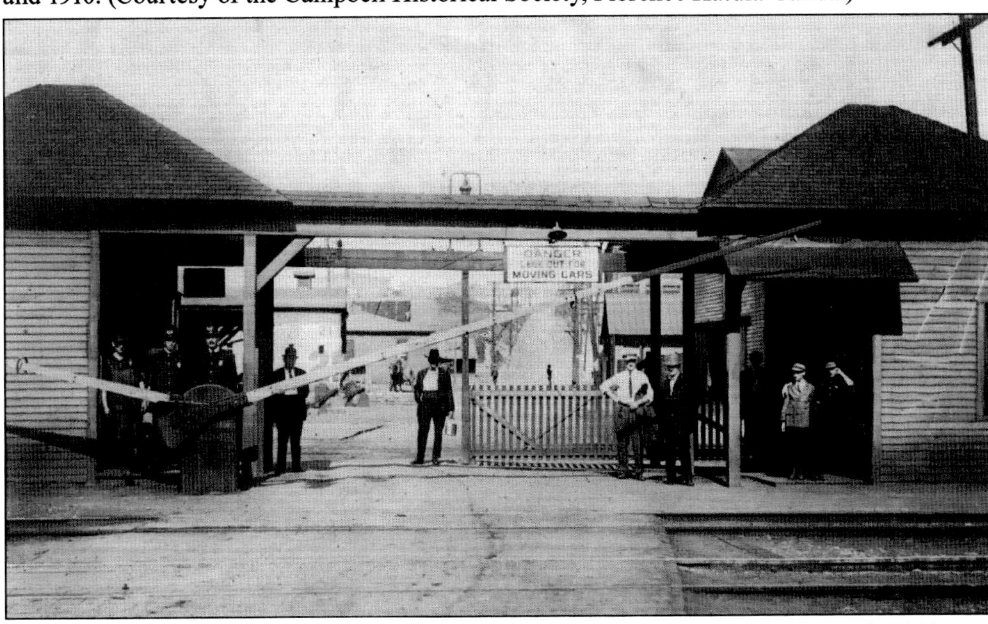

The Sharon Steel Company was built on the banks of the Shenango River, south of Sharon, Pennsylvania. Soon, several thousand emigrants from Eastern Europe settled there to work, raise families, and establish churches and schools. This community became known as Farrell, Pennsylvania. This photograph, dated 1913, shows the entrance to the Farrell Works in Farrell, Pennsylvania. (Courtesy of the Hostettler Collection, Mercer County Historical Society.)

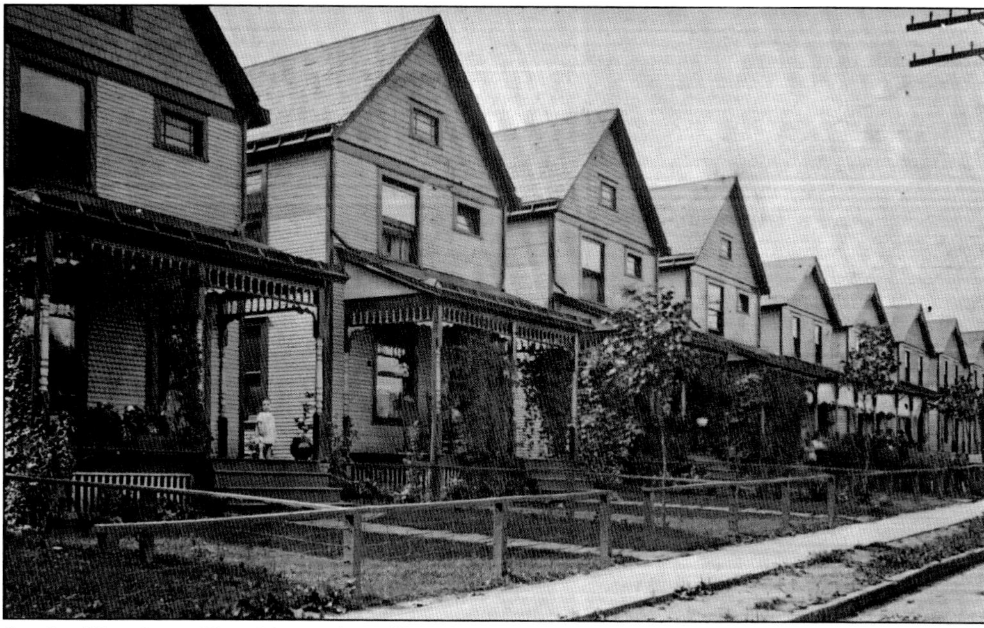

Steel mills often offered incentives like cheap housing to attract immigrant workers. These houses, built by the Farrell Works, were located on First Avenue and rented for $12.50 per month in 1913. They had six rooms, a hall, bath, cellar, and hot and cold water. The company paid the water bill. Similar houses were located on Fruit, Wallis, and Spearman Avenues. (Courtesy of the Hostettler Collection, Mercer County Historical Society.)

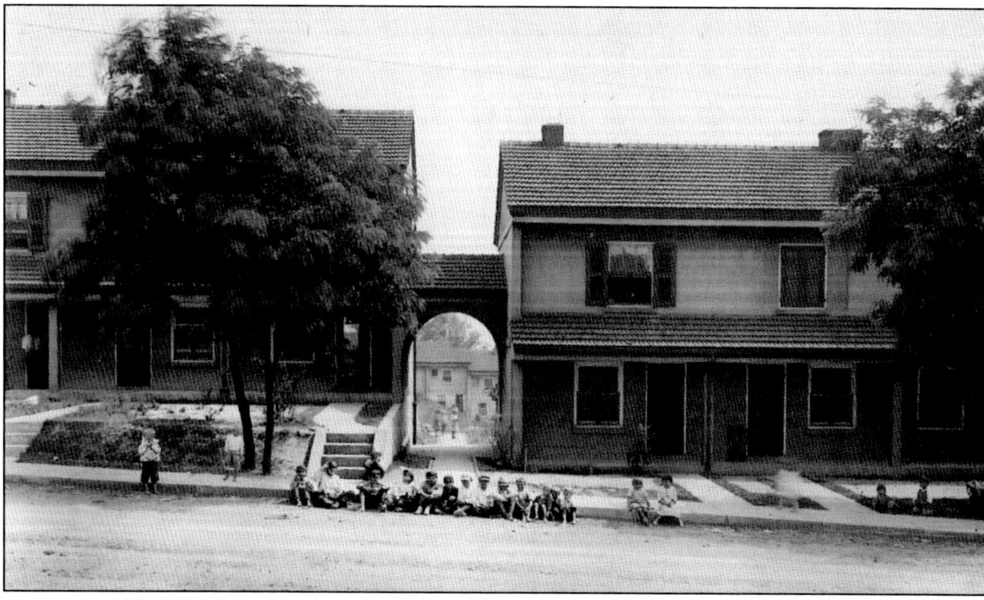

Constructed in 1918, these apartments were offered specifically to the "foreign-born workers" of Youngstown Sheet and Tube. They rented for $15, $18, and $20 per month, water included. There were also a park, playground, and four company stores. These homes were the first functional use of concrete in residential construction in the world and are now listed in the National Register of Historic Places. Interestingly, they were kept small to discourage the custom of taking in boarders. (Courtesy of the Campbell Historical Society, Florence Katula Galida.)

Two

All in a Day's Work

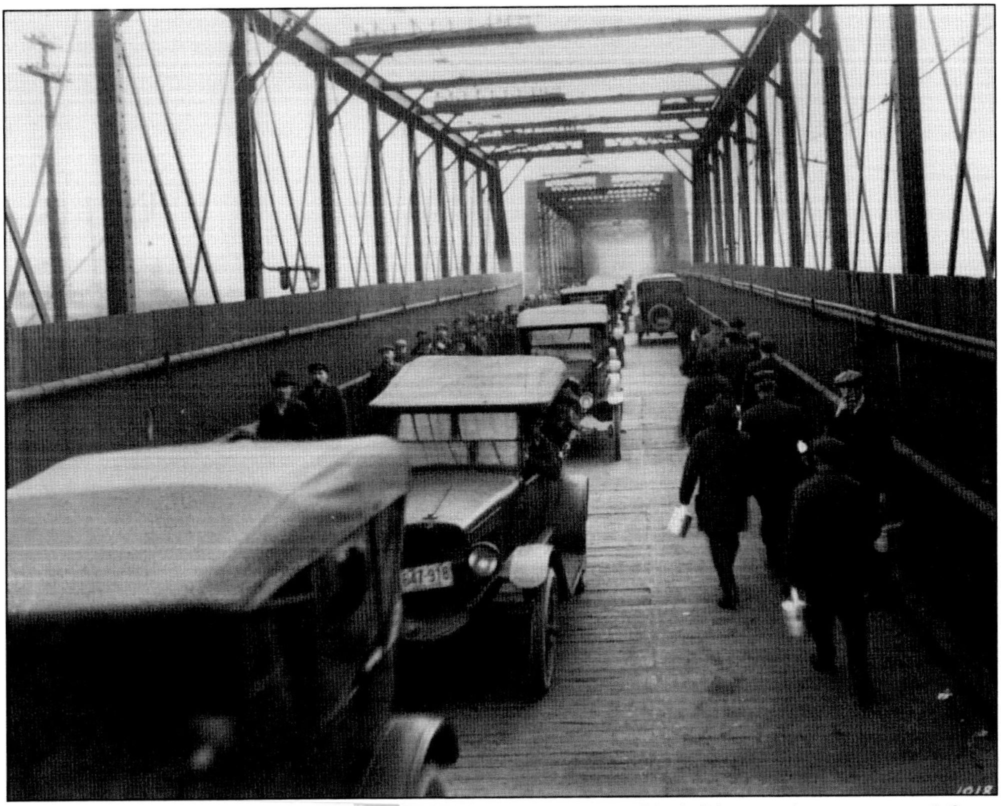

On a daily basis, thousands of footsteps were taken across this bridge on the way to and from work. Mill workers, with their lunch buckets in hand, enter and leave the old north gate of Youngstown Sheet and Tube's Campbell Works on Wilson Avenue in Campbell, Ohio. (Courtesy of the Campbell Historical Society, Florence Katula Galida.)

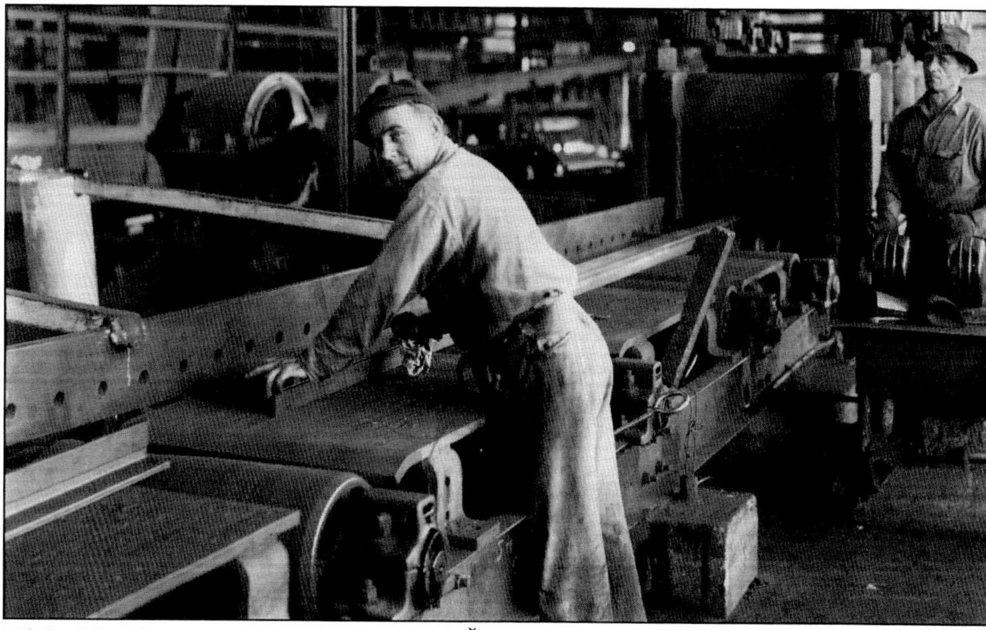

Michael L. Hovanes was born in Beloveža, Šariš, in 1891, the son of Joseph and Mary Varho Hovanec. He came to Johnstown, Pennsylvania, in about 1909 and to Youngstown in about 1920. He was employed as a machine operator in the bar mill of Republic Steel Corporation. He and his wife, Florence Komara, lived in Lansingville and attended St. Nicholas Greek Catholic Church. (Courtesy of Mary M. Hovanes.)

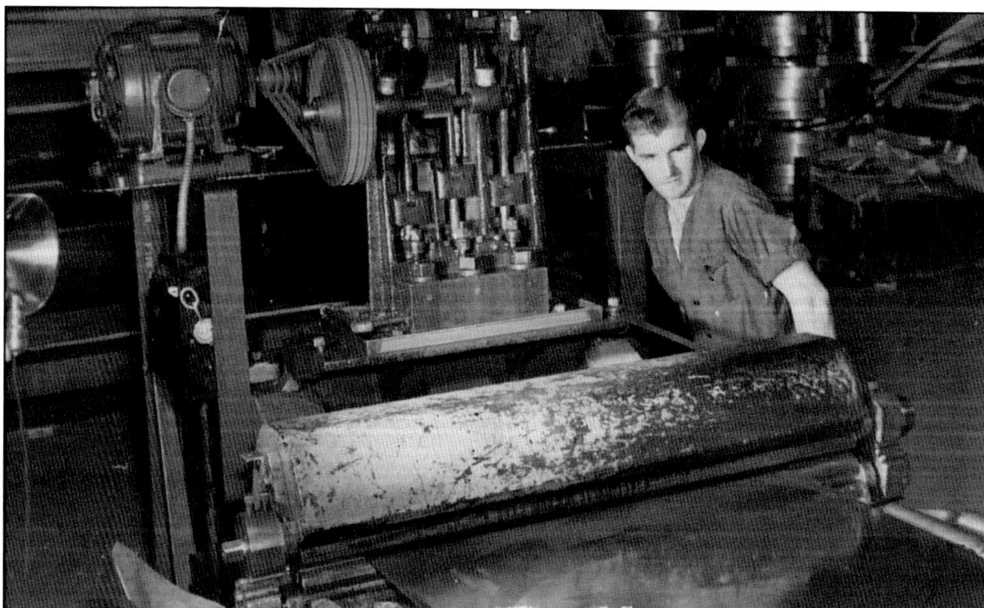

General Fireproofing was founded on the north side of Youngstown in 1902 and manufactured steel office furniture. They introduced their first four-drawer vertical file in 1910 and their first fireproof safe in 1912. During World War II, regular production ceased, and the plant was converted over to manufacturing aircraft parts for the war effort. Joseph Gubany, shown, worked at General Fireproofing as a stretcher leveler. (Courtesy of Susan Gubany Summers.)

Not everyone who came to the Greater Mahoning Valley worked in the mills. Slovaks worked in a wide variety of jobs; they were laborers, business owners, farmers, and professionals. Joseph Bartos spent many years as a policeman here. (Courtesy of Thomas J. Mrofchak.)

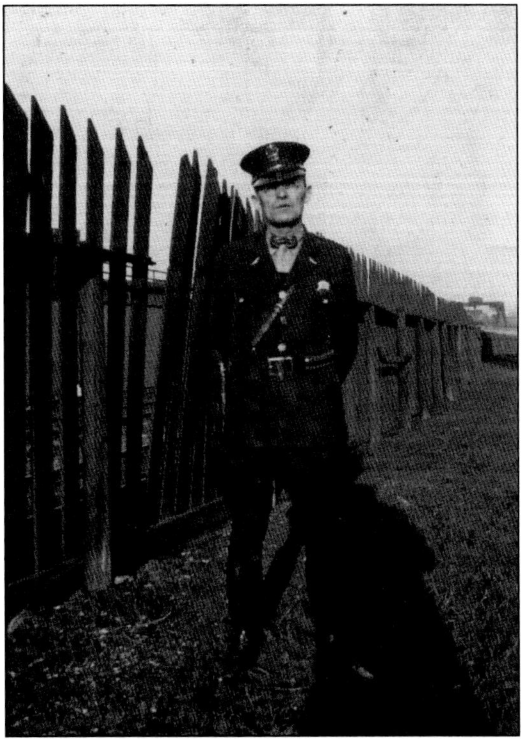

Campbell postmaster from 1966 to 1984, Paul Behun (center), and former postmaster from 1939 to 1966, John Galida (right), look on as Joseph Simboli punches out for the last time, starting his retirement. (Courtesy of the Campbell Historical Society, Florence Katula Galida.)

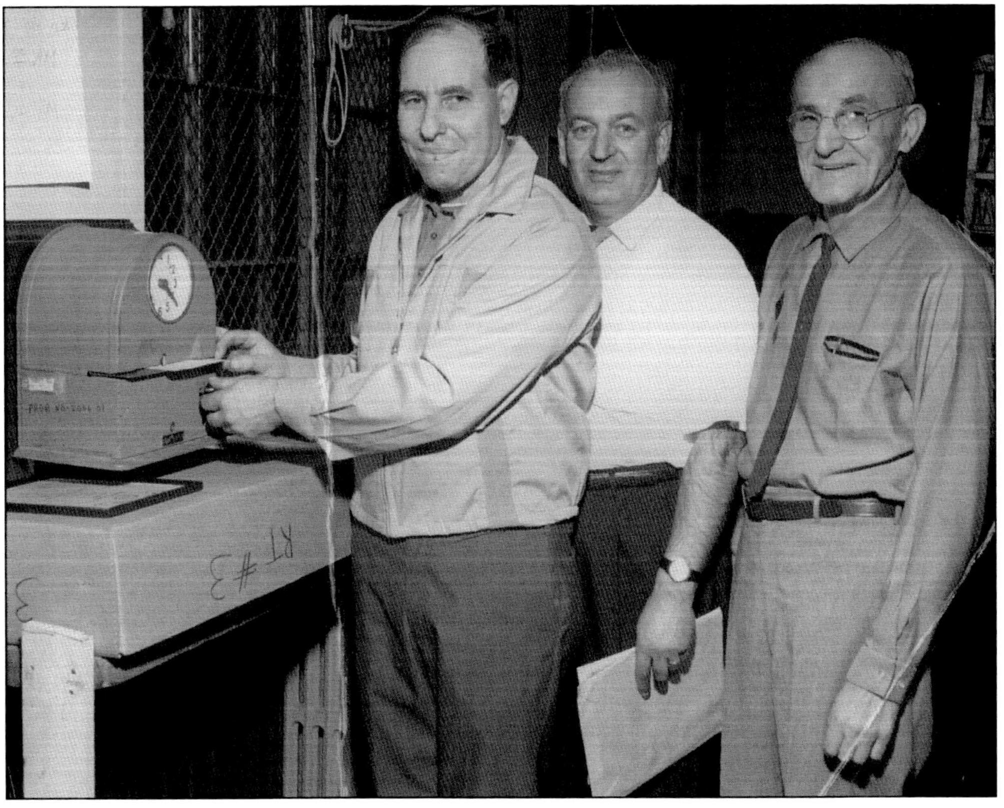

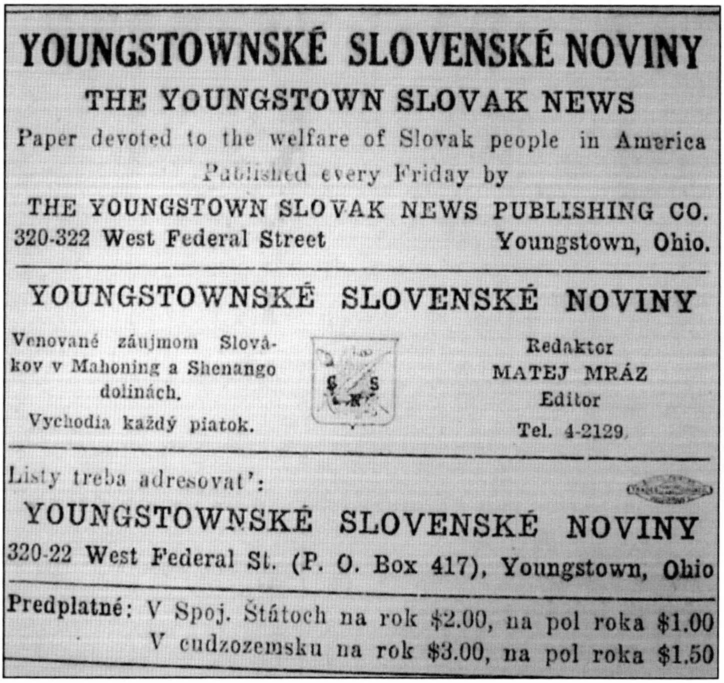

YOUNGSTOWNSKÉ SLOVENSKÉ NOVINY

THE YOUNGSTOWN SLOVAK NEWS

Paper devoted to the welfare of Slovak people in America

Published every Friday by

THE YOUNGSTOWN SLOVAK NEWS PUBLISHING CO.

320-322 West Federal Street Youngstown, Ohio.

YOUNGSTOWNSKÉ SLOVENSKÉ NOVINY

Venované záujmom Slovákov v Mahoning a Shenango dolinách.

Vychodia každý piatok.

Redaktor MATEJ MRÁZ Editor

Tel. 4-2129

Listy treba adresovať:

YOUNGSTOWNSKÉ SLOVENSKÉ NOVINY

320-22 West Federal St. (P. O. Box 417), Youngstown, Ohio

Predplatné: V Spoj. Štátoch na rok $2.00, na pol roka $1.00

V cudzozemsku na rok $3.00, na pol roka $1.50

Slovaks published their own newspapers to keep the community informed of local, national, and international events. The first paper, published every Friday until 1940, was started by the Reverend Oldrich Zlámal in 1900 and was "devoted to all of interest to Slovaks in the Mahoning and Shenango Valleys." (Courtesy of Joseph Hornack of the Slovak Institute, Cleveland, Ohio; photograph by James Stracensky.)

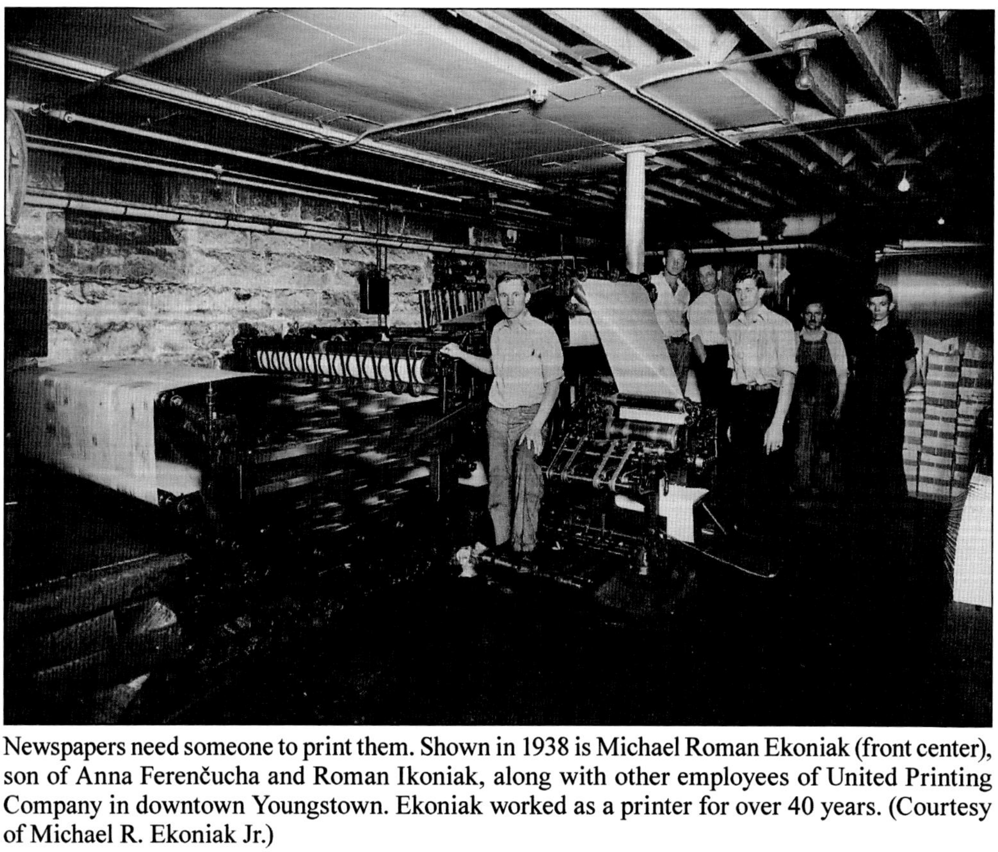

Newspapers need someone to print them. Shown in 1938 is Michael Roman Ekoniak (front center), son of Anna Ferenčucha and Roman Ikoniak, along with other employees of United Printing Company in downtown Youngstown. Ekoniak worked as a printer for over 40 years. (Courtesy of Michael R. Ekoniak Jr.)

George Tomko grew up in Sharon, Pennsylvania. In his youth, he would copy the funny papers and, sometimes, the whole Sunday comic section. In his backyard studio, he would draw his monthly cartoon for the *Sharon Herald* newspaper and give the people of the Shenango Valley a look at life in "the good ol' days." (Courtesy of the Mercer County Historical Society and Maurice Daniel.)

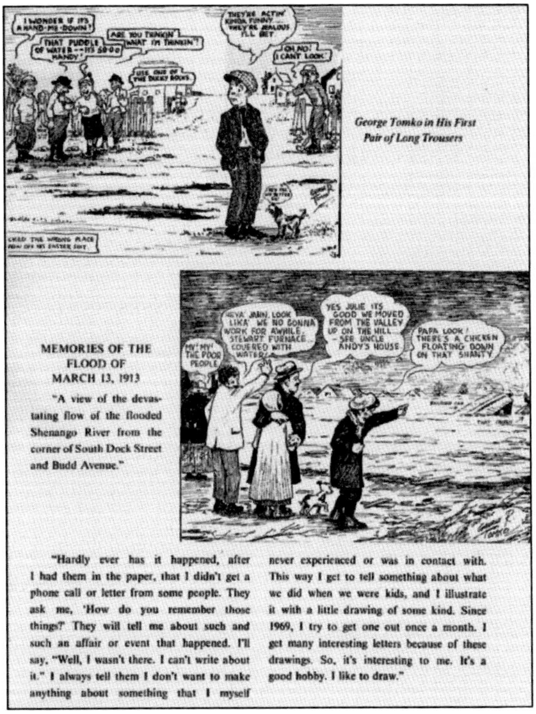

George Tomko in His First Pair of Long Trousers

MEMORIES OF THE FLOOD OF MARCH 13, 1913

"A view of the devastating flow of the flooded Shenango River from the corner of South Dock Street and Budd Avenue."

"Hardly ever has it happened, after I had them in the paper, that I didn't get a phone call or letter from some people. They ask me, 'How do you remember those things?' They will tell me about such and such an affair or event that happened. I'll say, "Well, I wasn't there. I can't write about it." I always tell them I don't want to make anything about something that I myself never experienced or was in contact with. This way I get to tell something about what we did when we were kids, and I illustrate it with a little drawing of some kind. Since 1969, I try to get one out once a month. I get many interesting letters because of these drawings. So, it's interesting to me. It's a good hobby. I like to draw."

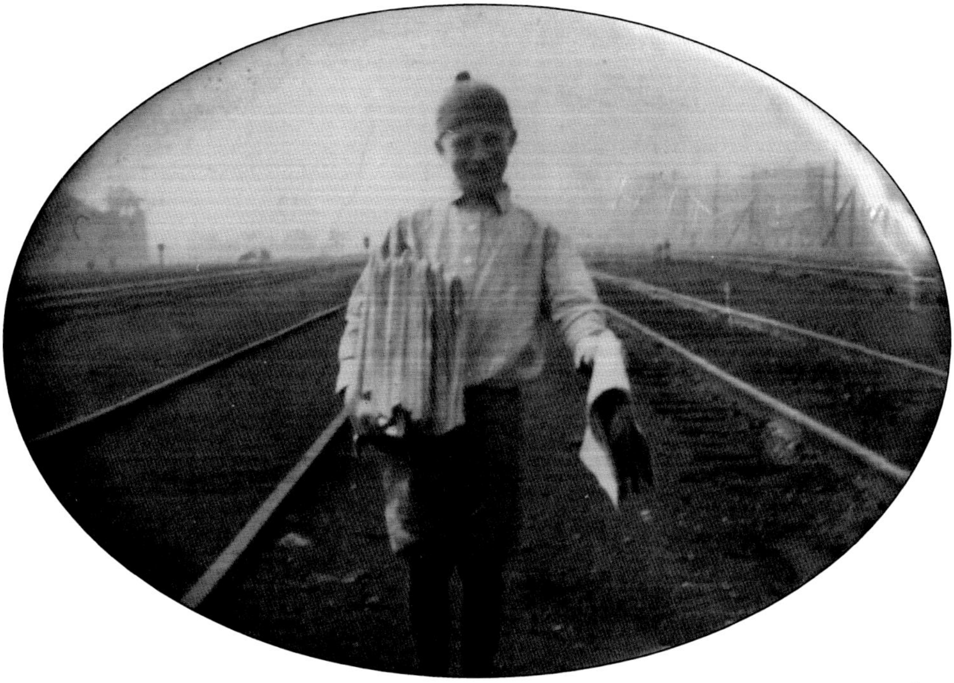

Joseph Sedzmak, son of Andrew and Anna Sedzmak, is shown in about 1920. He was one of many young boys who earned money for the family by delivering newspapers throughout the valley. Shown is an oval award pin he earned for the most papers delivered. He is pictured delivering the *Vindicator* along the railroad tracks through Youngstown Sheet and Tube. (Courtesy of Joseph Sedzmak.)

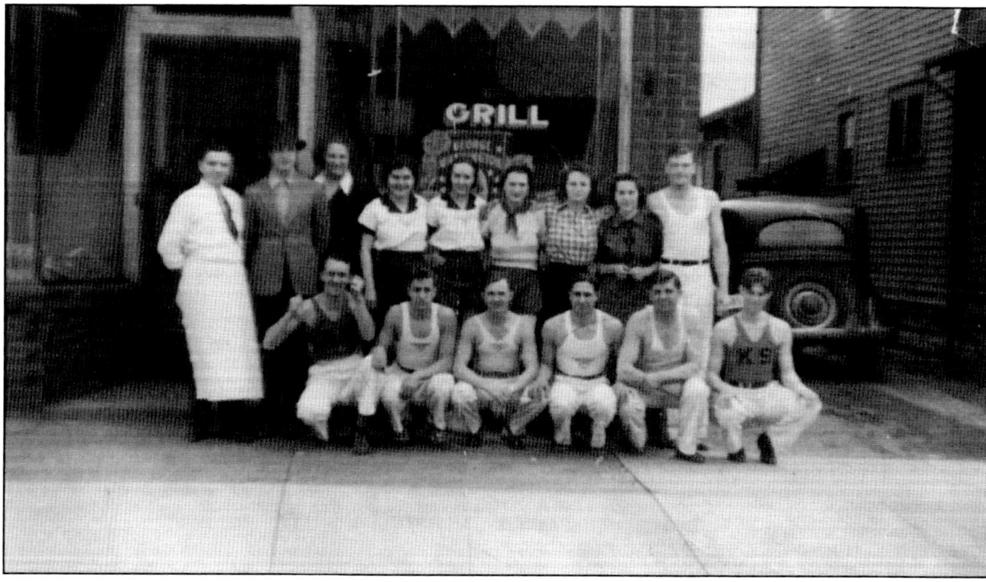

Local taverns in the valley were popular businesses where mill workers often stopped after their shifts. These taverns sponsored community events and teams. This photograph was taken in front of Little Hollywood Tavern on East Indianola Avenue when it opened in 1939. Standing in the second row are Joseph Maruskin Sr. (far left, in apron), son Joseph Jr. (in hat), and Joe Jr.'s second wife, Margita (third from left). They are shown with the Sokol team that they sponsored. (Courtesy of Lucille Martinko Kramer.)

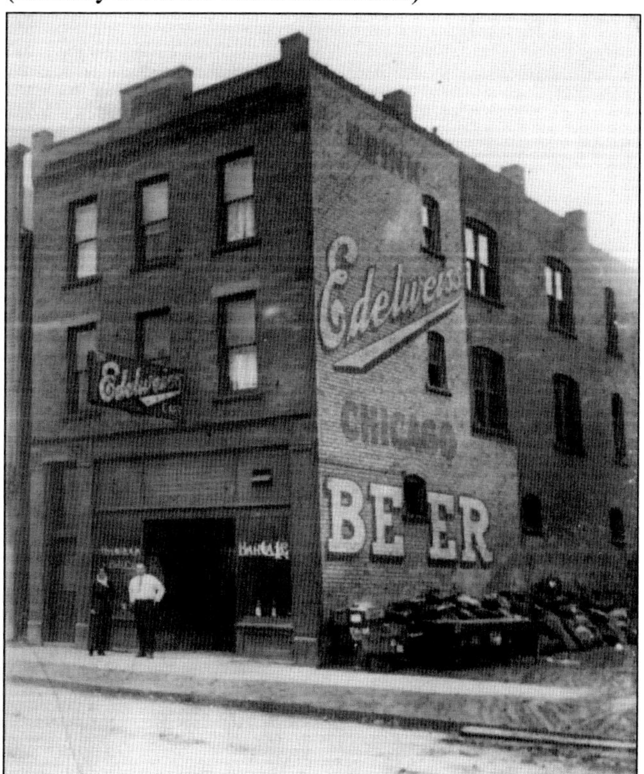

The Hamrock Brothers Edelweiss Bar and Café was located on Wilson Avenue in Campbell, Ohio. Mr. and Mrs. Hamrock stand outside, waiting to greet the customers. (Courtesy of the Campbell Historical Society, Florence Katula Galida.)

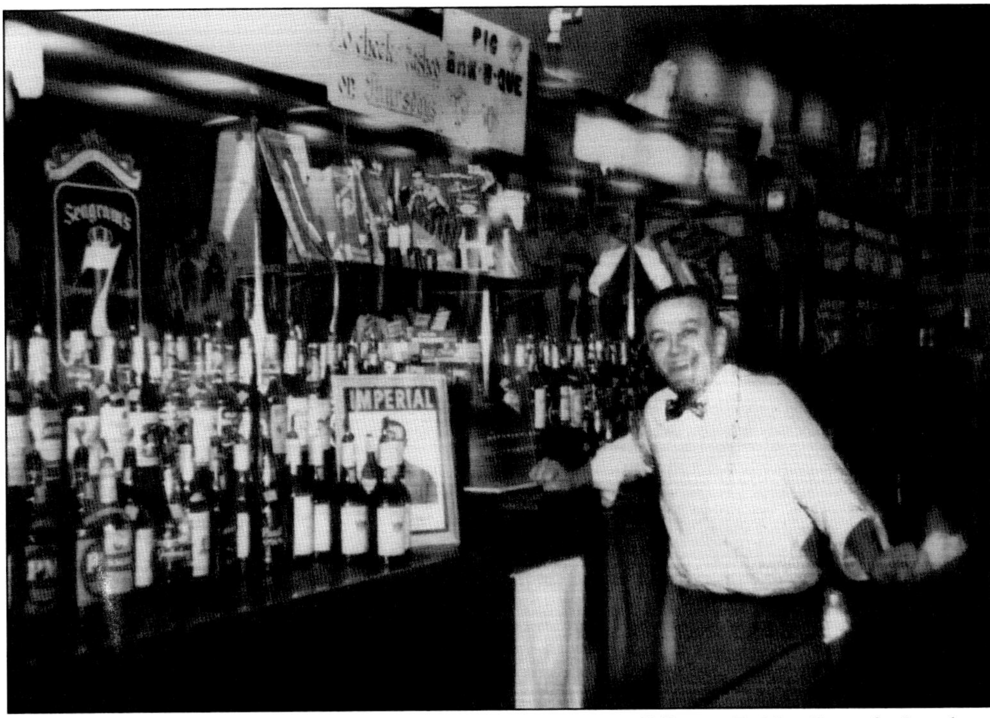

In 1933, John Repasky opened Rip's Cafe in the Henderson Building on Bridge Street in Struthers, Ohio. He received the first state liquor license for the sale of whiskey, wine, and ale by the glass in Struthers. In business after 77 years and now on Youngstown-Poland Road, the cafe is still operated by the Repasky family. Mike Repasky is shown in the late 1940s. (Courtesy of Janet Repasky Morris.)

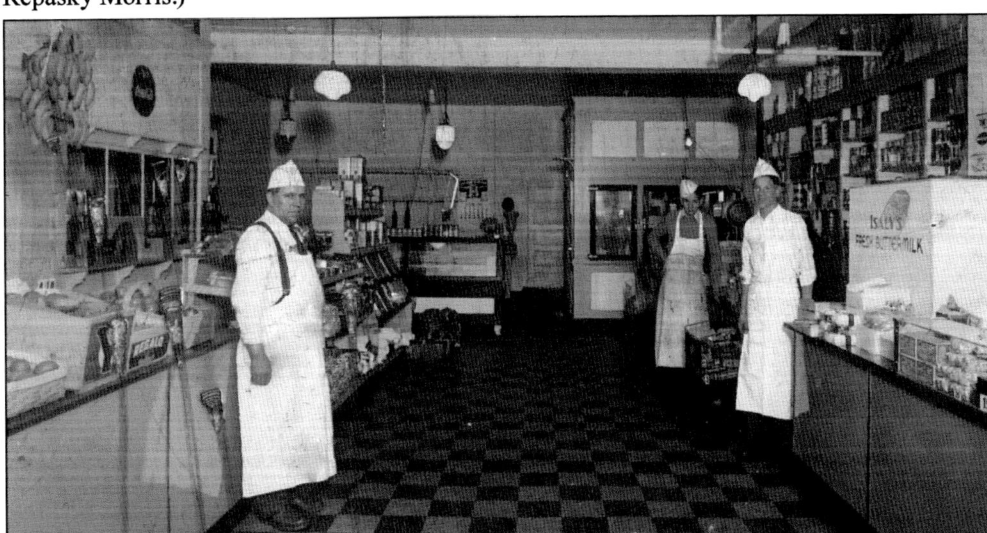

Of course, all of the businesses were not taverns. Pictured here is the first Isaly's franchise in Haseltine at 1814 Wilson Avenue. Owner Stephen Franko immigrated from Daňišovec, and his wife, Mary Sedlacko Franko, was from Odorin. Shown in about 1950 are, from left to right, Steve Franko, and his sons Frank R. Franko (a future mayor of Youngstown) and John W. Franko. The Frankos had two other sons, Steve Jr. and Andrew. (Courtesy of Kathryn Novotny Franko.)

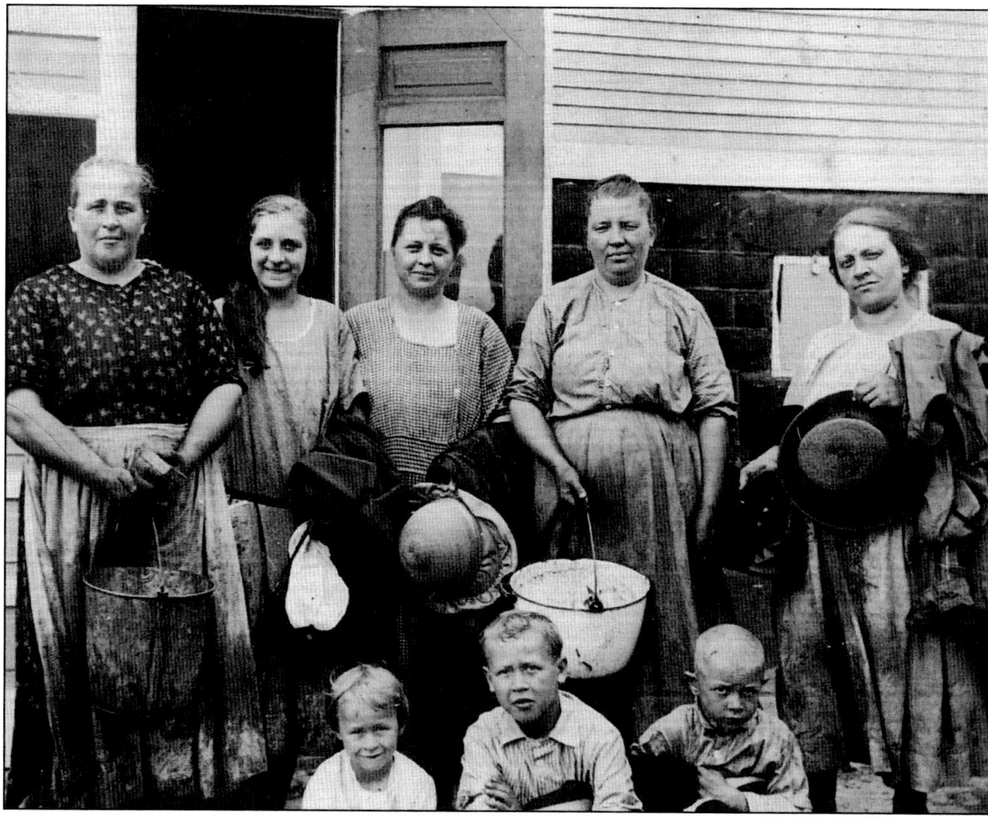

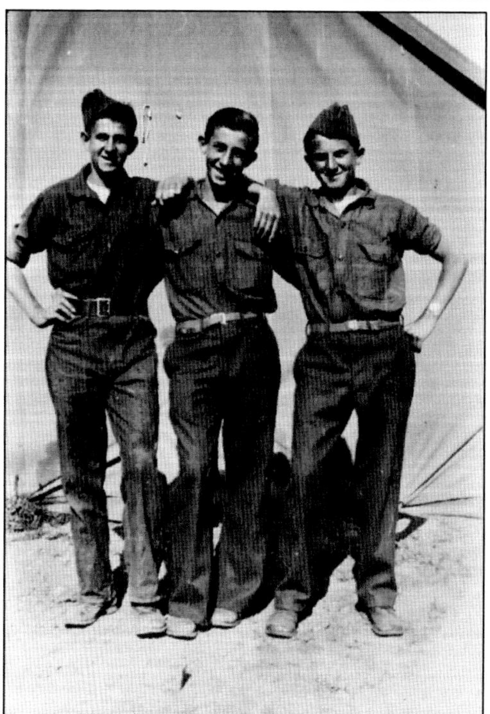

Women worked hard also, although many were volunteers, as were these women from Immanuel Slovak Evangelical Lutheran Church. From left to right are (first row) Annie Kovach, Mike Kovach, and Milan Pagac; (second row) Zuzanna Kovach, Kathryn Leporis, Anna Pagac, Suzanna Payer, and Anna Puhalla. (Courtesy of Mark Miller, Concordia Lutheran Church.)

During the 1930s, many of the unemployed, unmarried young men were happy to find the work offered by President Roosevelt's Depression-era Civilian Conservation Corps (CCC), which paid $30 per month, $22 to $25 of which was automatically sent their families. Shown from left to right are Mickie, Johnny, and Babe Babik at a CCC camp in Minnesota. (Courtesy of Gene Babik.)

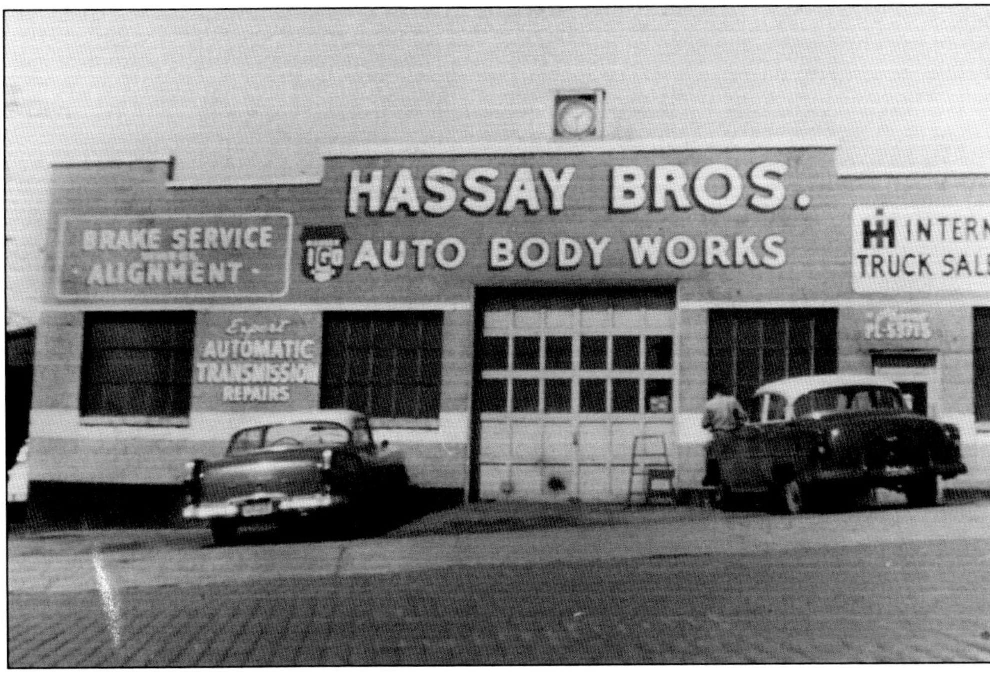

Brake service, alignment, and transmission repairs were the specialties of the Hassay brothers. They operated their automobile repair shop at the bottom of Coitsville Road and Wilson Avenue in Campbell, Ohio, during the 1950s. (Courtesy of the Campbell Historical Society, Florence Katula Galida.)

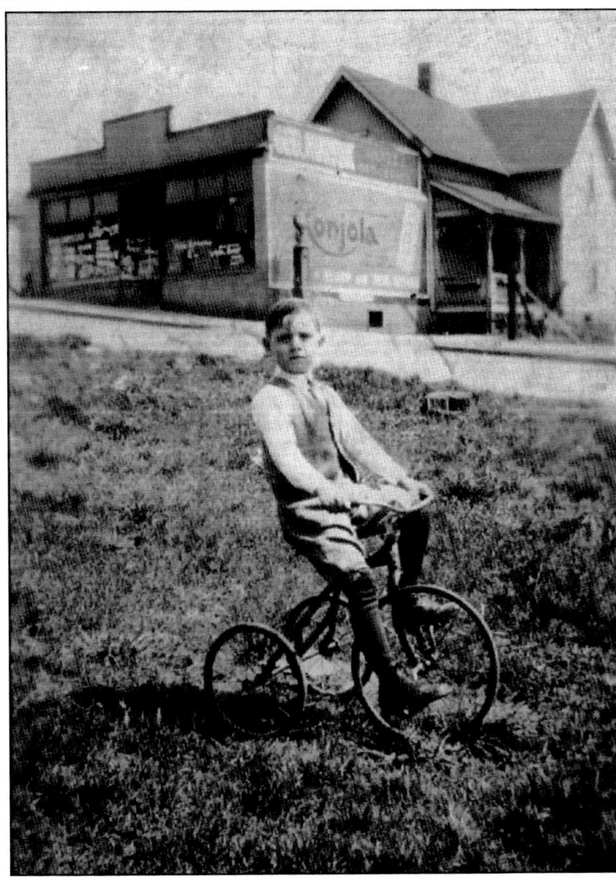

Before the supermarkets came along, neighborhoods had family-owned grocery stores, which usually served specific ethnic groups, providing them with groceries and dry goods at a convenient location. Hurtuk's Market at 38 Bridge Street, north of the Mahoning River in Struthers, Ohio, was known for its meats. Joseph Sokol is pictured across from the store on his tricycle. (Courtesy of the Struthers Historical Society, Marian Kutlesa.)

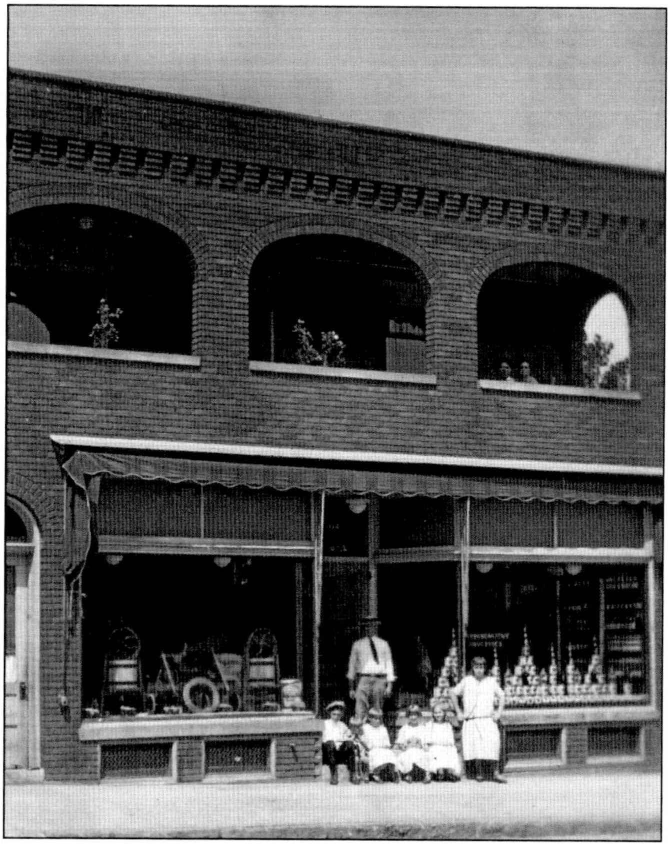

Shown at left is the John Novotny Grocery located on the corner of Taylor Street and Indianola Avenue in Lansingville. John Novotny was one of the sponsors of the 1922 census of Slovaks in the Mahoning Valley. He and his wife lived above the store. Shown below is the interior of the store. John Novotny is in the center; behind the far left counter in back is his son Joseph, and around the right-hand counter are, from left to right, daughter Millie Novotny, Joseph Novotny (no relation), unidentified, and son Mike Novotny. The customers in the back are unidentified. John's grocery had one of the first refrigerated meat cases in the area. It cost almost $5,000—a huge amount in the 1930s. (Both, courtesy of Michael R. Ekoniak Jr.)

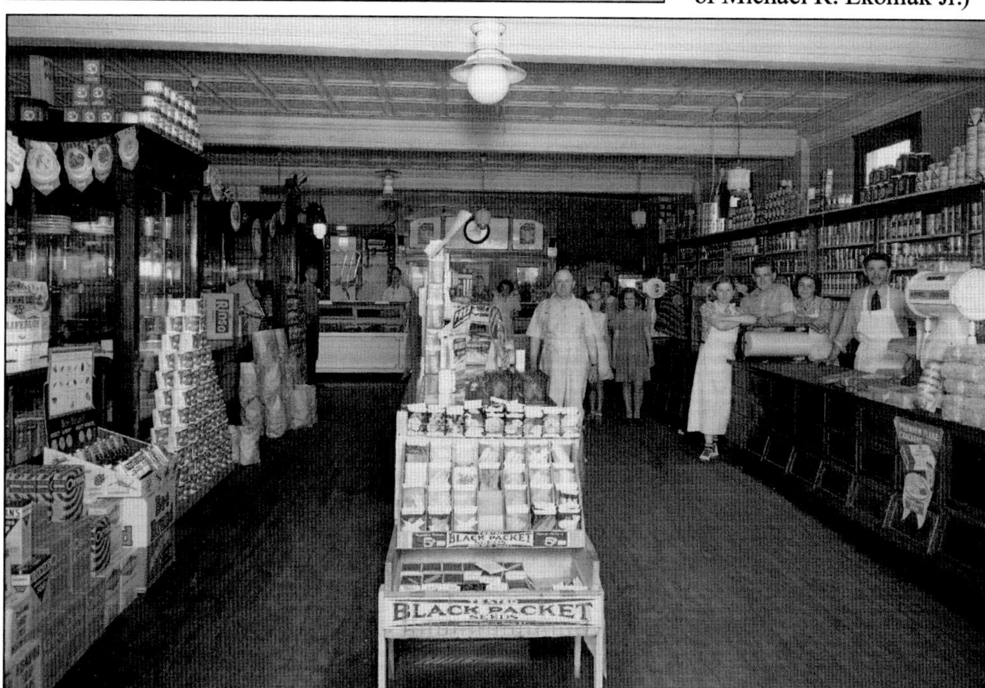

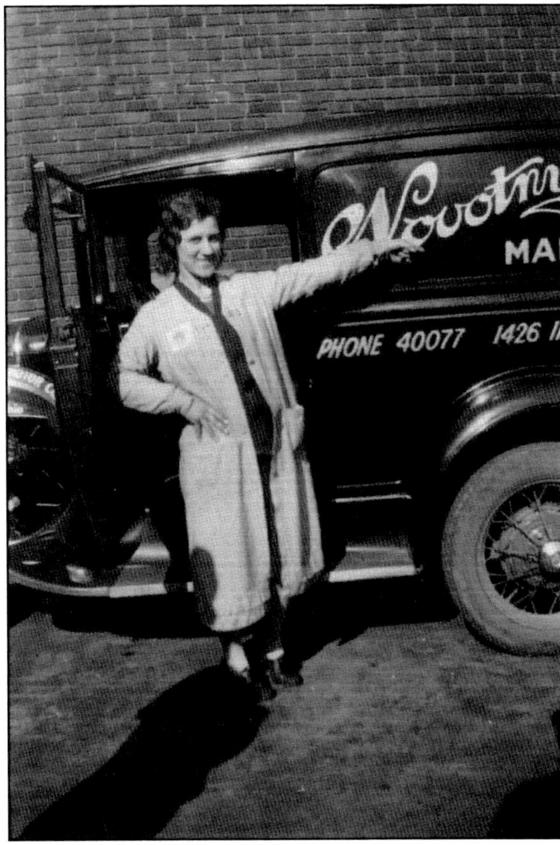

Not only did the grocers provide goods, they also delivered to their customers. Daughter Agnes Novotny is shown with their new 1931 delivery truck. These stores often let their customers carry a tab, especially during the Great Depression. John Novotny was proud that all of his customers paid what was owed as soon as they were back on their feet. (Courtesy of Michael R. Ekoniak Jr.)

Located on the corner of Twelfth Street and Reed Avenue, Peter Resetar's store offered dry goods and notions. This store was located in what was then known as East Youngstown (now Campbell), Ohio. The Resetar family is shown outside their store in the early 1900s. (Courtesy of the Campbell Historical Society, Florence Katula Galida.)

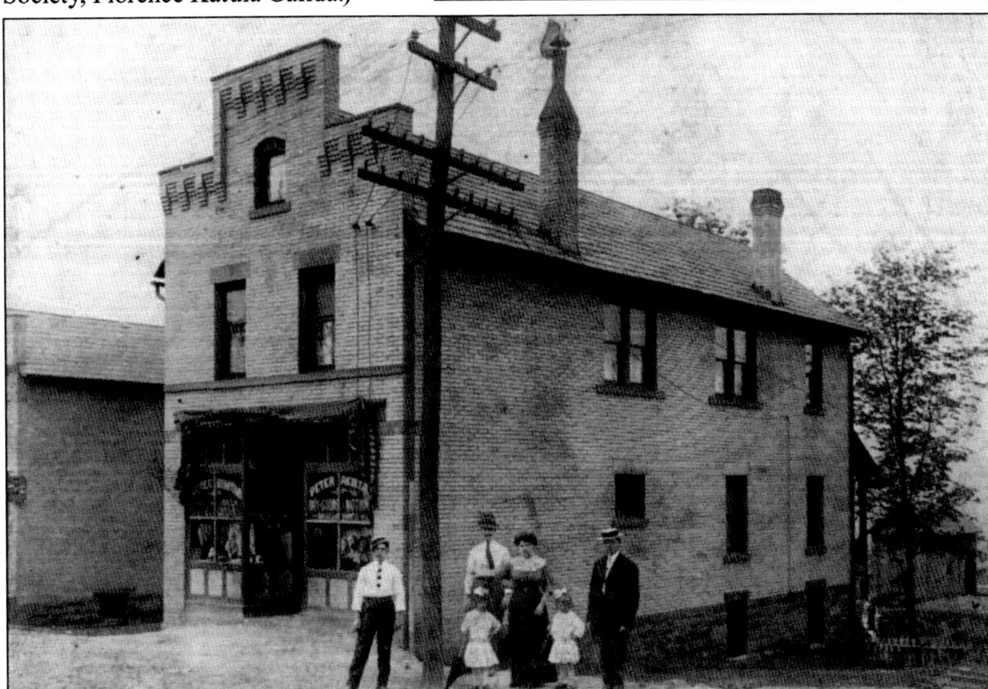

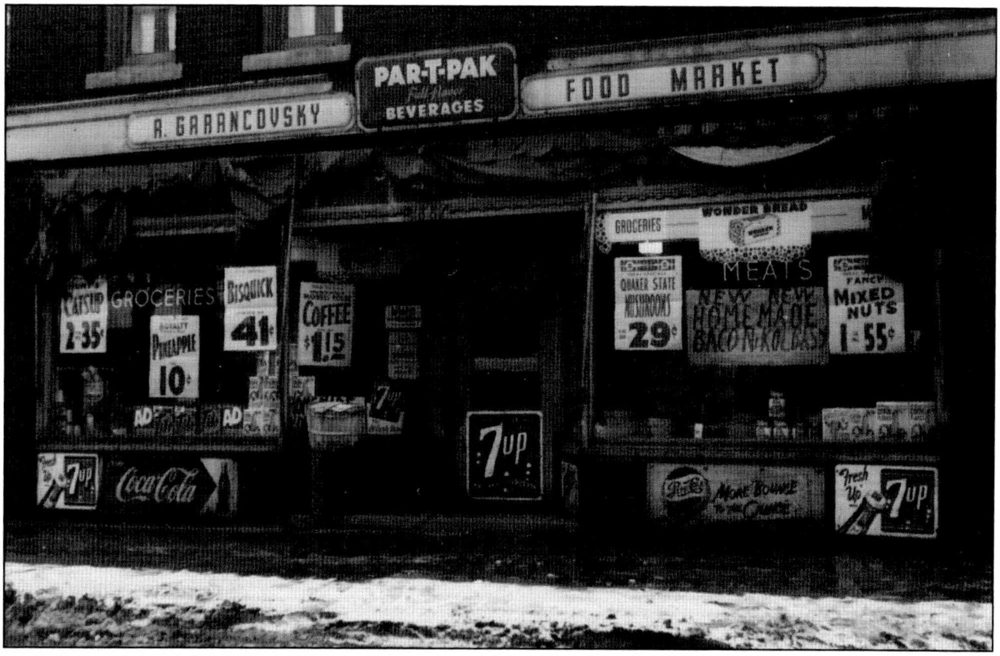

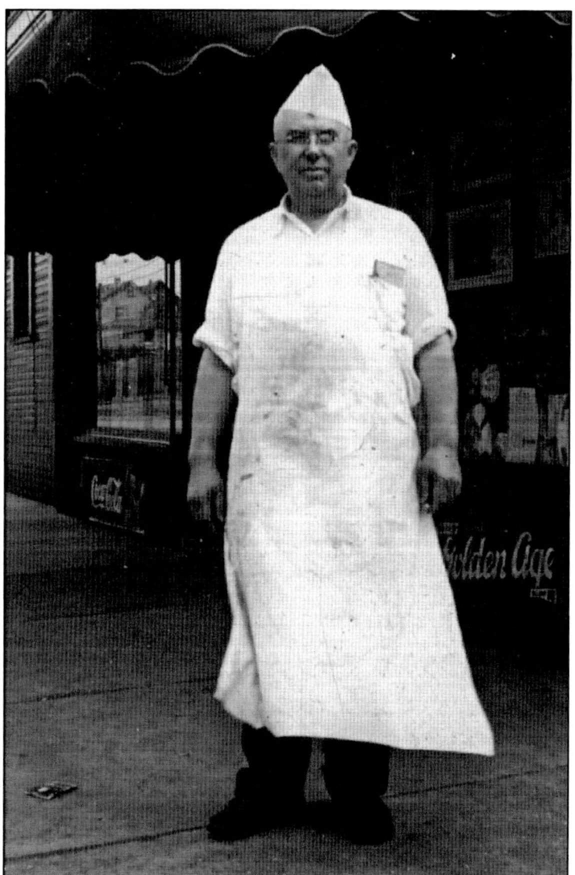

In 1923, Andrew Garancovsky opened a small meat and grocery store on Wilson Avenue in East Youngstown. The store was near Cold Metal Products and directly across from St. Nicholas Byzantine Church. He and son John delivered milk, sodas, and snacks to the mill workers daily. From the age of nine, John had the job of collecting empty pop and milk bottles while his father supplied the workers with fresh milk and cakes. The Garancovsky Food Market, operated by Andy and his sons John (until he went to work at Cold Metal Products) and Frank (who became a mailman in the area), was open for 40 years. (Both, courtesy of Andrew Garancovsky.)

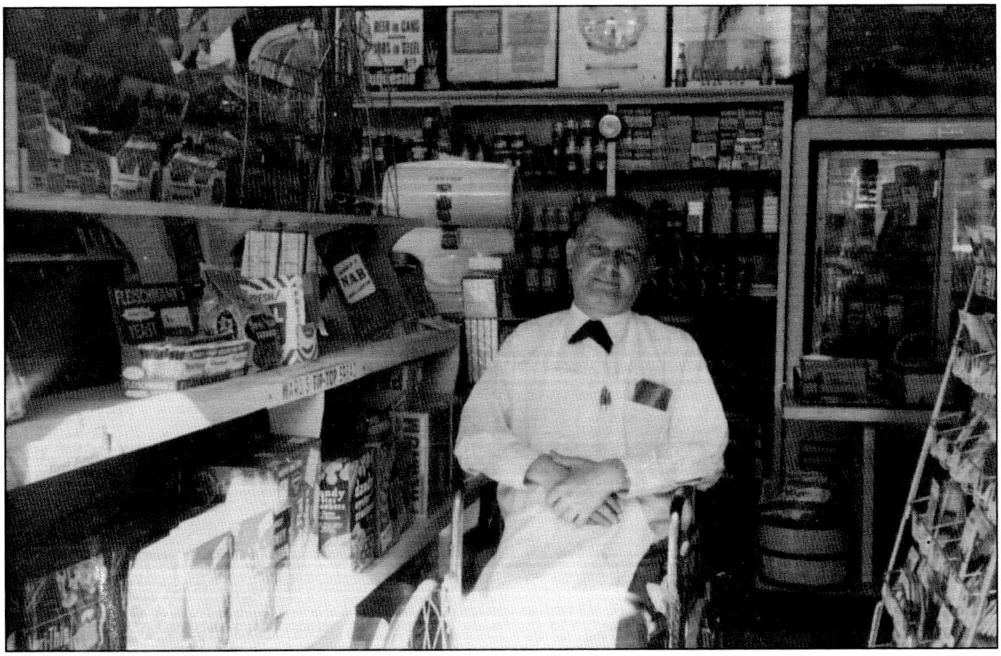

Stephen J. Novotny and his brother John operated Novotny Brothers Grocery at 2435 Shirley Road in the Lansingville area of Youngstown. Shown in 1948, Stephen Novotny was confined to a wheelchair because of childhood polio, but he never let that stop him from being a successful businessman and serving his community. (Courtesy of Kathryn Novotny Franko.)

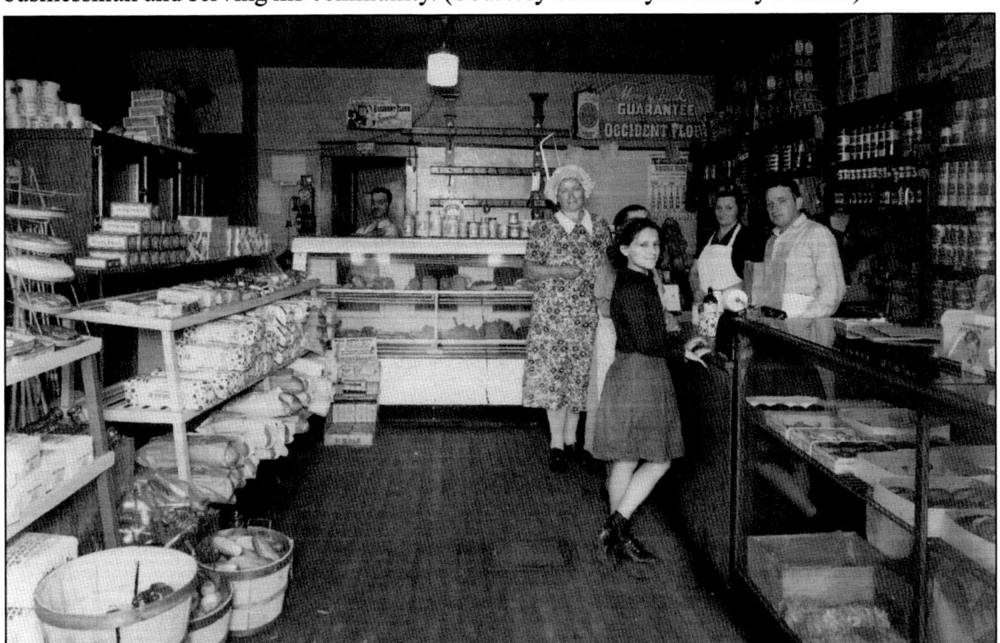

The Textoris family from Gemerská zupa owned the Midland Avenue Grocery in the Steelton area of Youngstown's West Side. Shown serving three of their customers in 1938 are, from left to right, Paul Textoris behind the meat case; Mary Textoris Stefanoff, his sister; and her husband, Thomas Stefanoff. (Courtesy of Margaret Textoris Tomo.)

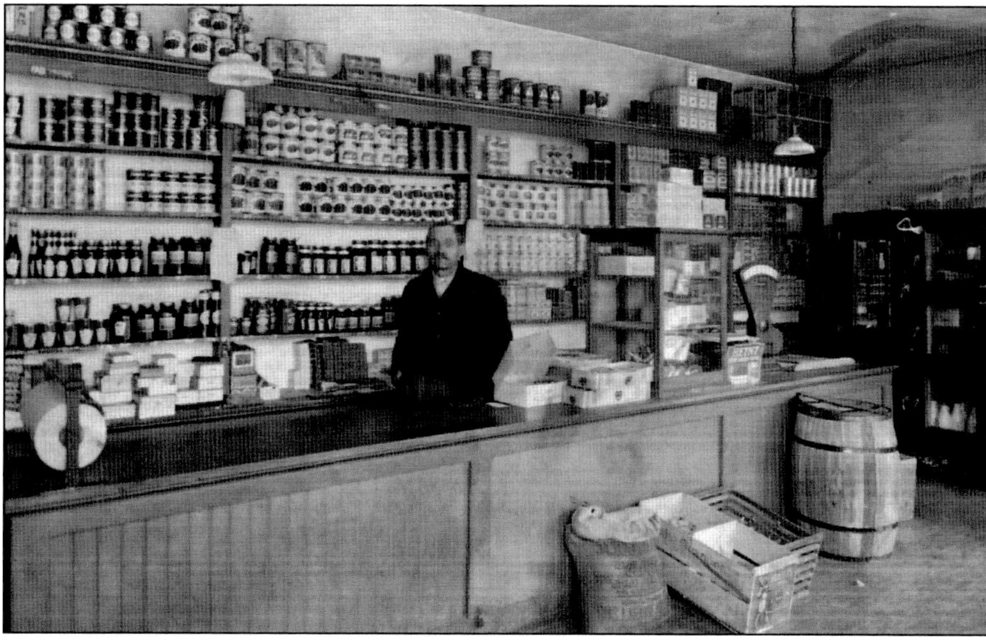

Stephen Backus (Bakos) is shown in his store, which was located in the front of his home at 16 Coitsville Road in Campbell. Backus came to the United States in 1882 from Poráč, Špiš. He and his wife, Anna Lisko Bakos, had 12 children. He was one of the founding members of St. Nicholas Byzantine Catholic Church in Youngstown, Ohio. (Courtesy of Mary Jane Backus.)

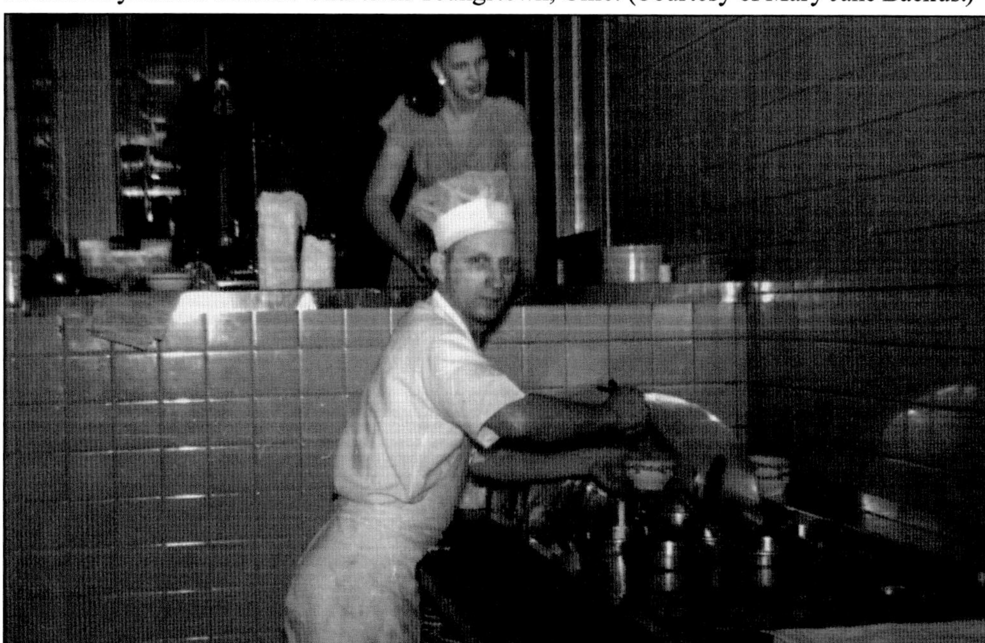

John Zajac Adams, son of Suzie Adam and Michael Zajac, who both emigrated from Pitrovce, Zemplinská zupa, worked at Stone's Grill in downtown Youngstown after World War II until the mid-1950s, when he became the cafeteria manager at the Youngstown Sheet and Tube offices at Stop 5. (Courtesy of David Adams.)

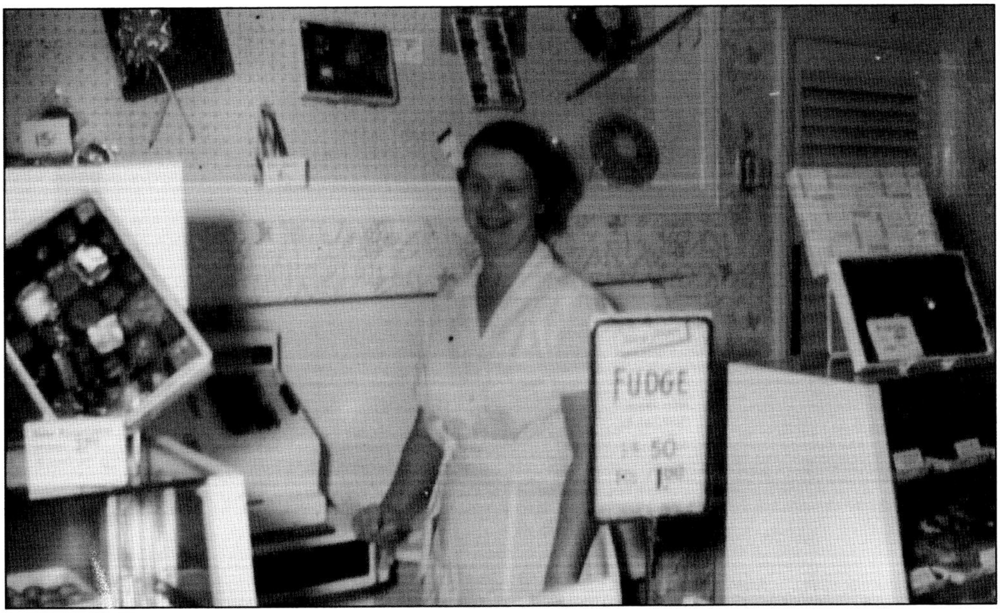

The Fanny Farmer candy store was located on the corner of Federal and Hazel Streets in the heart of the business district in downtown Youngstown, Ohio. Directly next door was the Paramount Theatre, and many theatergoers would stop in to buy their sweets before going to the movies. Shown in 1956 surrounded by boxes of chocolates and treats, Helen Gurella Gubany managed this candy store for over 25 years until her retirement. (Courtesy of Susan Gubany Summers.)

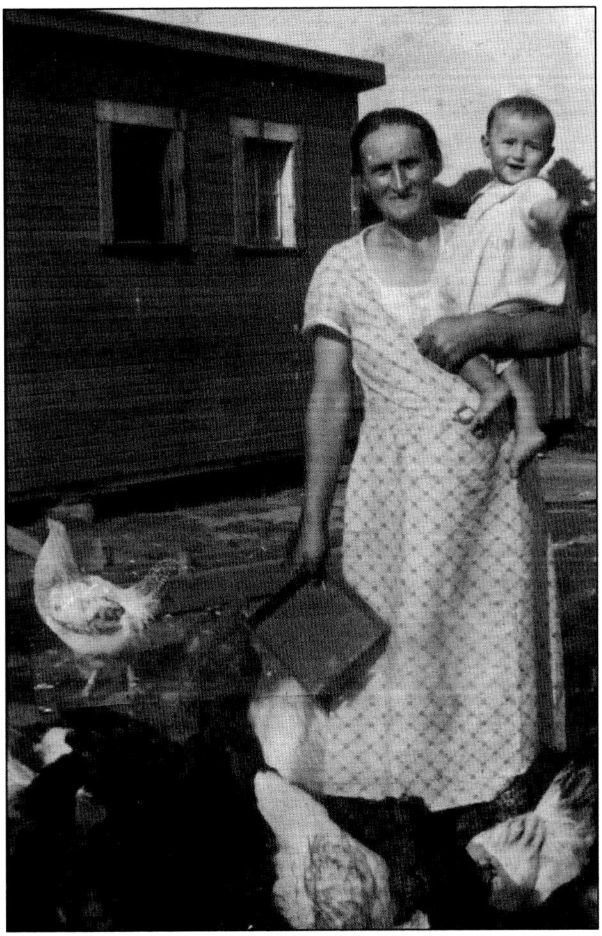

Mary Slanina and daughter Bernadette are pictured on their farm in North Jackson. Many Slovaks chose to buy land and operate farms rather than working in the steel mills. Others who opted to farm were the Kurtas, the Romyaks, the Chizmars, the Yohmans, and the Peterchaks. (Courtesy of Bernadette Slanina Demechko.)

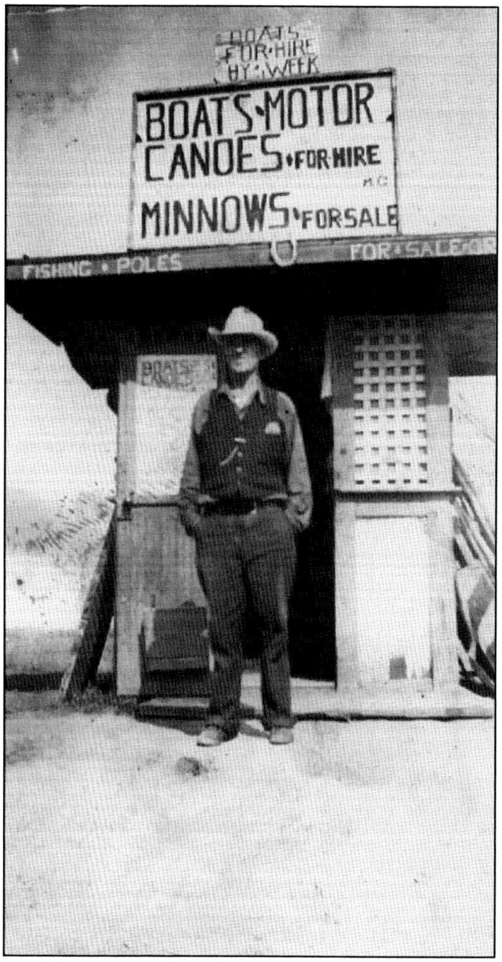

Between 1910 and 1913, a 1,640-acre reservoir was formed when a 2,800-foot-long dam was constructed in the Mahoning River at Lake Milton, Ohio. Lake Milton was a recreational destination with a small amusement park (including a roller coaster, midway, and boat trips) at Craig Beach. On the east side of the lake were taverns, a dance hall, and a skating rink. Pictured in this photograph is Stephen Gubany in the early 1930s in front of his boathouse. (Courtesy of Susan Gubany Summers.)

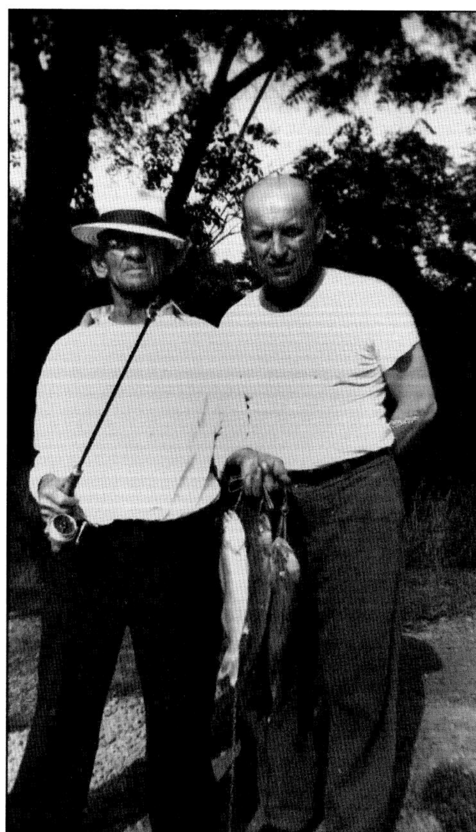

Roman Ekoniak and his son Joseph "Joe" Ekoniak are shown at Joe's farm on Turner Road, in Austintown, Ohio. Joe was a foreman at US Steel, and the farm was his retreat. It backed onto Meander Reservoir. He loved fishing and hunting there, where he and his wife, Ethel Ference Ekoniak, had nut trees, fruit trees, chickens, and a huge garden. (Courtesy of Michael R. Ekoniak Jr.)

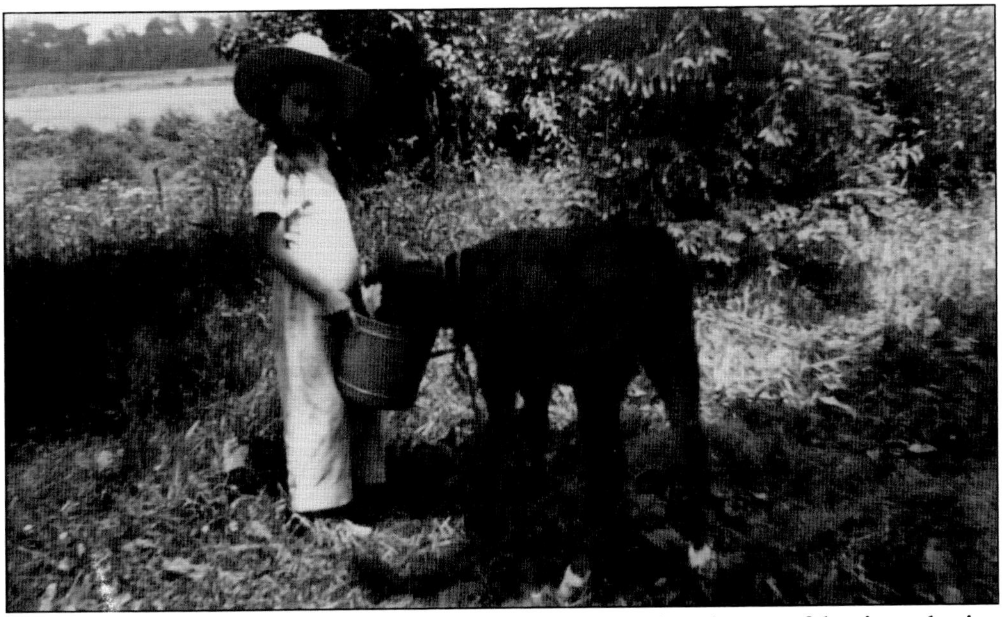

Marie Ekoniak is shown at her uncle's farm. The children loved getting out of the city and going to the farm, which seemed so far out in the country and so different from their city lives. Feeding the animals, fishing, and helping in the garden and farmhouse were adventures to look forward to. (Courtesy of Michael R. Ekoniak Jr.)

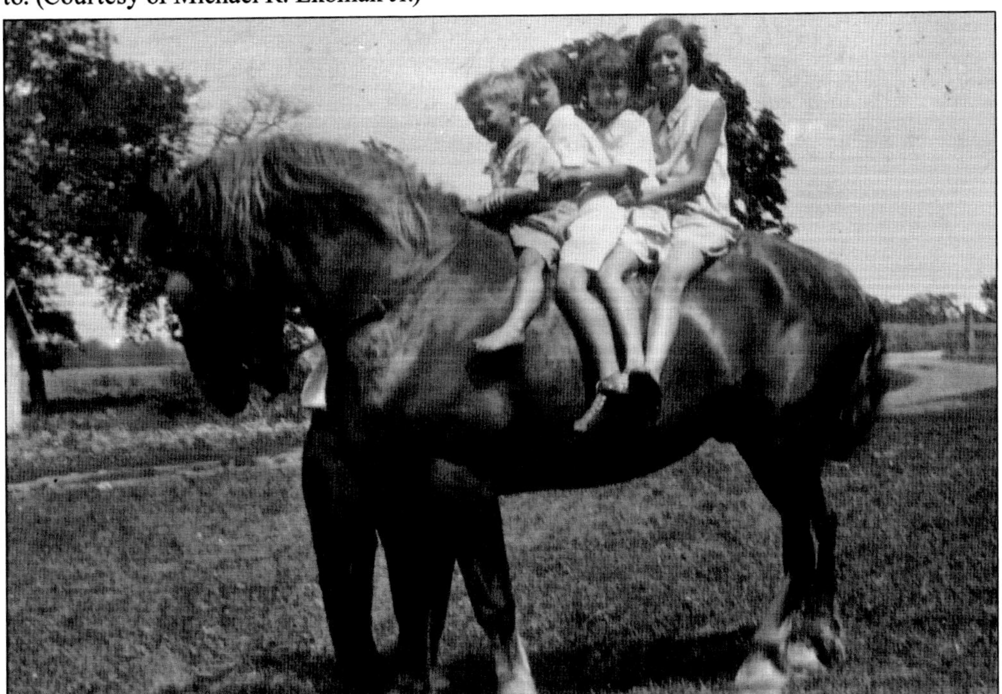

The Unchak farm in Cortland, Ohio, was a getaway for the children of Michael and Anna Baker, who lived in Campbell. While their parents visited cousins or helped on the farm, Joe, Ethel, Helen, and Margaret enjoyed sitting on Wilson, the Unchak family's draft horse. (Courtesy of Loretta Hanuschak Ekoniak.)

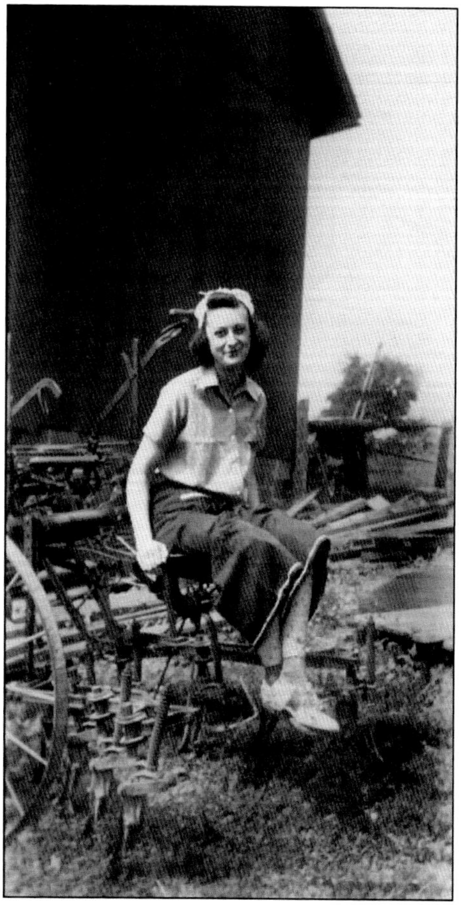

In 1930, Mildred Odrobinak takes a break on her friends' (John and Anna Mijavec) farm, which was located on Cherrywood Road in Pulaski, Pennsylvania. The family still owns and operates the farm and runs the Mijavec Feed and Supply Store. (Courtesy of Lillian Bigley Johnson.)

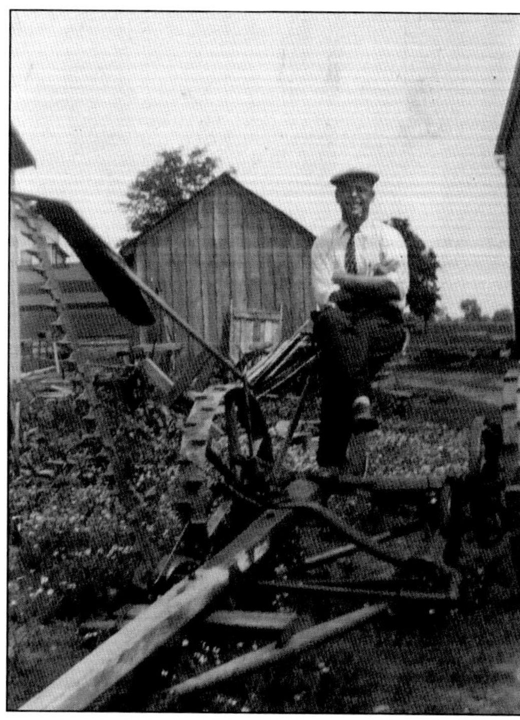

Michael Baker is shown at the Unchak farm in Cortland, Ohio. Going for a Sunday visit to his cousin's farm in the country was a welcome break for Michael and the entire Baker family. Even the work was a big change from the mills. Michael's daughter Eleanor "Allie" loved capturing it all in photographs. (Courtesy of Loretta Hanuschak Ekoniak; photograph by Eleanor Baker.)

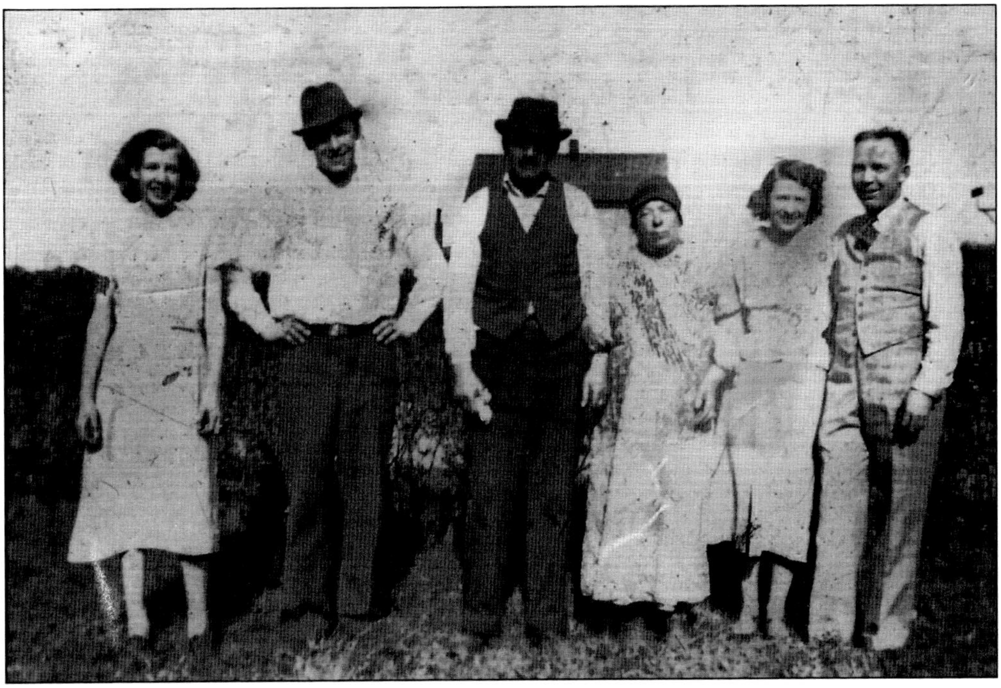

Anton Kopanic from Ruskinovce came to America in 1906. His wife, Juliana Kovalčiková from Harichovce, came in 1907 with their daughter Mary. In 1919, they bought property in the East Side neighborhood (Sharon Line) of Youngstown, and their farm eventually had 150 cows. Pictured in the 1930s are, from left to right, Petronella Kopanic, Michael J. Kopanic Sr., Anton Kopanic, Juliana Kopanic, Helen Kopanic Evans, and William Evans. (Courtesy of Michael J. Kopanic Jr.)

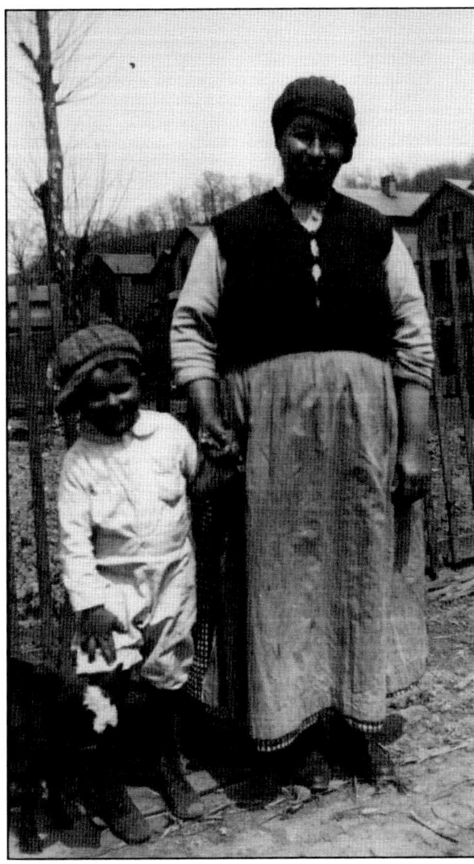

Anna Harbula holds her grandson's hand on her farm in about 1919. He was thrilled to run around the farm and play with animals, like the young goat pictured with him. (Courtesy of Elizabeth Semyan Williams.)

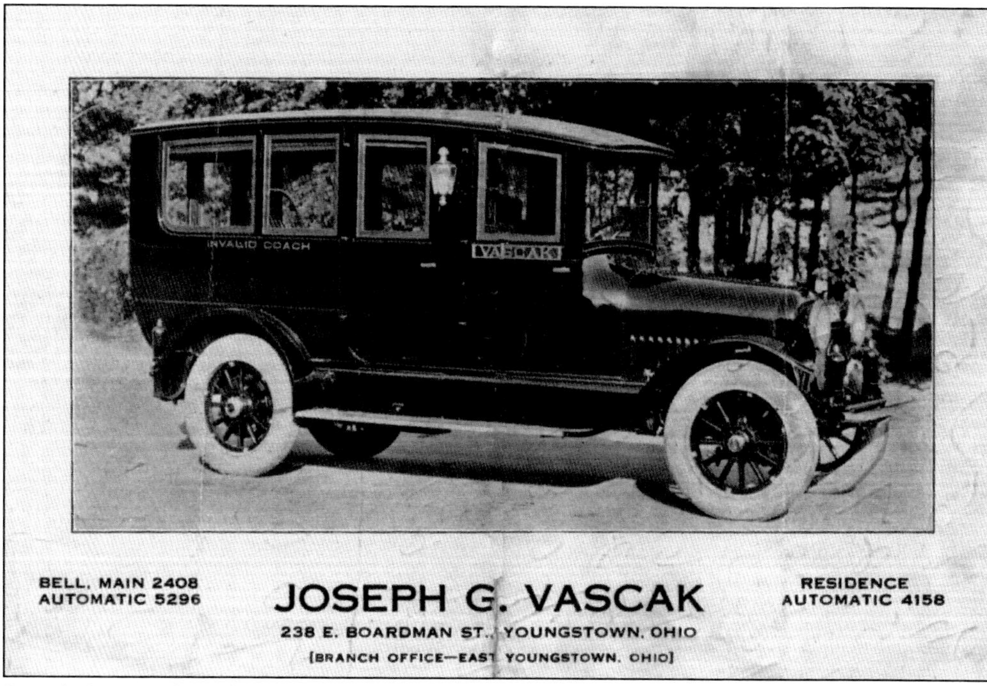

Joseph G. Vasčak Sr. from Richnava was the first Slovak funeral director in the Mahoning and Shenango Valleys and founded the Vasčak Funeral Home in Youngstown, Ohio, in 1907. His first funeral cost $19. Of the 153 funerals held in 1907, most of the deceased were under five years of age. From Front Street, Vasčak moved to the former Burdman home on Lincoln Avenue. In 1981, the Vaschak Funeral Home combined with the Michael Kirila Funeral Home. (Courtesy of Vaschak-Kirila Funeral Home.)

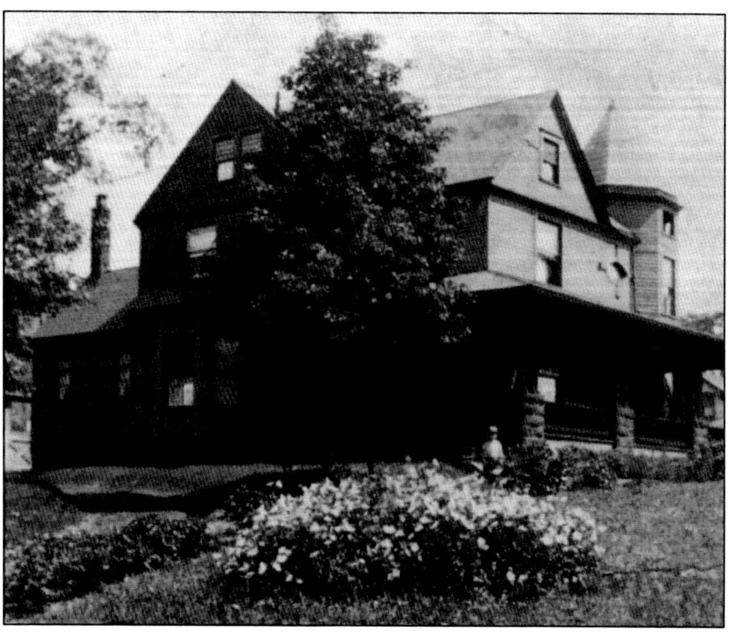

The Wasko Funeral Home was established in 1931 by John Putko, Carl Rich, and John Wasko Sr. In 1937, they moved the business to the old Milligan home on Coitsville Road in Campbell, Ohio, and the partnership remained in effect until 1968. From 1968 to the present, the home has been under the guidance of the Wasko family. (Courtesy of the Wasko Funeral Home, Jaquelyn Wasko.)

Three

Od Srdce ("From the Heart")

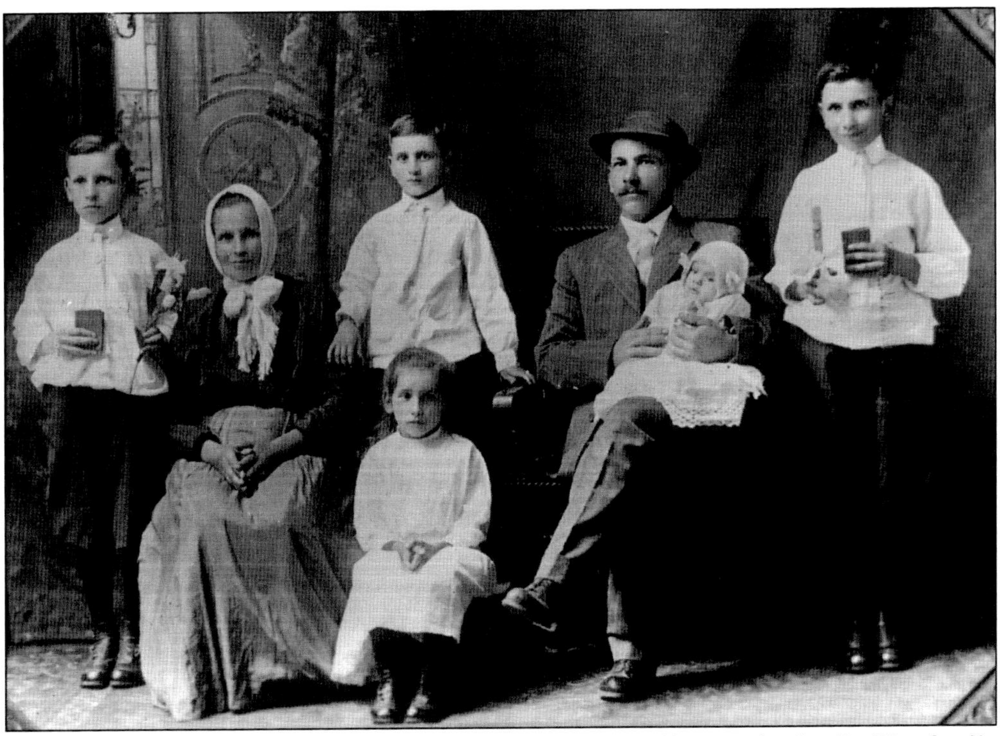

Faith, work, celebration, and sorrow revolved around the effect on the family. The family was from the heart, or *od srdce*. This is the family of Roman Ikoniak from Javorky and Anna Ferenčucha from Vojkovec. Immigrating around 1899, Roman worked at the Anna Furnace in Struthers, later the Pittsburgh & Lake Erie Railroad (P&LE). From left to right are Joseph, Anna, Michael, Ann (sitting in front of Michael), Roman, and Paul. The baby shown died in infancy, and another daughter, Kathryn, was not born when this photograph was taken. (Courtesy of Michael R. Ekoniak Jr.)

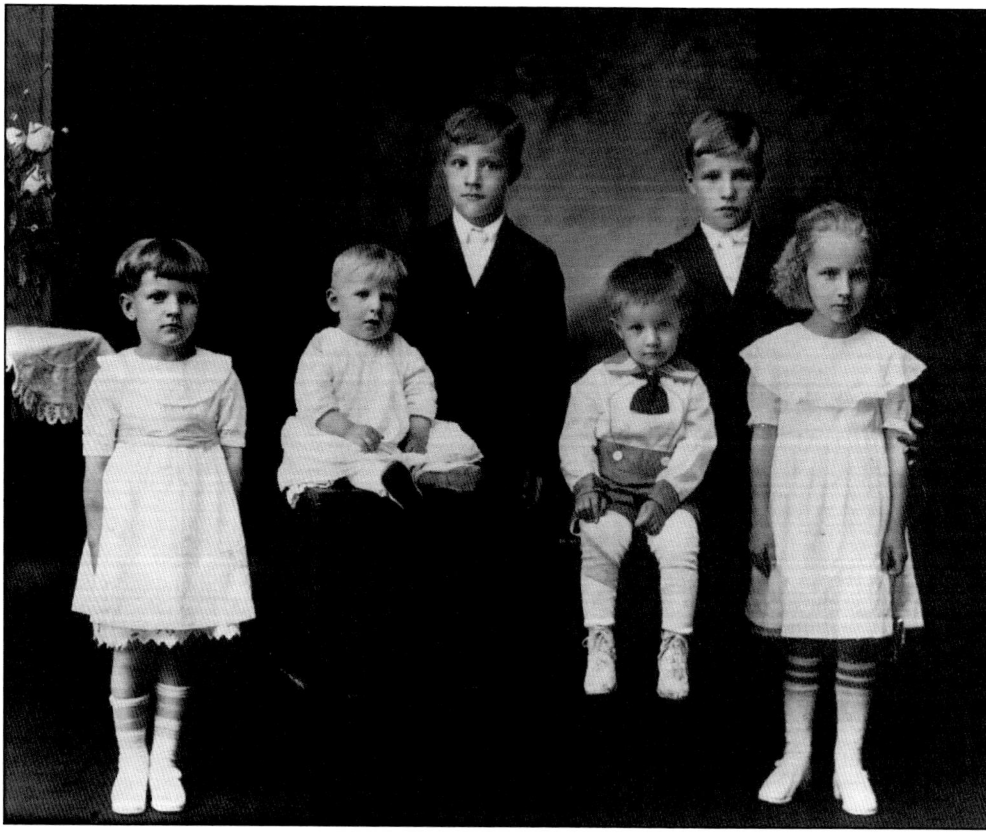

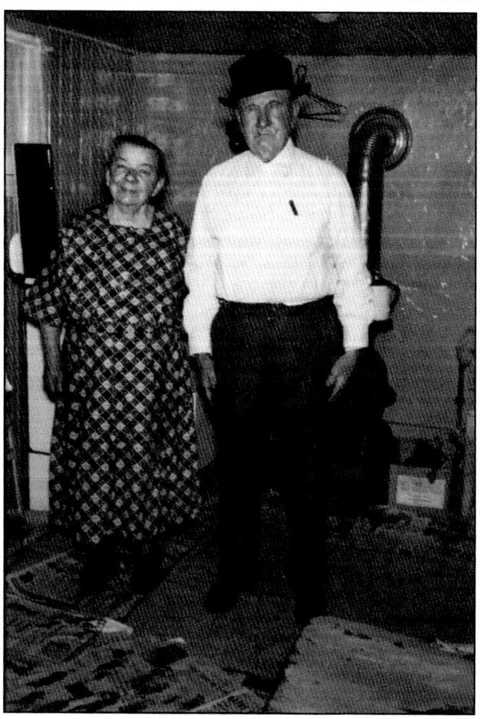

Paul Sedzmak, from Chrast nad Hornadom, and Catherine Ondrus, from Klčov in Spišská zupa, married in Connellsville, Pennsylvania, and then came to Youngstown in the 1920s, eventually moving to Bruce Street in the Steelton area. Their six children are, from left to right, Elizabeth, Steven, Paul, Andrew, Joseph, and Clara. (Courtesy of Joseph Sedzmak.)

Andrew Swantek emigrated from Bardejov, Šariš, in 1884, and his wife, Mary Kalafut, came to the United States in 1891 from Poráč, Spiš. He worked at US Steel while they lived on Reed Avenue in Campbell, Ohio. Their five children were George, Jacob, John, Mary, and Ann. (Courtesy of Joseph Swantek.)

Paul Antal was born in Klenovec, Gemer, Slovakia, in 1912 and came to the United States at age 13. Johanna Kolesar, also from Klenovec, came in February 1921. They married in May 1921 at John Hus Evangelical Lutheran Church. The couple had seven children and was married for 59 years. (Courtesy of Janice Kovach.)

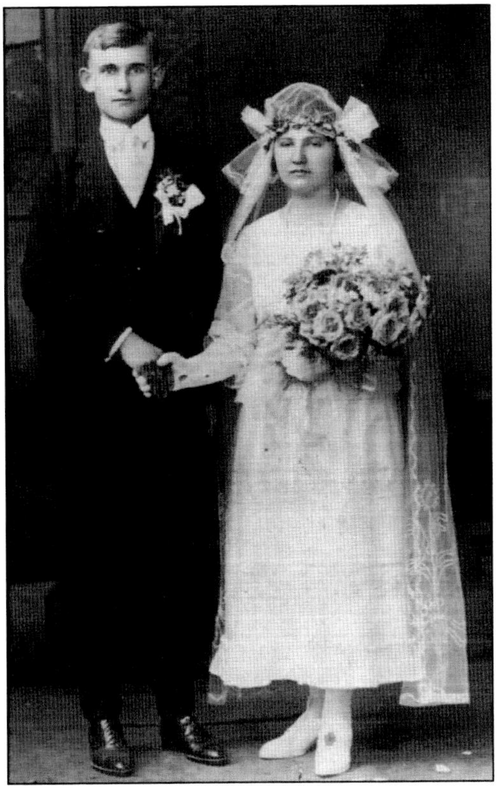

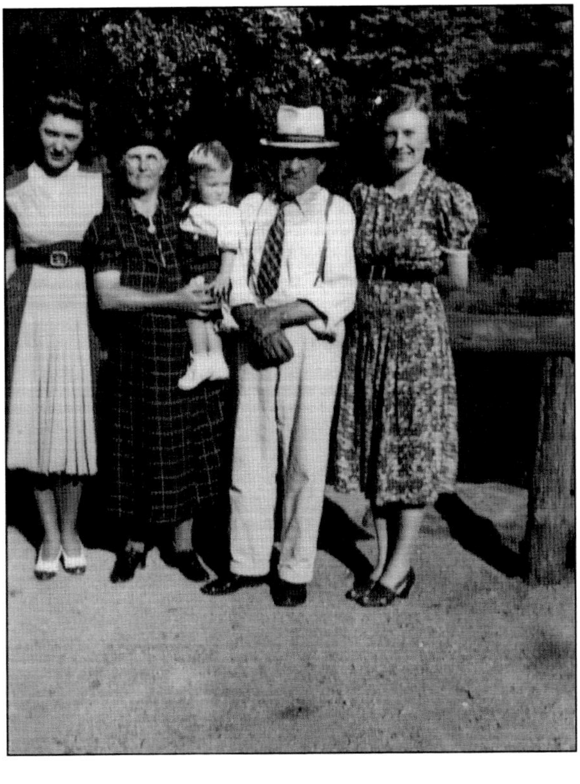

What is better than a day at Mill Creek Park with Baba and Dzedo? Shown in 1941 are, from left to right, Aunt Mary Dutko, Mary Vasko holding grandson Jack Vasko, Joseph Vasko, and Aunt Betty Petrek. (Courtesy of Jack Vasko.)

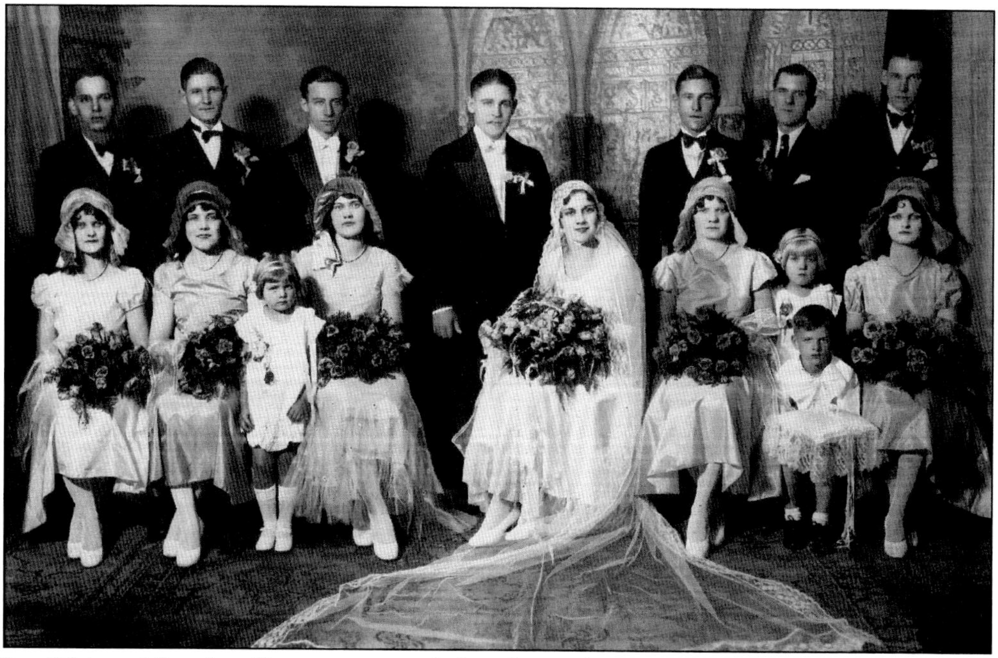

Leo Dietz and Sue Ann Kozar were married on September 21, 1930, in the first St. Elizabeth's Church in Youngstown, Ohio. They lived in Youngstown, Ohio, and raised a family of four children: Leona, twins Leo and Loretta, and Susan. Leo retired from Republic Rubber. (Courtesy of Susan Kozar Scheetz.)

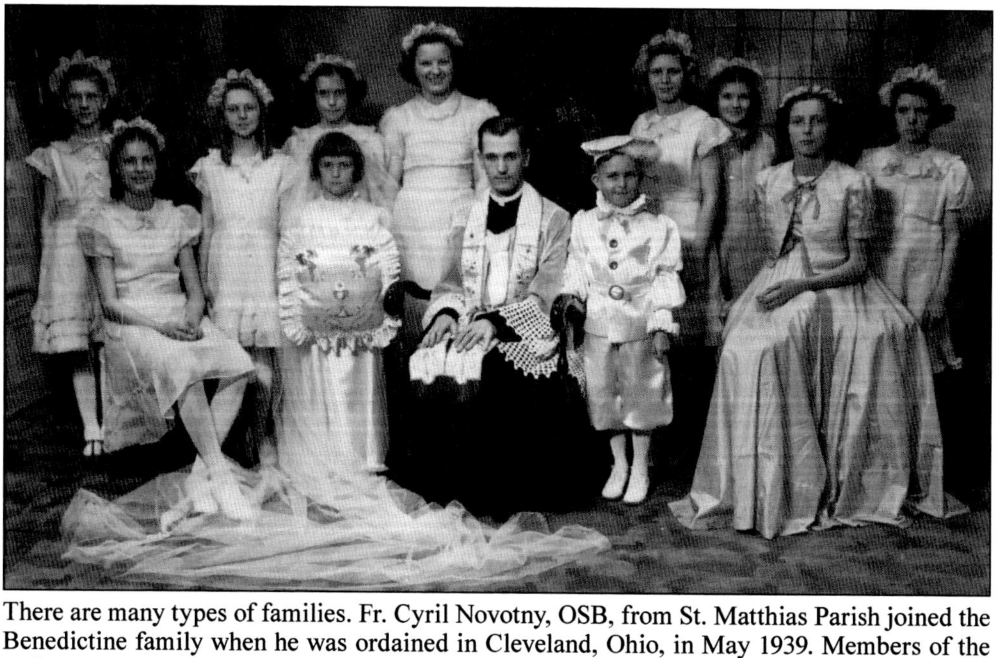

There are many types of families. Fr. Cyril Novotny, OSB, from St. Matthias Parish joined the Benedictine family when he was ordained in Cleveland, Ohio, in May 1939. Members of the ordination court are, from left to right, (first row) Jennifer Komara, Cecelia Schlosser, Father Novotny, Edward Skokan, and Margaret Schlosser; (second row) Mary Louise Krempasky, Helen Skokan, Elizabeth Schlosser, Rosalie Corpa, Margaret Sarisky, Ann Pachuta, and Ann Tokarsky. (Courtesy of Kathryn Novotny Franko.)

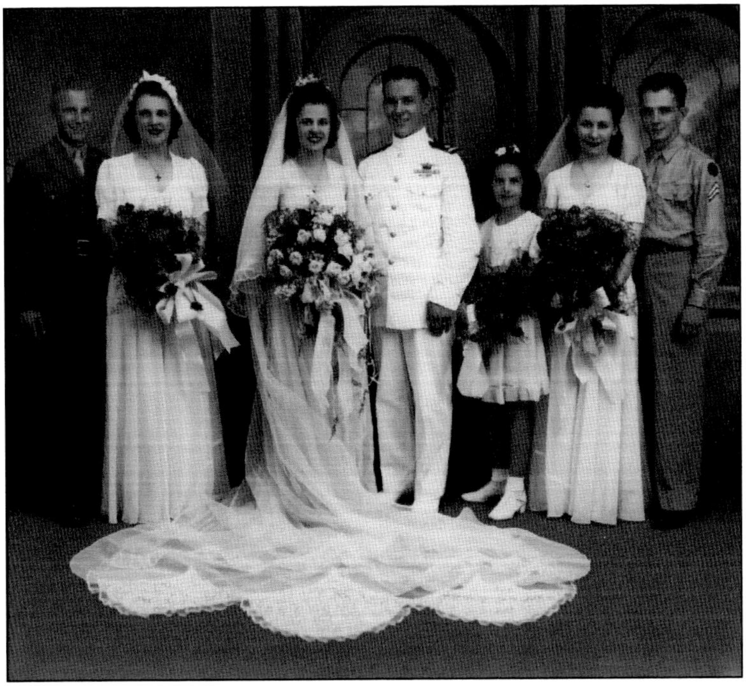

The military forms another close-knit family. Stanley Martauz and Kay Niemzura had a very diverse military wedding. Pictured in the wedding party are, from left to right, Herbie Martauz, US Marine Corps; Wanda Pasek; bride Kay Niemzura; groom Stanley Martauz, US Navy; Mary Rodzen; Henrietta Martauz; and Joseph Niemzura, US Army. (Courtesy of the Campbell Historical Society, Florence Katula Galida.)

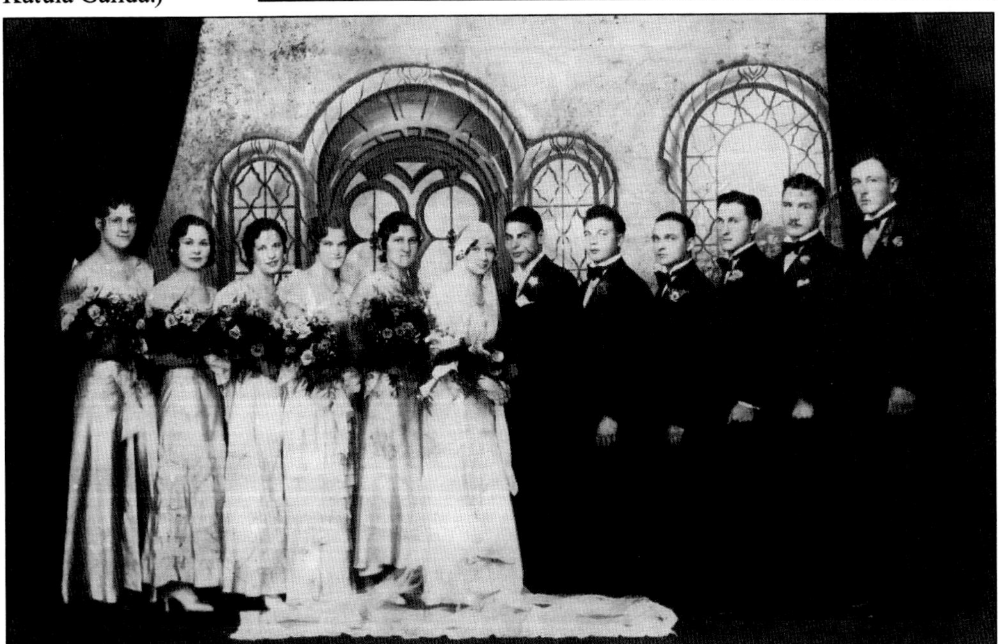

Michael J. Katula, whose family was from Závadka (present-day Slovakia), and Ann R. Solic, whose family was from Zagreb (present-day Croatia), were united in marriage on September 26, 1931, at SS. Peter and Paul Croatian Roman Catholic Church in Youngstown, Ohio. The wedding party includes, from left to right, Maddeline Papalko, Betty Kulik, Eleanor Martin, Mary Lucas Kopey, Barbara Pundak, bride Ann Rosalyn Solic, groom Michael J. Katula, Stephen Solic, Mose Opretza, Mike Maro, John Petruska, and Ben Kunicki. (Courtesy of the Campbell Historical Society, Florence Katula Galida.)

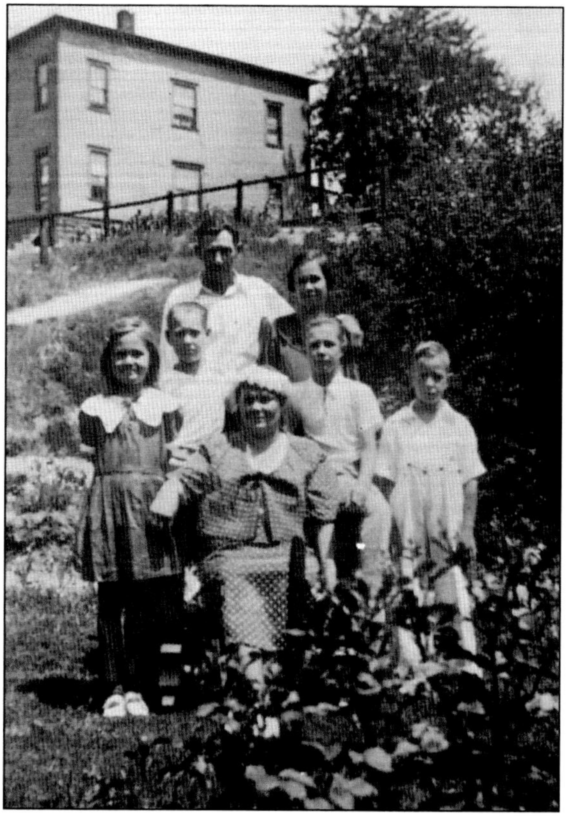

The Sanders family lived in the Schwebel flats and attended St. Elizabeth Slovak Church and school. The family members are pictured while visiting friends and relatives on Wilson Avenue in Campbell, Ohio, and include, from left to right, (first row) Ethel and Mary (seated); (second row) Lawrence, John, and Eugene; (third row) John Sr. and Josephine Sanders. (Courtesy of Carol Sanders Shiminsky.)

Stephen Kovach (seated) was born in Klenovec, Slovakia, and came through Ellis Island in 1907. His wife, Maria Dovica (seated), was from Malá Paloma, in Gemer, Slovakia, and came to the United States in 1912. She and Paul had eight children. The children shown are, from left to right, Susan, Julia (little girl in white dress), Mary, baby John, and Steve. Stephen and Maria had been married for 60 years when Stephen died in 1972. (Courtesy of Janice Kovach.)

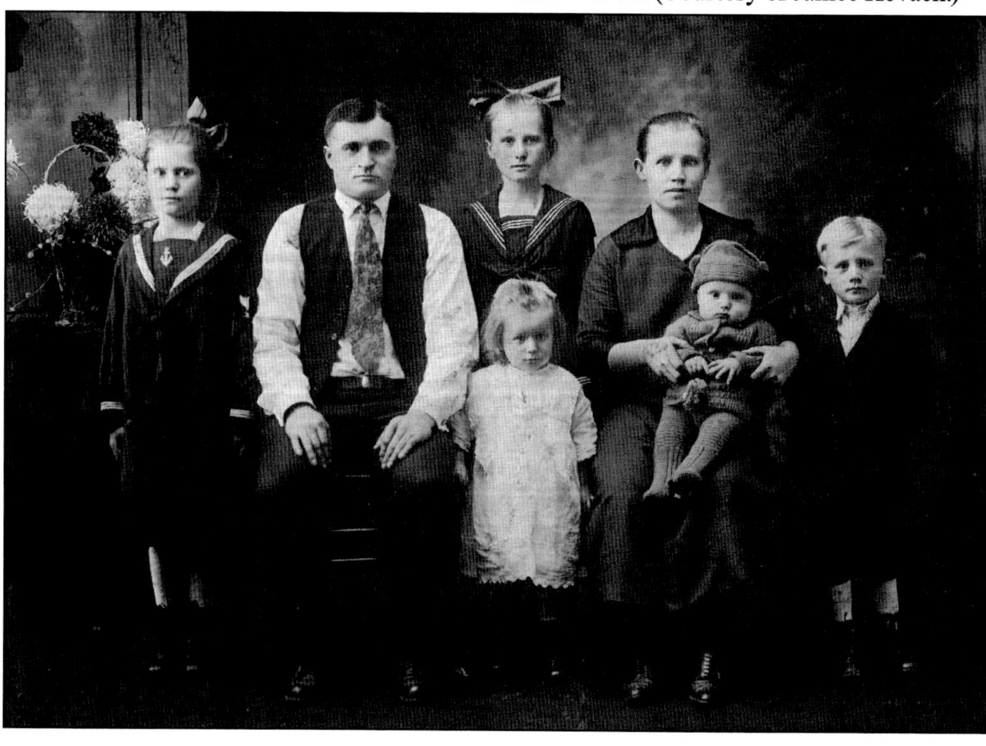

Andrew Hirt and his wife, Mary Sič-Yergus, came to the United States when their son Andrew was three. Mary was born in Pennsylvania, but her family returned to Pohorela. Andrew was a shoemaker in Pohorela and continued his trade here. Pictured are, from left to right, mother Mary, John, Andrew Jr., Ann, and father Andrew Sr. (Courtesy of Florence Tessari Hirt.)

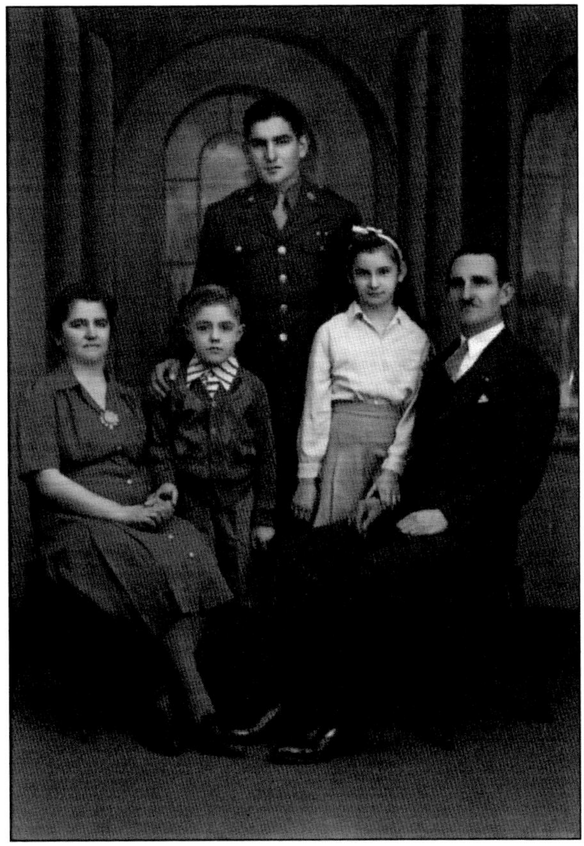

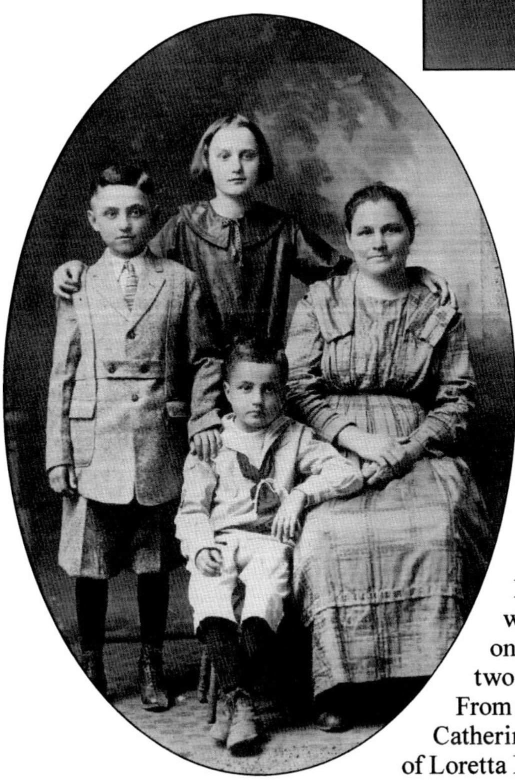

Catherine Kolesar Hanusčak came to the United States from the village of Poráč in Spiš to join her husband, Maftje (Matthew), who had come shortly before her in 1899. They lived on Gladstone Avenue in Campbell and were members of St. Nicholas Byzantine Church on Wilson Avenue. They had five children. The two oldest, Catherine and Mary, are not shown. From left to right are Nicholas, Michael, and mother Catherine. Standing behind them is Helen. (Courtesy of Loretta Hanuschak Ekoniak.)

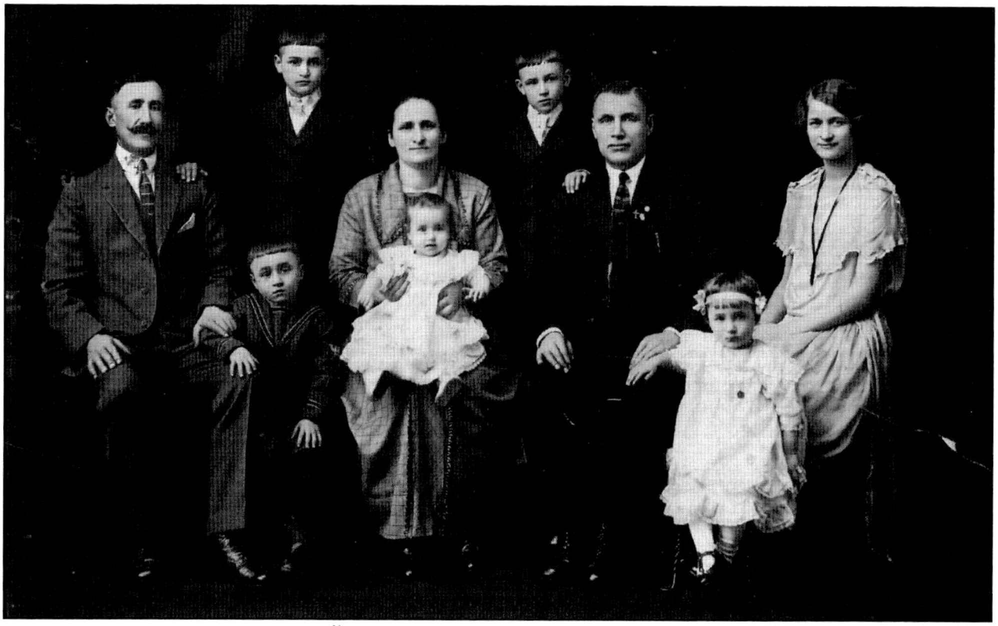

The Slaninas came from Spišský Štvrtok, Slovakia. John worked as a bricklayer with brother-in-law Michael Gresh. In the 1920s, they built many of the buildings on Youngstown's Indianola Avenue. John's sons founded Poling and Bacon Construction. From left to right are (first row) Michael Gresh, Joseph Slanina, Mary Gresh Slanina holding daughter Anastacia, John Slanina, and daughters Veronica and Mary; (second row) sons Steve and John. (Courtesy of Bernadette Slanina Demechko.)

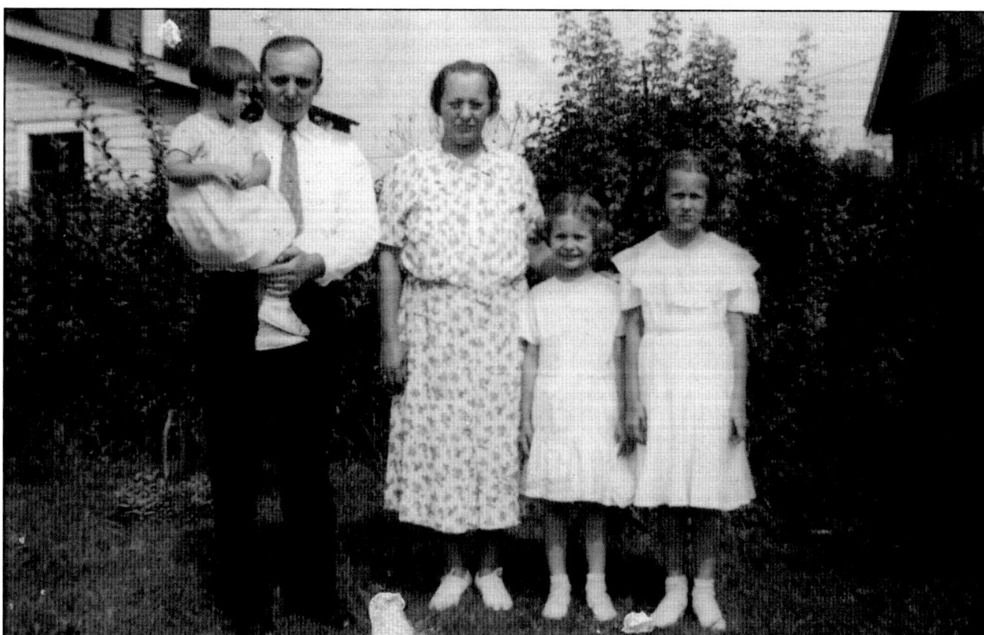

Shown at their home on Indianola Avenue in Lansingville, John G. Yalch (Jalcs) came from Markušovce, and his wife, Mary Bartos, was born in Závadka. From left to right are John holding daughter Genny, Mary, and daughters Eleanor and Gertie. (Courtesy of Thomas Mrofchak.)

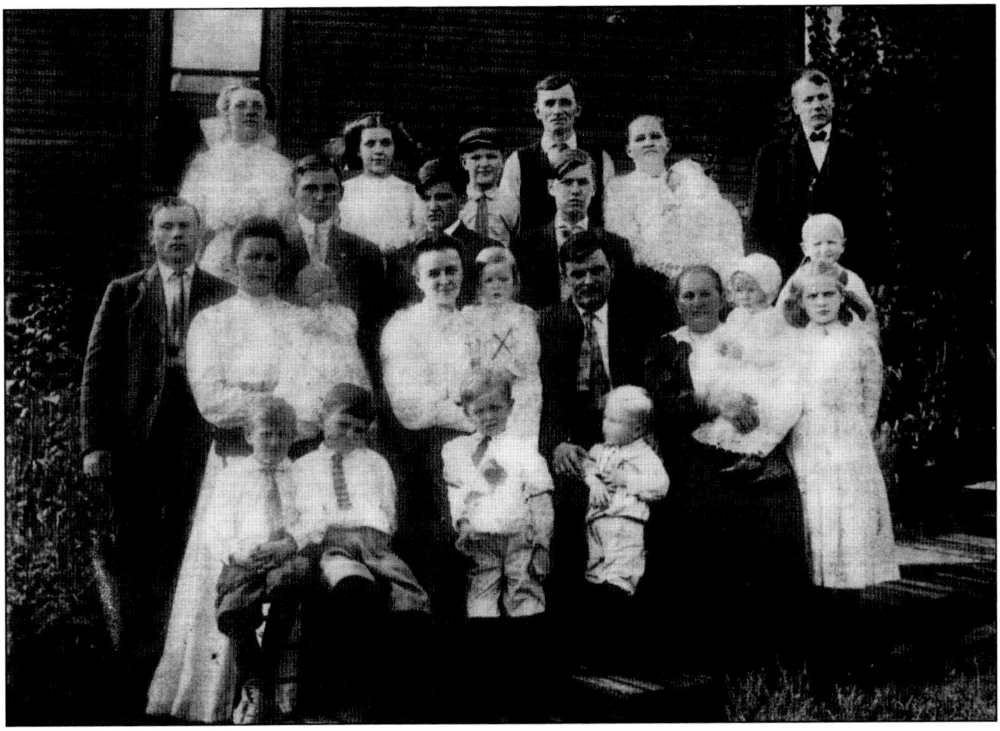

The Lucas family from Struthers, Ohio, include, from left to right, (first row) Joseph Bobby, John Repasky, Joseph Repasky, and John Gura; (second row) John Michael Gura, Anna Gura holding Juliana, Mary Lucia Repasky holding George, Nicholas Lucas, Anna Lucas holding Alex, Martha Mickler, and Michael Bobby (behind Martha); (third row) Nicholas G. Lucas, John Lucas, and Peter Bobby; (fourth row) Elizabeth Gura, Kathryn Slanina, John Bobby, Mr. Valiovsky, Mrs. Bobby holding Elsie, and Peter Bobby. (Courtesy of Janet Repasky Morris.)

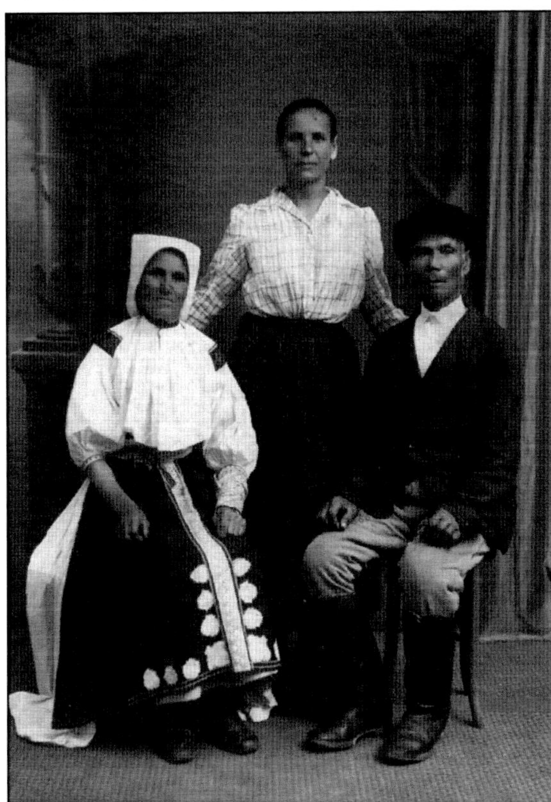

In 1906, the Zametz family left their village in Lieskovec, destined for the port of Antwerp, Belgium. Crossing the Atlantic Ocean and arriving weeks later at Ellis Island, they finally reached their new country, the United States of America. Pictured are mother Eva Zametz (left), daughter Mary (center), and father Stephen Zametz. (Courtesy of Mary Margaret Kochis DeCrescentis.)

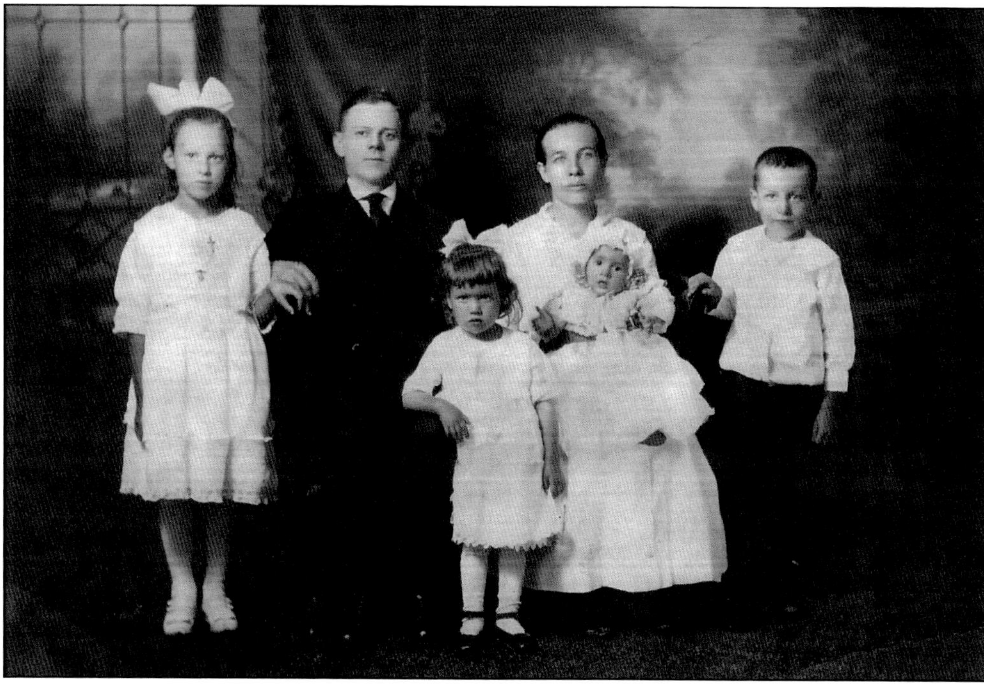

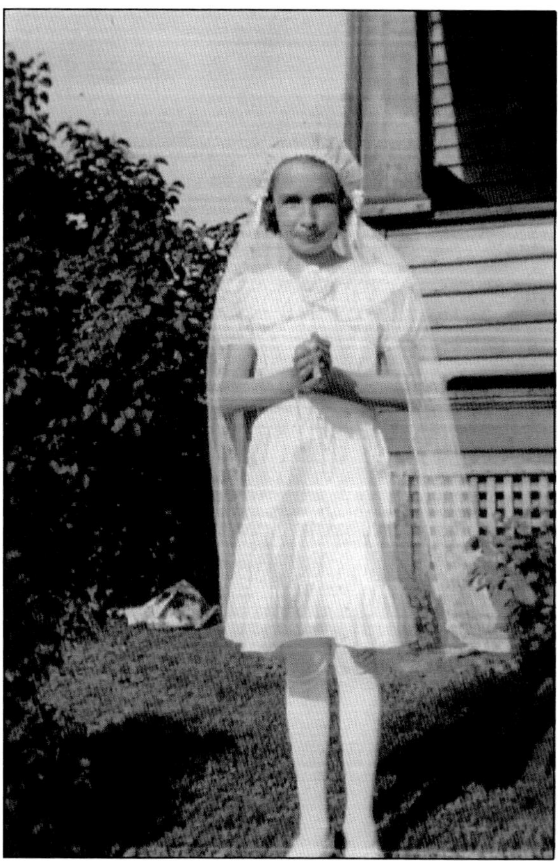

John Hruby from Markušovce and his wife, Maria, were married in Connellsville, Pennsylvania. They bought a farm in New Middletown, eventually moving to Campbell, Ohio, where John worked at Youngstown Sheet and Tube. From left to right are Mary, John Sr., Catherine, Mary holding Michael, and John Jr. (Courtesy of a Hruby granddaughter.)

Dorothy Tomko grew up in Struthers, Ohio, with her parents, George and Sophie Tomko, and brothers George Jr. and Thomas. The family attended Holy Trinity Church in Struthers, Ohio, where Dorothy received her First Holy Communion. She married Harry Haddox, and together they had three children: Nancy, Colleen, and Holly. (Courtesy of the Haddox family.)

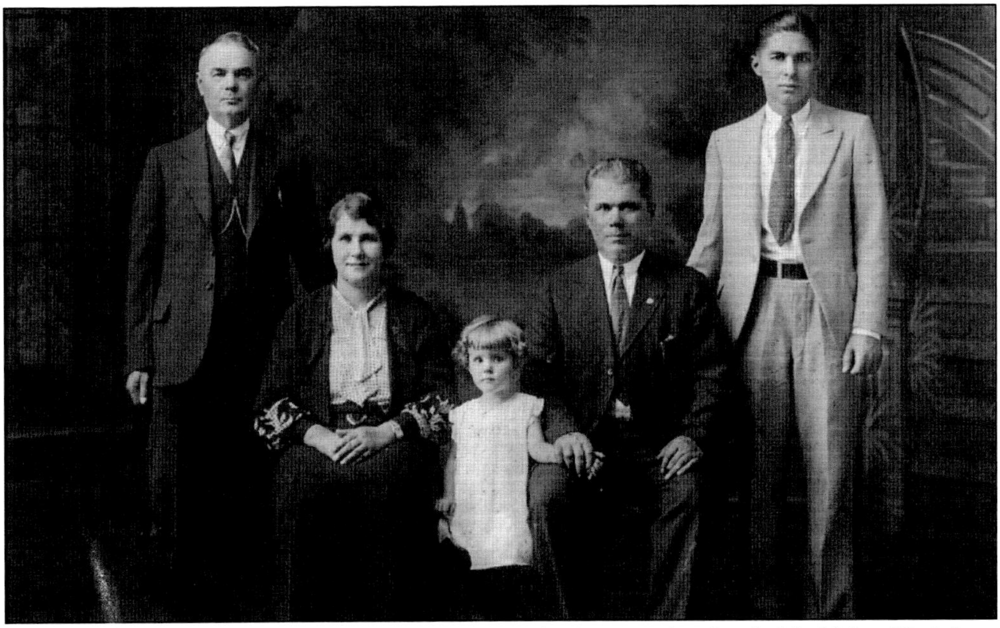

In 1913, Zachary Maximov immigrated to the United States, leaving behind his wife, Mary, and their young son, Vasil. He was reunited with them 13 years later on December 14, 1926, in Campbell, Ohio. Gathered for this photograph are, from left to right, Mary's brother-in-law Alex, Mary (Semeniuk) Maximov, daughter Ann, Zachary Maximov, and son Vasil. (Courtesy of Carol Sanders Shiminsky.)

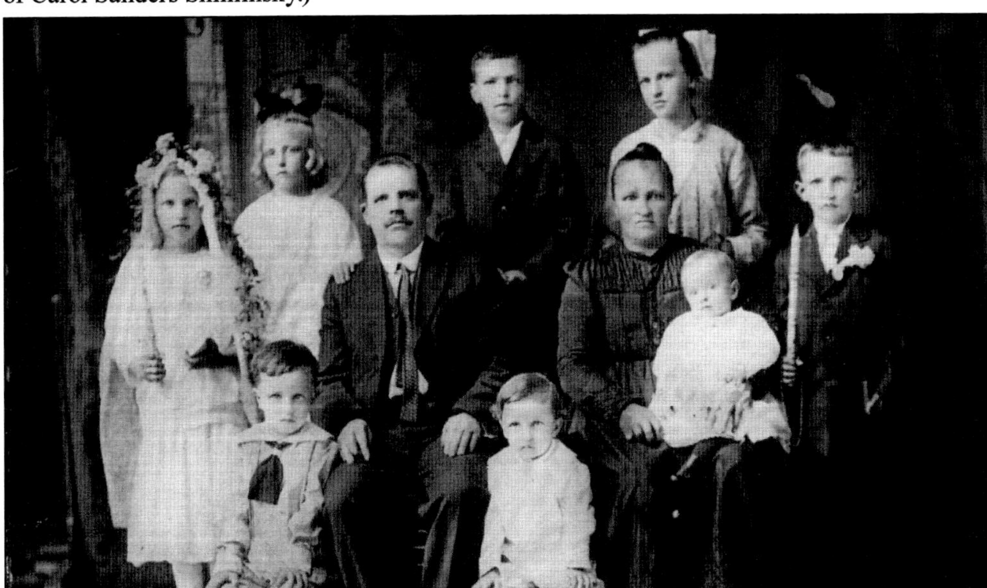

Frank Janci from Štvartek, Slovakia, worked as a blacksmith from his home on Taft Avenue. He is shown with his wife, Mary (Kubinsky) Janci, who was from Nová Ľubovňa, and eight of their nine children when Anna and John received their first Holy Communion. From left to right are (first row) Anna, Frank Jr., father Frank, Victor, mother Mary with Stephen on her lap, and John; (second row) Mary, Michael, and Veronica. Helen was not born yet. (Courtesy of Lucille Martinko Kramer.)

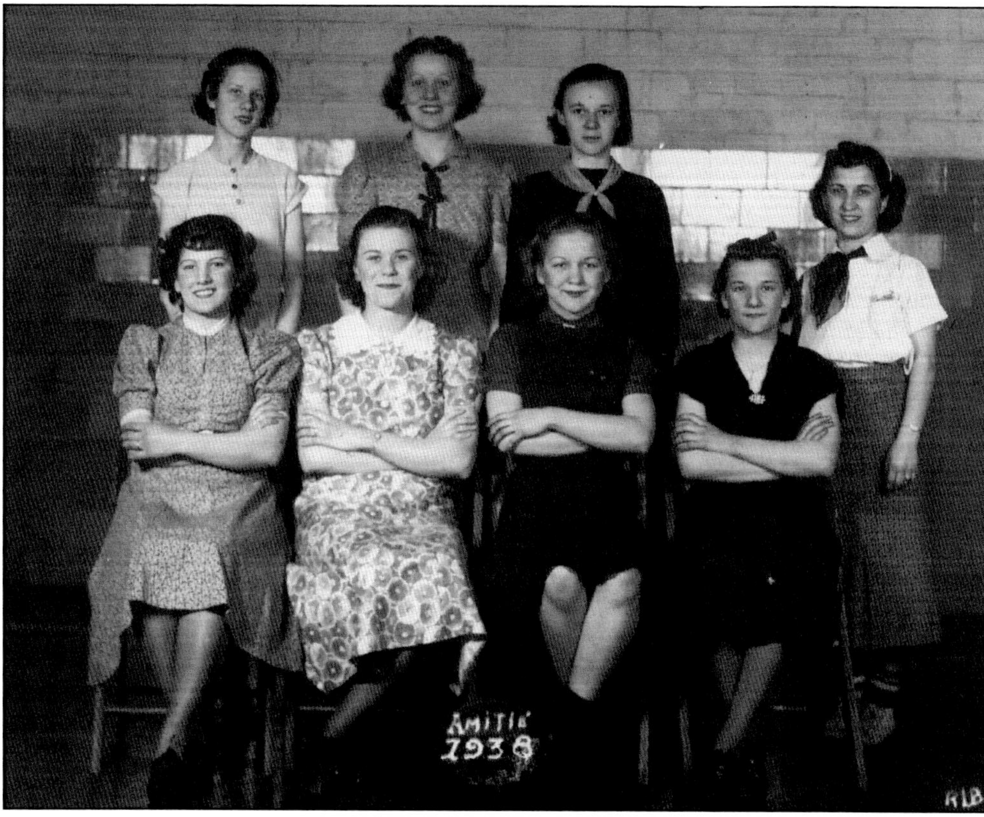

Close school friendships provided another type of family for many young people. The Campbell Memorial High Class of 1938 Amitié ("Friendship") Club is shown. From left to right are (first row), Frances Lepischak, Margie Baker, Katherine Kacenga, and Mary Megela; (second row) Martha Blasko, Evelyn Kubick, Margie Banjo, and Nancy Fitori. (Courtesy of Loretta Hanuschak Ekoniak.)

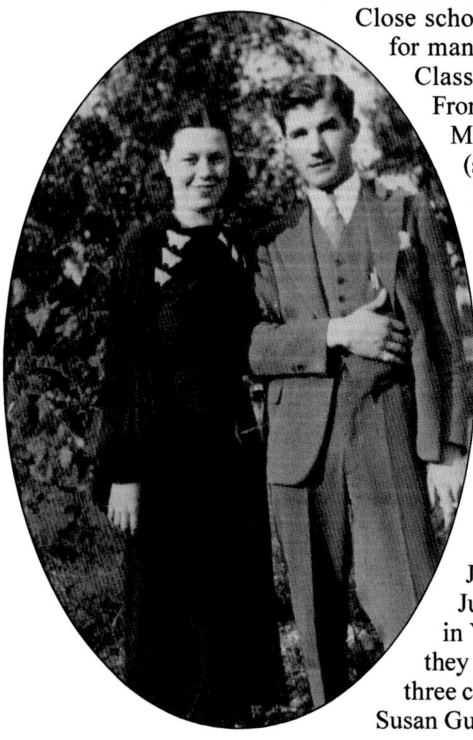

Joseph Gubany and Helen Gurella were married on June 19, 1936, at SS. Cyril and Methodius Church in Youngstown, Ohio. For most of their married life, they lived in Campbell, Ohio, where they raised their three children: Patricia, Donald, and Susan. (Courtesy of Susan Gubany Summers.)

Emigrating from Domaňovce, Zemplin, George Gurella came to America and settled in Struthers, Ohio. He married Mary Tomko at Holy Trinity Church on November 17, 1915. Officiating at the ceremony was Rev. Joseph Zalibera, with witnesses Michael Shafko and Maria Fangula. (Courtesy of Susan Gubany Summers.)

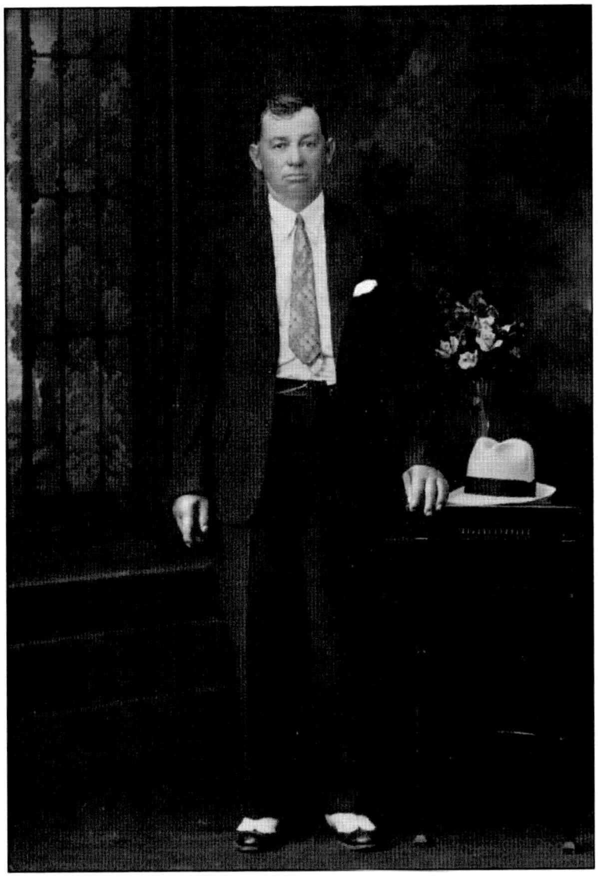

Michael and Mary (Billen) Kessel are shown with daughters Elizabeth (standing on chair) and Mary; Michael was born in Veľky Ruskov and came to America in the 1890s. Mary was born in Pennsylvania. They were married in 1902 at St. Mary's Greek Catholic Church in Youngstown. Daughter Mary was born in Slovakia while Michael and Mary were visiting their parents after their marriage. Their other children, Michael and Anna, had not yet been born when this picture was taken. (Courtesy of Marilyn Bross Mickholtzick.)

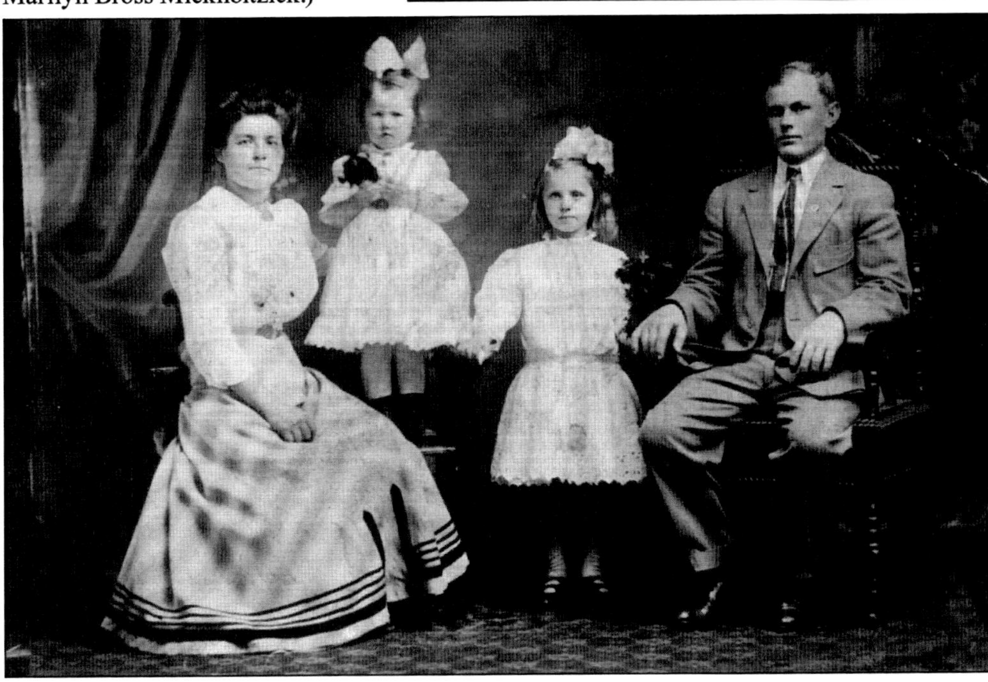

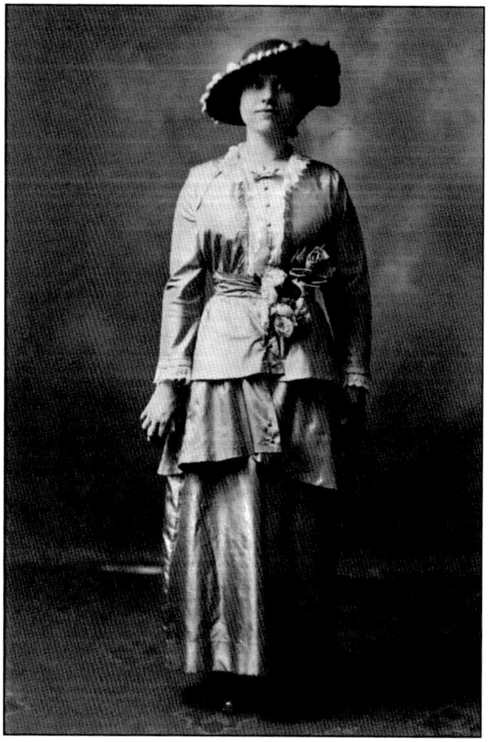

Four members of the Dudaš family from Žalobin, Zemplinská zupa, immigrated to the Mahoning Valley in the early 20th century: Pavla, Anny (Stanovčak), Terézia Dudaš (Horni), and Heleny Dudaš (Račok). Pictured shortly after her arrival is Terézia at age 15. On January 12, 1914, she and Ján Horni, who immigrated to the valley from Jasenovce, Zemplin, were married at SS. Cyril and Methodius Church. (Courtesy of Msgr. Peter Polando.)

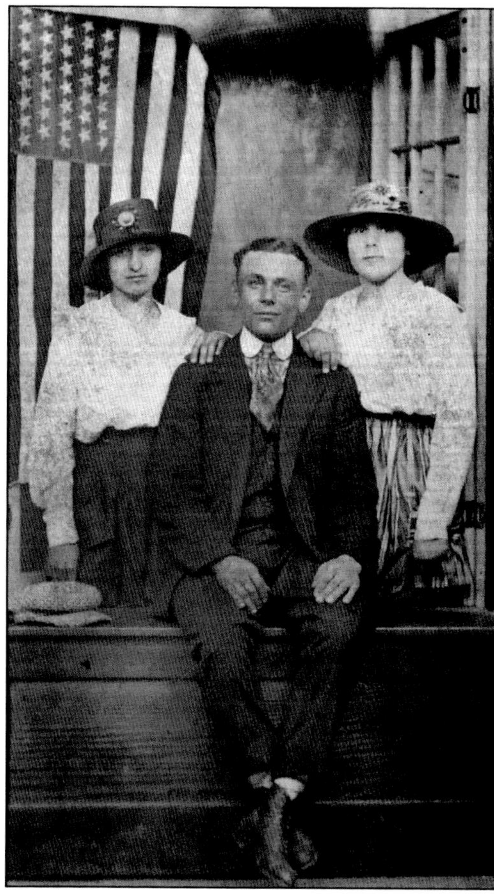

Michael Baker (Pekar) came to the United States in June 1912 at age 16. He first went to Minnesota where his brother Joseph lived, but he eventually settled in Campbell, Ohio, where he worked as a millwright at Youngstown Sheet and Tube. He received his citizenship papers on June 26, 1925, in Mahoning County. (Courtesy of Loretta Hanuscak Ekoniak.)

Mary Helen Maceyko was the oldest of 10 children born to John Maceyko from Jamník, Spišská zupa, Slovakia, and Mary Filakowsky from Braddock, Pennsylvania. They lived in Campbell, Ohio, on Picadilly Street. When she was 14, Mary Helen started working as a domestic for the Skinner family, who lived on the North Side. They encouraged her to go to Kent State University, where she received her teaching degree in 1937. (Courtesy of Barbara Furin Sloat.)

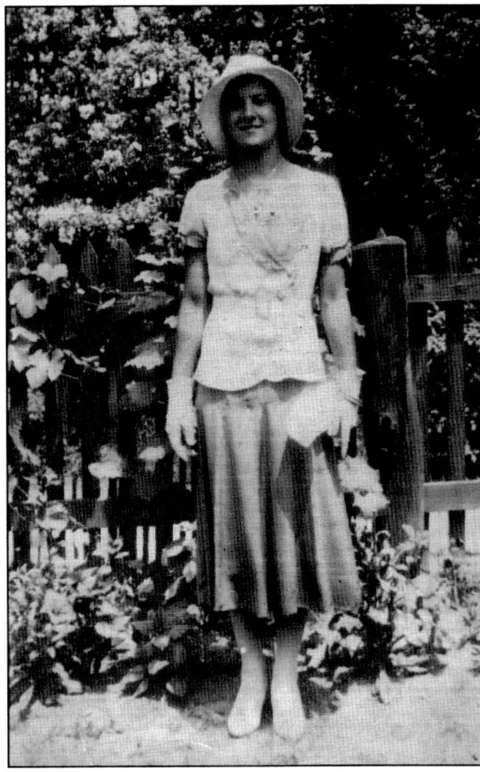

John and Mary Pastier immigrated to America around 1900. They first settled in western Pennsylvania, where John had relatives, but soon moved to Salem, Ohio, where John was employed as a foundry worker. The Pastier family is shown with their children, from left to right: (first row) Susan, father John, Julia, mother Mary, and Elizabeth; (second row) Mary, John, and Anne. (Courtesy of Janet E. DelBene.)

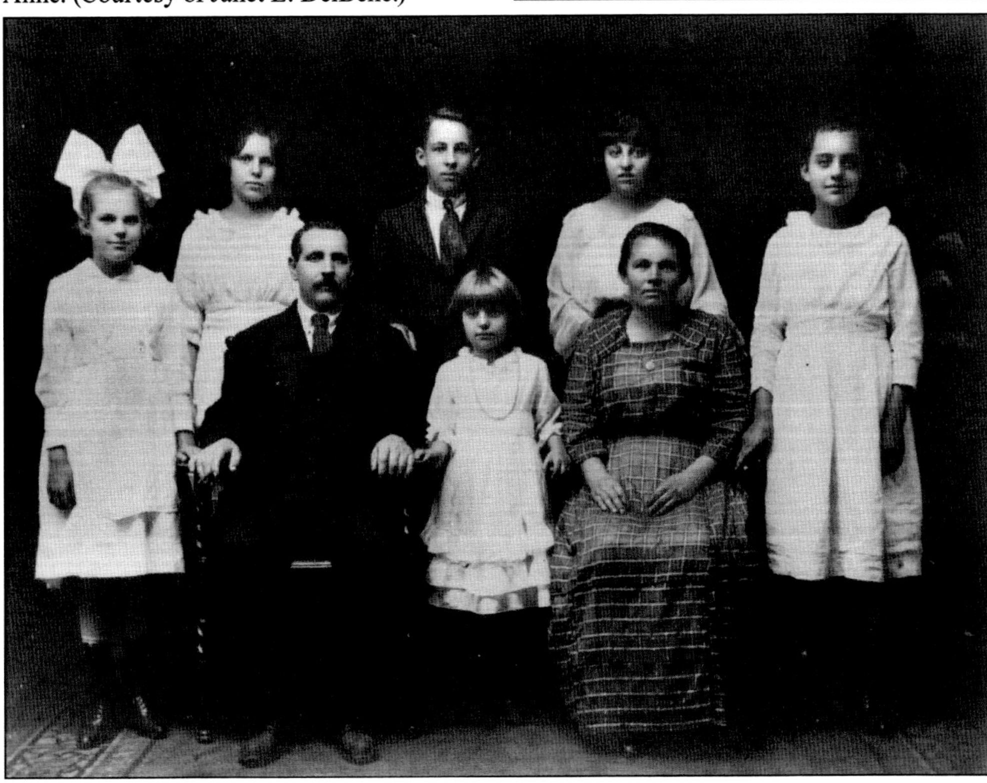

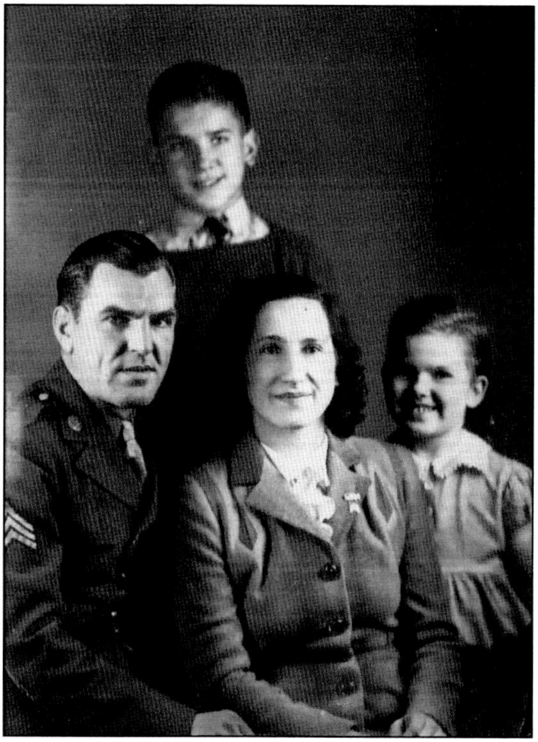

Michael Zupko from Campbell married Ann Ekoniak from Struthers in 1931. He worked as a train engineer for Youngstown Sheet and Tube. When Michael was in the Army, everyone called him Mitchell to avoid confusing him with another Michael Zupko, who outranked him. The Zupkos had two children, Lucille and Frank. Michael's cousin Walter Zupko married Ann's sister Katie. (Courtesy of Michael R. Ekoniak Jr.)

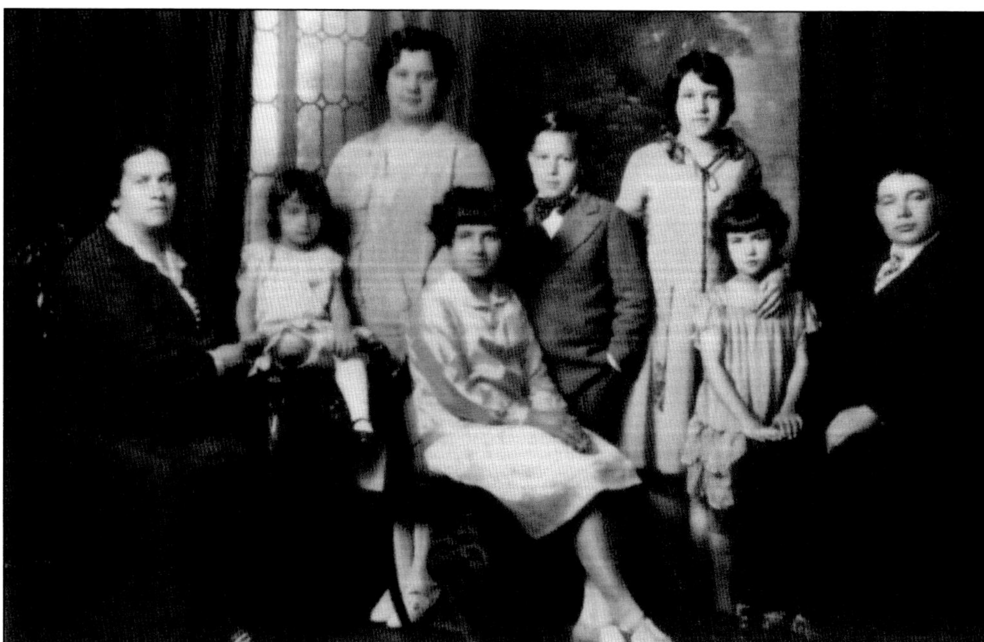

Barbara Zetts and John Judin emigrated from Spišská zupa. They owned and operated Judin's Market at 71 Thirteenth Street in Campbell, Ohio. John was also a founding member of St. John the Baptist Slovak Church in Campbell, Ohio. The family members are, from left to right, (first row) Barbara (Zetts) Judin, Dorothy (on table), Betty (sitting), Marie (standing next to her father), and John Judin; (second row) Ann, Stephen, and Helen. (Courtesy of Charlotte Judin Davolio.)

In 1906, Andrew Jurica (Yurick) and Anna Liptak were married in Reading, Pennsylvania. They moved to the Youngstown area of Hazelton and then to Lansingville. They came from Šariš zupa; Andrew was from Pekľani, and Anna was from Jakubovany. They had seven children: Ann, Victoria, Mary Lou, Helen, Joseph, Margaret, and Edward. (Courtesy of Eileen Bacha.)

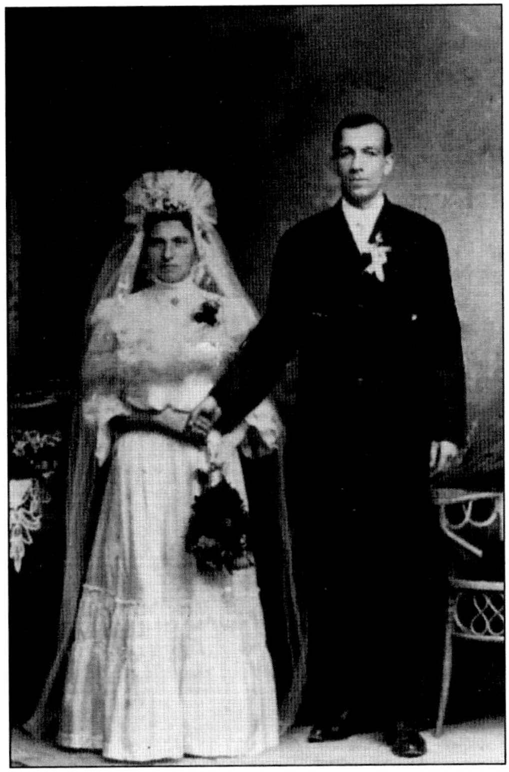

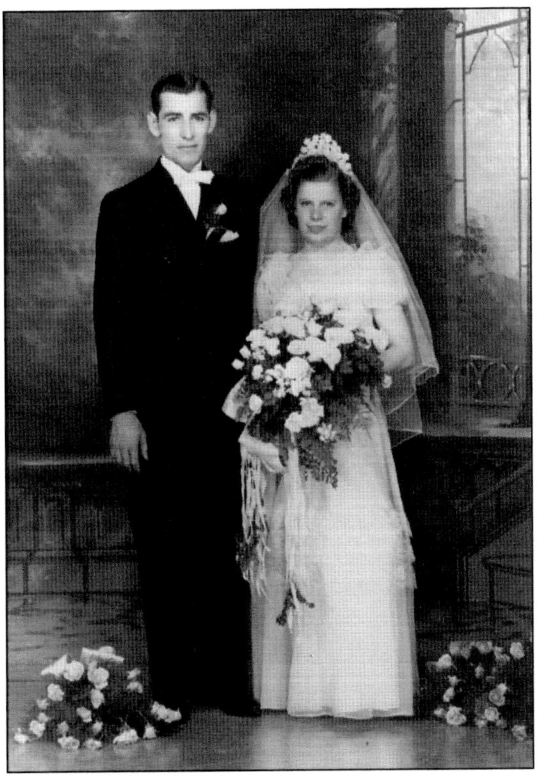

On August 15, 1940, Andrew and Margaret (Swantek) Leschinsky were married in Campbell, Ohio, at St. John the Baptist Slovak Church. Shortly after their marriage, Andrew left his new bride and entered the US Marine Corps. He fought in the Battle of Iwo Jima and was there when they raised the US flag on top of Mount Suribachi. When he returned to civilian life, he and Margaret raised a family of seven children: Marjorie, Carol, Thomas, George, Dorothy, John, and Mary. (Courtesy of Carol Leschinsky Misik.)

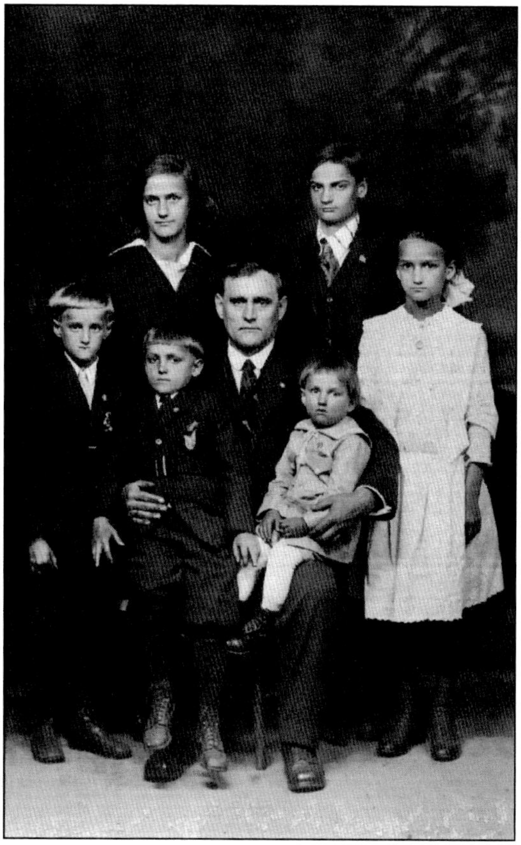

John Palguta and his wife, Mary Kramer, came looking for a better life in the United States. They settled first in Pennsylvania and then came to Youngstown, Ohio, where John worked in the steel mills and Mary worked as a housemaid. Mary died, leaving John to raise their six children. From left to right are (first row) Edward, Emil, father John, Joseph, and Ethel; (second row) Catherine and Frank. (Courtesy of Dorothy Palguta Tesner.)

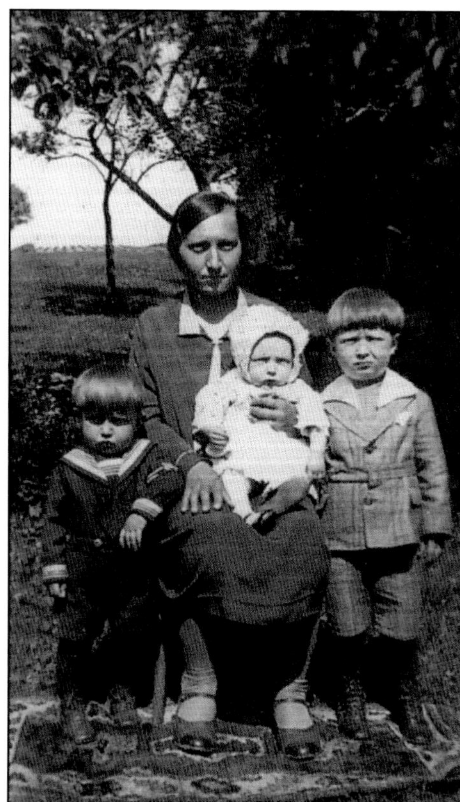

This photograph was taken in 1930 in Strâže, now Slovakia. Anna Bartos returned to Strâže while pregnant with her son Andrew to help her parents. She remained for eight years before returning to the United States to rejoin her husband, Andrej Michal Bartos. Pictured from left to right are John, Andrew, and Joseph Bartos with Anna. (Courtesy of Andrew Bartos.)

Andrew Holecko was from Markušovce, Slovakia, and came to Youngstown in 1904. Anna Hlavchak was from Spišský Štiavnik, Slovakia, and came to Youngstown in 1905. They were married at SS. Cyril and Methodius Church in 1907. Andrew was a rigger at Youngstown Sheet and Tube, and they were charter members of St. Matthias Church. Shown with children John (on Anna's lap) and Catherine, they had four other children not pictured here: Andrew, Thomas, Helen, and Joseph. (Courtesy of Joseph Sedzmak.)

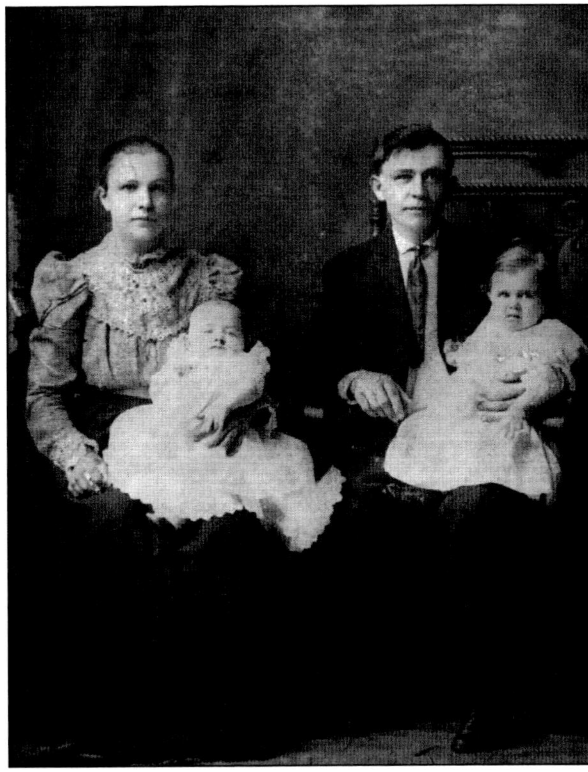

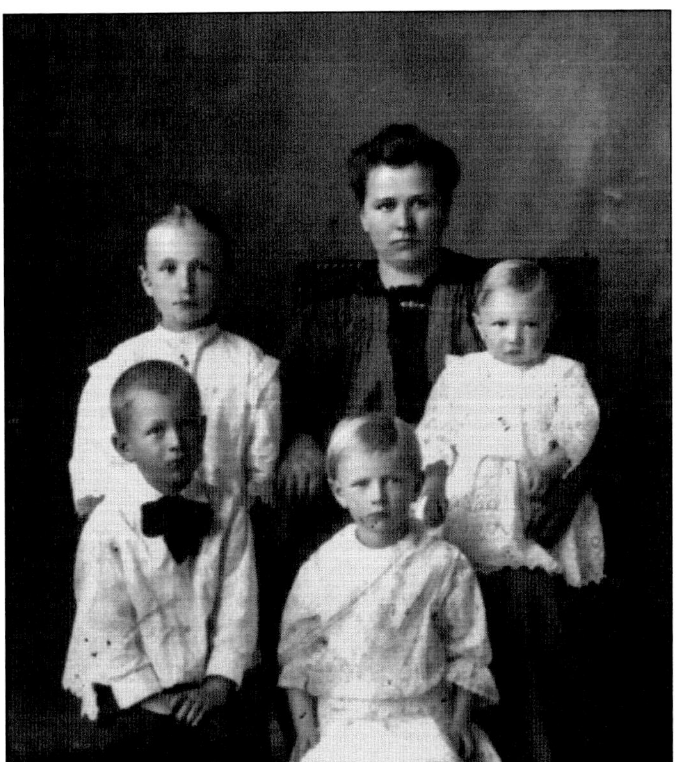

John and Anna Gbur arrived from Hervartov, Šariš, in 1905. They had a farm in New Middletown, Ohio, where they raised their family. Anna Gbur is shown with their four children, who are, from left to right, Mary (standing), George, Annie, and Helen. (Courtesy of Ilene Minhinnett Miller.)

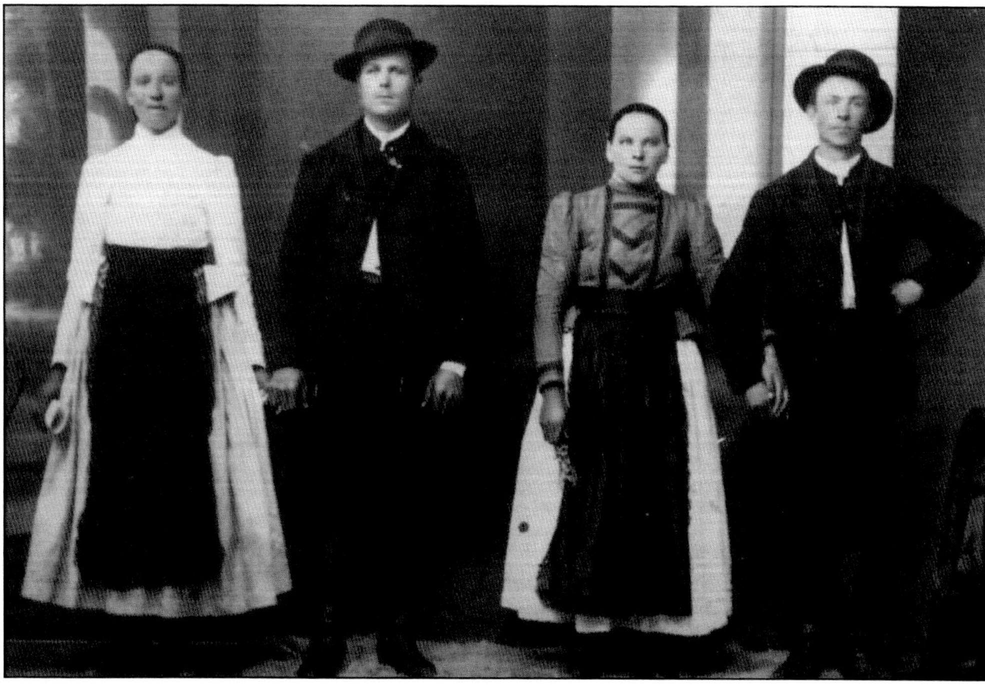

On the left, Johanna Duncko Petrek and husband John came from Letanovce, Spiš, to Hubbard, Ohio, in 1926. On the right are Johanna's brother Joseph Duncko and his wife, Anna Kubalec Duncko. Joseph and Anna had four children: Joseph (born before they immigrated), Anna and Steve (born in the United States), and Millie (born in Slovakia, where Anna had returned during the Great Depression). Anna returned to America in 1936. (Courtesy of Steven Duncko.)

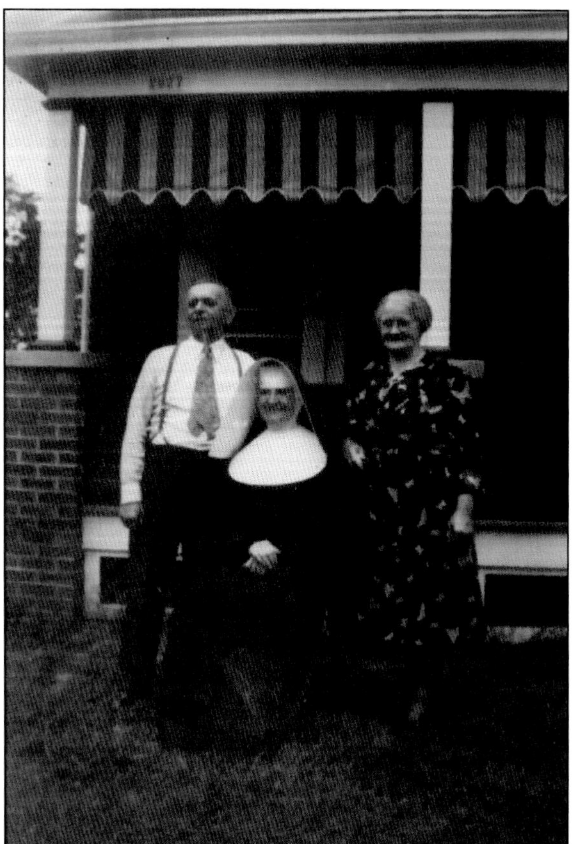

Stephen and Veronica Horvat are shown in their front yard in Lansingville with their daughter Sr. Mary Hermina, VSC, a Vincentian sister who was a teacher at St. Matthias School. Slovak families felt great pride when one of their sons or daughters dedicated his or her life to God's work. (Courtesy of Jack Vasko.)

Joseph Almasi, pictured on the right, came to the United States from Spišská zupa in the early 1880s. J. Jancisin is on the left. When Joseph was able to bring his wife, Anna Uhrin Almasi, and his young family to join him, they settled in the Coitsville Township area. Joseph was one of the first Slovak emigrants to come to the Youngstown area. (Courtesy of John Almasy.)

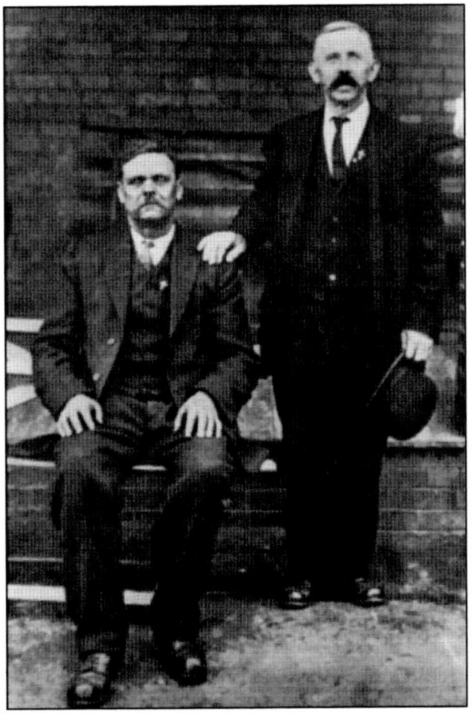

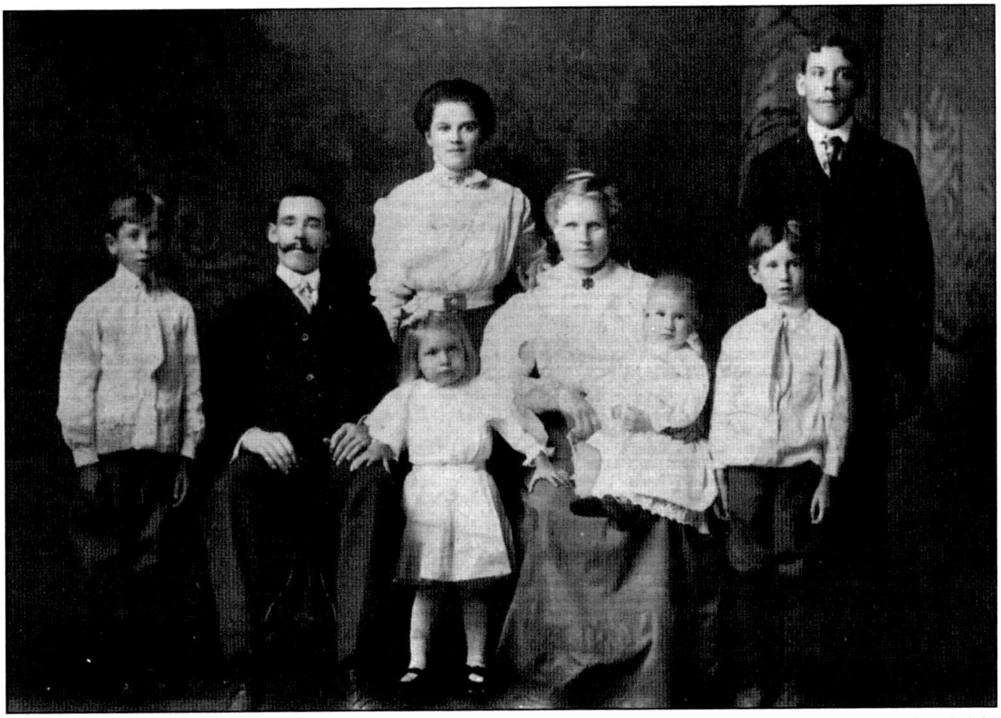

Anna Gall Zelinsky and her husband, Matthew Zelinsky, are shown standing in the back of this photograph of the family of Matthew's brother. Matthew Zelinsky was born in Červenica pri Sabinove near the town of Pečovská Nová Ves, and Anna Gall was born in Ražňany. (Courtesy of Barbara Macalla Jennings.)

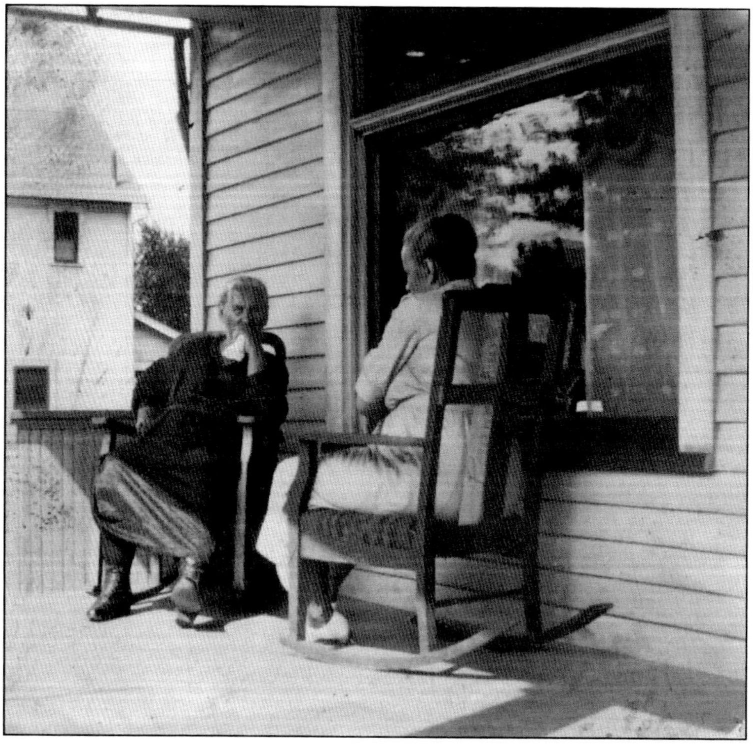

Anna Backus (left) and Susannah Korchnak are seated on the front porch. In the little spare time that a Slovak woman had, sitting on the porch and exchanging news with her friends was a welcome break. Outside of the kitchen, the porch was probably the center of the neighborhood social scene. (Courtesy of Mary Jane Backus.)

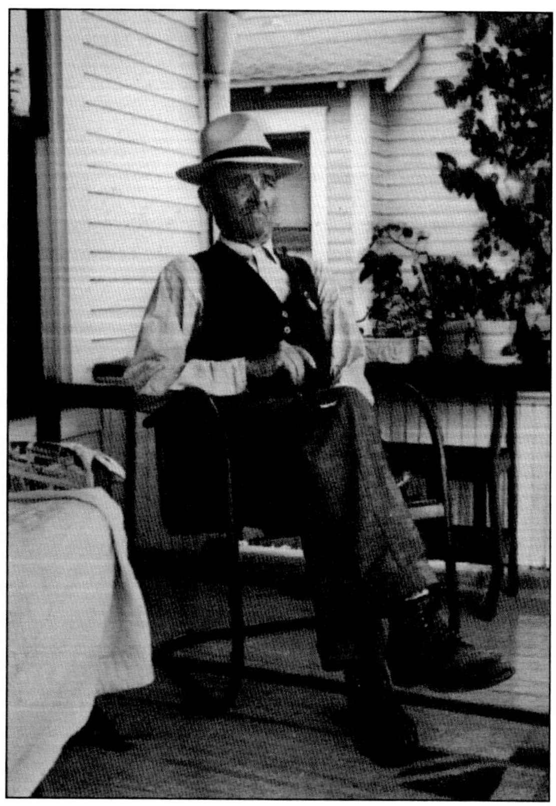

Just passing the time of day, Nicholas George Lucas—or "Grandpa Lucas," as he was called by the Repasky children—is sitting on the front porch of his Katherine Street home in the Nebo (meaning "heaven") neighborhood of Struthers, Ohio. (Courtesy of Janet Repasky Morris.)

Before television, it was a common practice for families to gather on the weekend for visits. Helen Gubany appears with her children, who are, from left to right, Patricia Gubany (Felger), Susan Gubany (Summers), and Donald Gubany. (Courtesy of Susan Gubany Summers.)

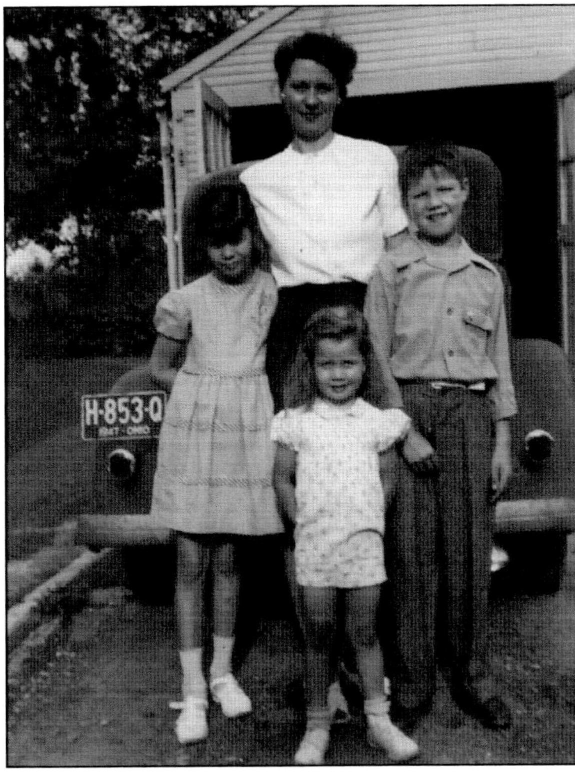

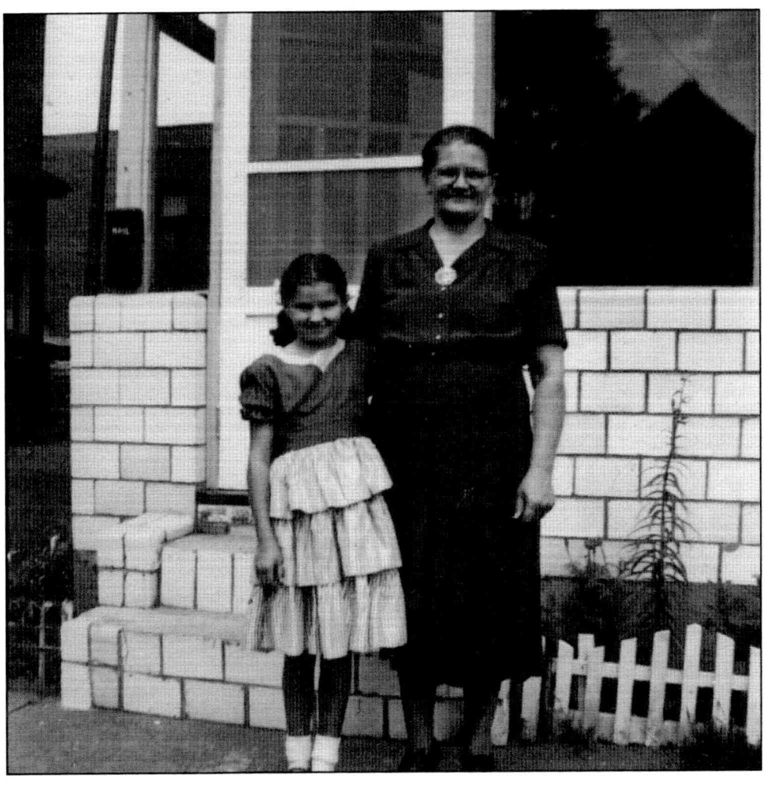

Carol Fecko and her mother, Anna Komara Fecko, are standing in front of their house on Myrtle Avenue. In 1926, Anna and her husband, Stephen, came to Leetonia, Ohio, from Brutovce and Spišské Vlachy. Their first four children—John, Steve, Mary, and Annie—were born in Slovakia, and the last four—Betty, Dorothy, Eleanor, and Carol—were born in the United States. (Courtesy of Carol Fecko.)

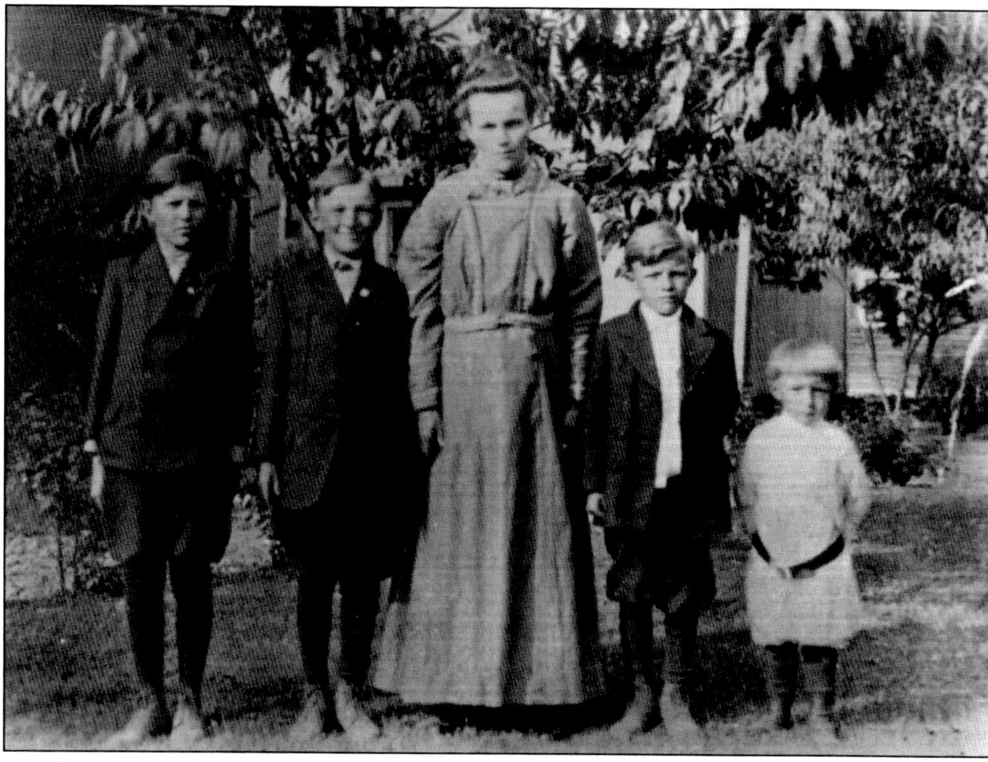

Joseph Bacha (Bacsga) came to the United States in 1890 from Hrabušice, and Mary Cerviniak came in 1902. They were married in Sharon, Pennsylvania, living in Farrell before coming to the Steelton area of Youngstown, Ohio. In this picture from July 1914 are, from left to right, Joseph, John, Mary, Andrew, and Albert. Mary is pregnant with their fifth son, Michael. Her husband died in October, two months before Michael was born. (Courtesy of Eileen Bacha.)

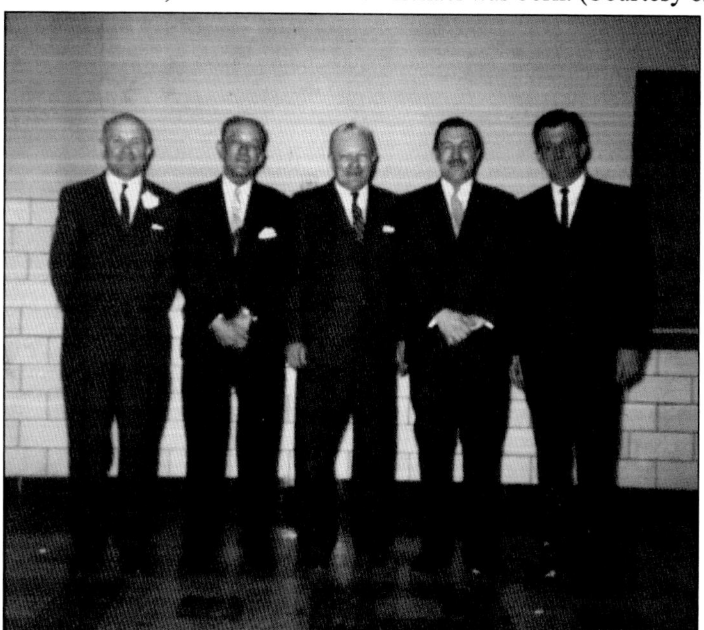

The five Bacha brothers were brought up by their widowed mother, who supported them by cleaning houses and working at a rest home. The boys became successful businessmen, starting Bacha Brothers, a coal delivery and general hauling business. From left to right are Joseph, John, Andrew, Albert, and Michael. (Courtesy of Eileen Bacha.)

The sons, daughters, brothers, and sisters of John and Ann Mijavec gathered together in 1939. Pictured from left to right are, Margaret (in polka dot dress), John, George, Helen (with corsage), Anna (Lillian Bigley Johnson's mother), and Alex. (Courtesy of Lillian Bigley Johnson.)

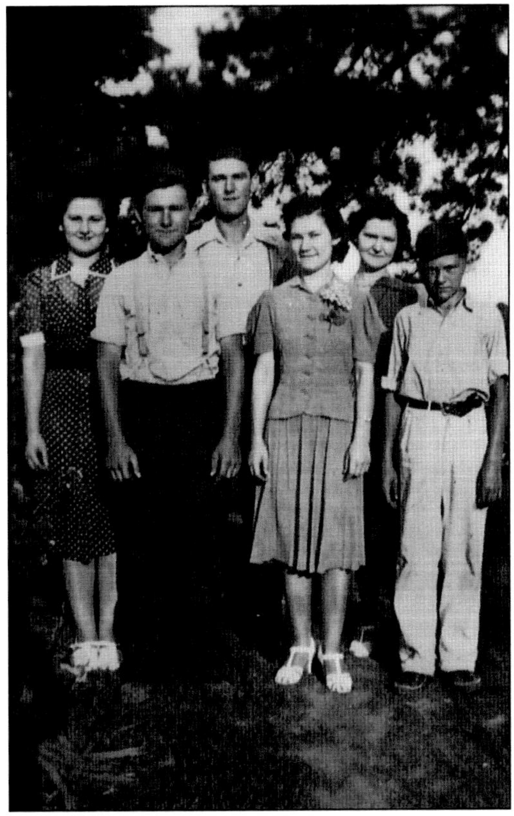

John Novotny from Koterbachy, Slovakia (now known as Rudnany), married Mary Kalafut from Olšov in January 1899 in Markušovce. He came to America in 1900. After Mary joined him, he worked as a coal miner in Pennsylvania before moving to Youngstown, Ohio, where he had a grocery store in Lansingville. From left to right are Angeline Mary, Mildred, John Jr., mother Mary, Justine "Jay," John Sr., Joseph, Agnes, and Michael. (Courtesy of Michael R. Ekoniak Jr.)

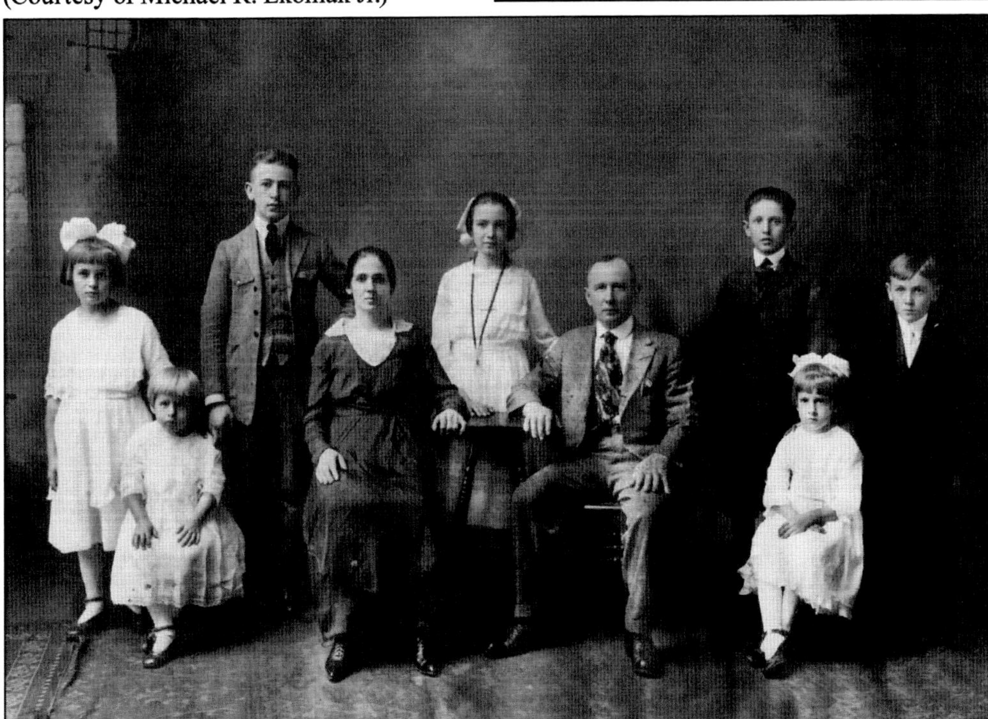

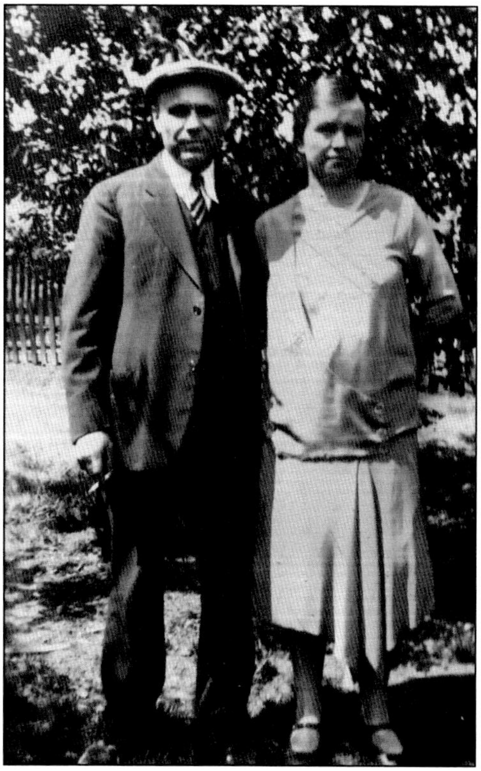

In 1918 while in Hazelton, Pennsylvania, Michael (Pekar) Baker from Kelča Zemplin married Anna Dill from Stockton, Pennsylvania. Her parents were from Kelča. They lived in Campbell, Ohio, on Morley Avenue. Michael worked in Minnesota on a farm and sawmill and in North Dakota as a logger before moving to Campbell, where he worked in the Youngstown Sheet and Tube mill. They had six children: Margaret, Helen, Ethel, Eleanor, Joseph, and Raymond. (Courtesy of Loretta Hanuschak Ekoniak.)

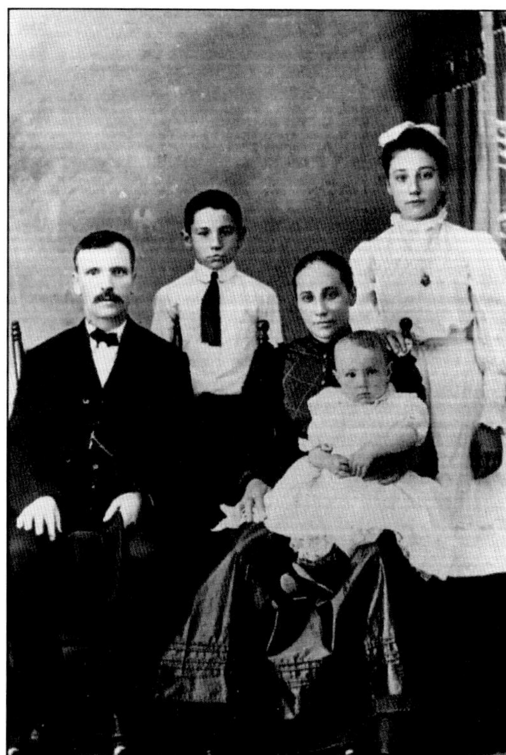

John Martinko came with his parents to the United States from Štiavnik, Spiš, in 1904. Pictured here with his family are, from left to right, John Sr., John Jr., wife Mary Janci holding Stephen, and Mary. (Courtesy of Lucille Martinko Kramer.)

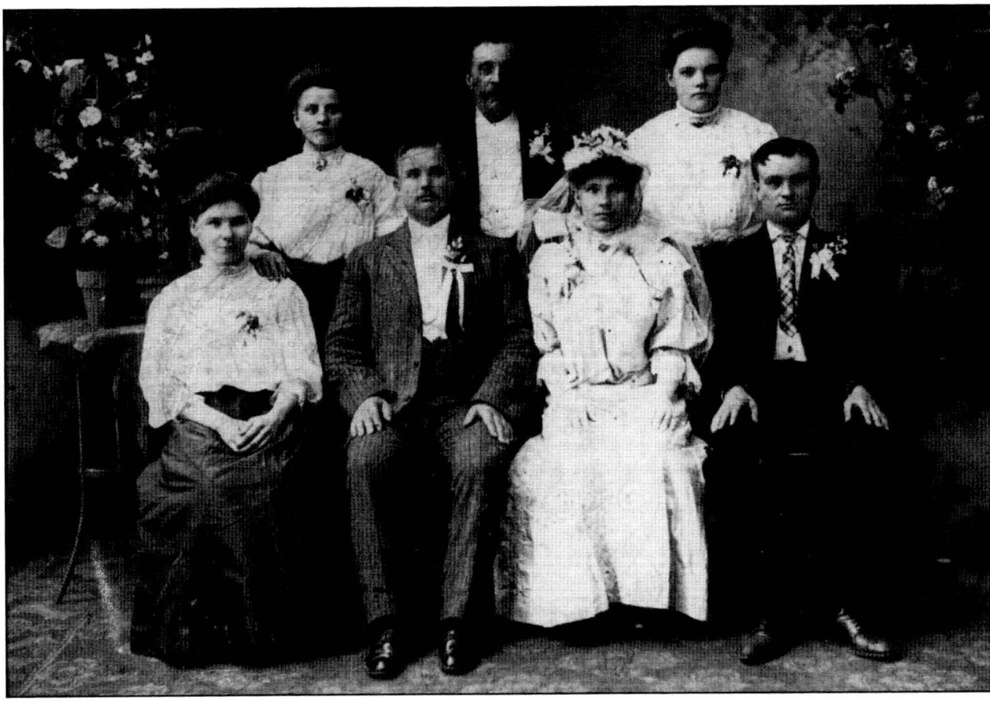

Michael Butsko (the groom) came from Toriska, Spiš, in 1906. His bride, Catherine Cherpak from Nižné Repaše, and he were married in 1907 in Pittsburgh, Pennsylvania. Michael worked at the US Steel blast furnaces in New Castle, Pennsylvania, and in Warren, Leetonia, and Lowellville, Ohio. He and Catherine were married for 52 years and had four daughters: Anna, Catherine, Elizabeth, and Eileen. (Courtesy of Eileen Pepperney.)

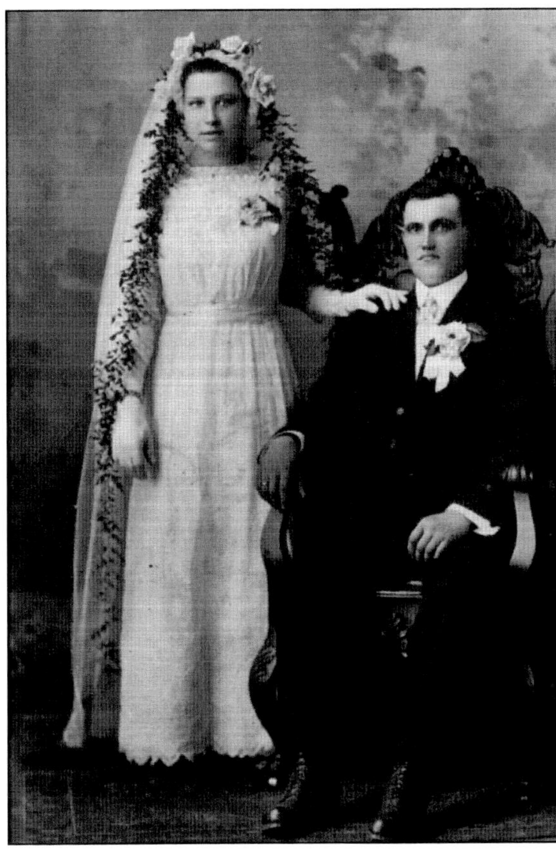

Andrew Tomaskovic came from Letanovce, Spiš, to the United States as an indentured railroad worker; he later worked as a coal miner and then at the US Steel Ohio Works. He was married at SS. Cyril and Methodius Church in June 1913. He and his wife, Mary, made their home and raised 10 children on Ridgeview Avenue in the Steelton neighborhood of Youngstown. (Courtesy of Robert Tomaskovich.)

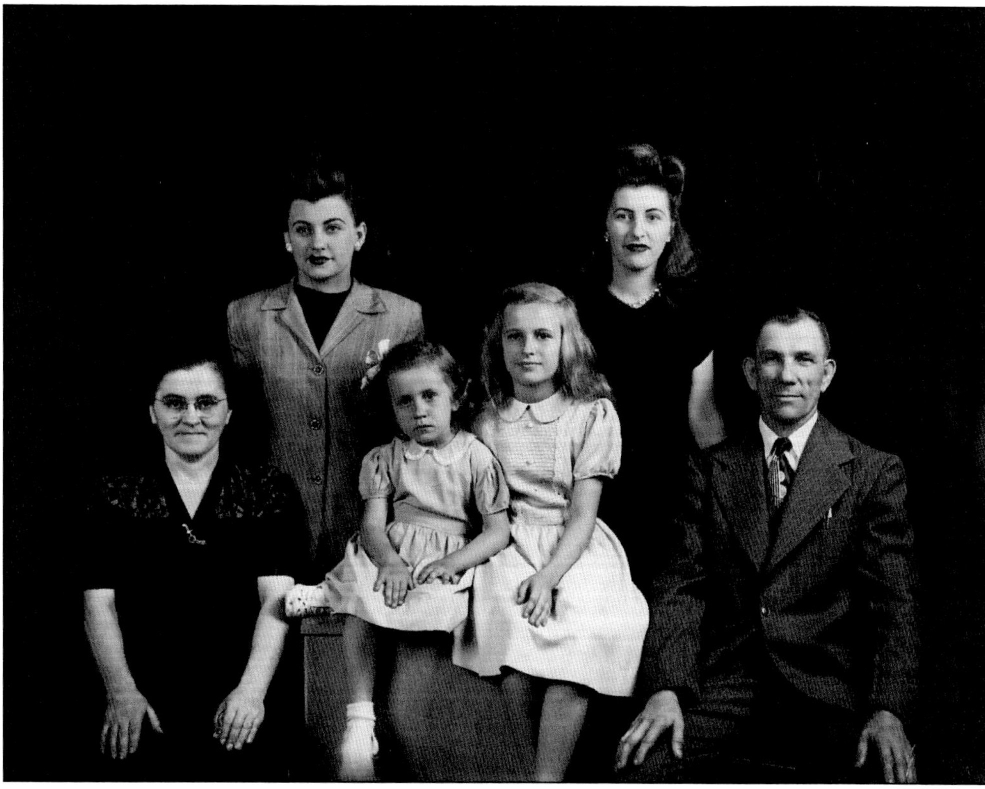

Michael Dzurnak came from Danišovce, Spiš, in 1924 and married Veronica Kicos in 1926. He was a crane operator for 40 years with Youngstown Sheet and Tube. Pictured in 1947 are, from left to right, Veronica; daughters Veronica, Agnes, Mary, and Helen; and Michael. (Courtesy of Joseph Bachani.)

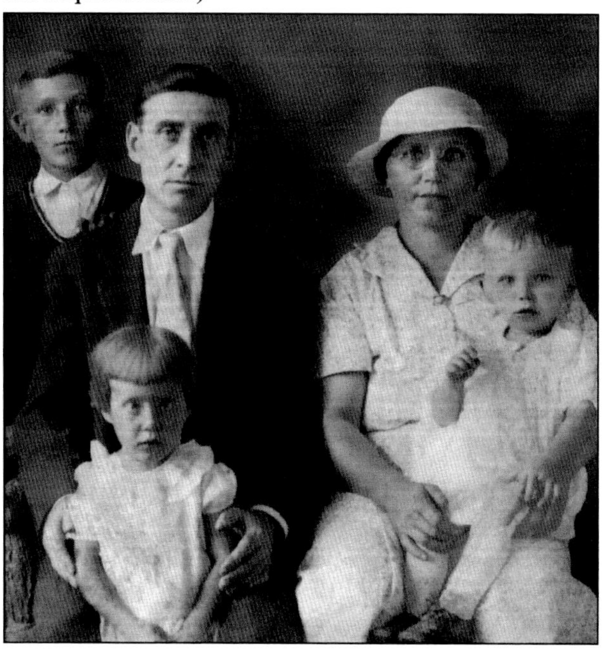

Stefan Bator married Kristina Anna Halko, who was born in 1898 in the United States but returned to Slovakia with her mother as a child. After his marriage, Stefan immigrated to the United States and worked as a coal miner in Whitney, Pennsylvania, and then at US Steel in Youngstown. Kristina joined him in 1927 with their son. Pictured in about 1934 are, from left to right, Stefan Jr., Stefan Sr. holding Anna, and Kristina holding Frank. (Courtesy of Frank Bator.)

Gali and Susanna Biroschak Korchnak came to the United States from Brutovce in Spiš in about 1907. They owned a farm in Poland, Ohio, on the corner of Arrel Road and Youngstown-Pittsburgh Road (known as Smith Corners), where they raised their seven children. (Courtesy of Mary Jane Backus.)

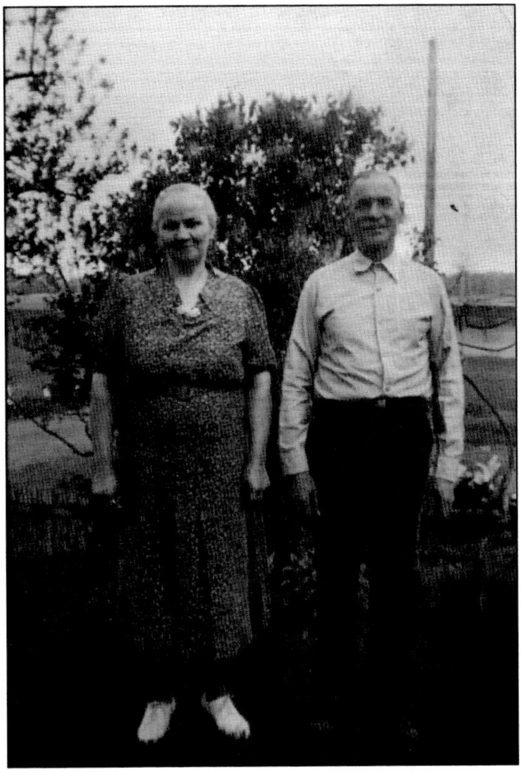

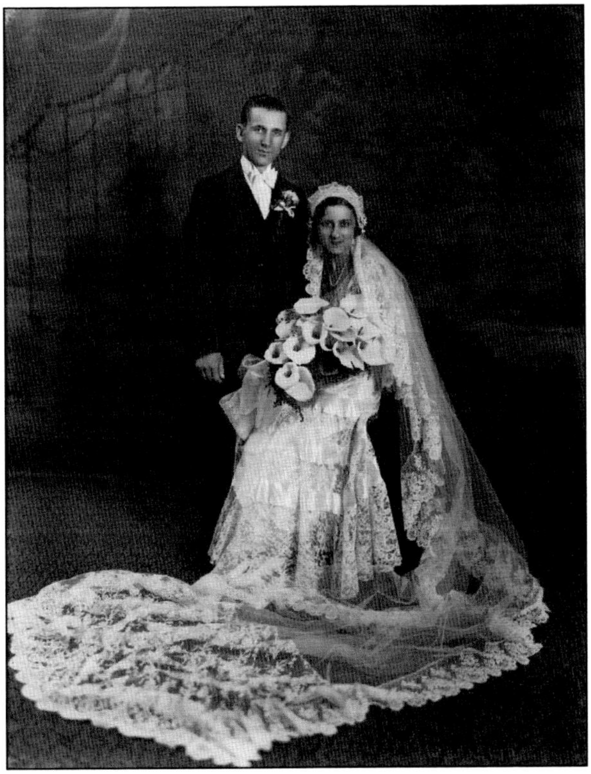

Michael Roman Ekoniak and Agnes Novotny were married in May 1932 at St. Matthias Church in the Lansingville neighborhood of Youngstown. Michael, son of Roman Ikoniak and Anna Ferenčucha, worked as a printer at United Printing in Youngstown. Agnes, daughter of John Novotny and Mary Kalafut, worked at her father's grocery store until she married. They had three children: Eleanore, Marie, and Michael. (Courtesy of Michael R. Ekoniak Jr.)

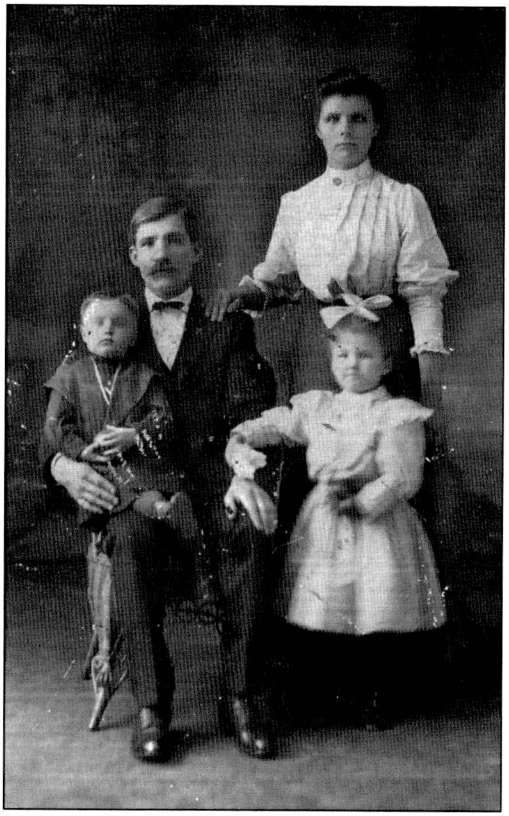

Leaving his home in Zipov, Zemplin, behind, Stefan Gubany headed for Bremen, Germany, where he boarded the passenger ship *Friedrich J. Grosse* on September 20, 1902. After arriving in New York, he traveled to Pittsburgh, Pennsylvania, where he and Anna Jacob, also from Zipov, married and started their family before eventually moving to Youngstown, Ohio. Pictured are, from left to right, Stephen Jr. sitting on the lap of Stephen Sr., daughter Anna and wife Anna. (Courtesy of Susan Gubany Summers.)

John Semyan from Bánovice came to the United States in 1911. Elizabeth Harbula from Trhovište came in 1909. She and John married in 1914 and moved to Youngstown, where John worked at US Steel. They are shown in 1928 on the Fabry farm near Petersburg. From left to right are (first row) Betty, Michael, and George Semyan; (second row) John Semyan, *cetka* ("aunt") Helen Harbula, Elizabeth (Harbula) Semyan, and John Semyan. (Courtesy of Judy Semyan Bayus.)

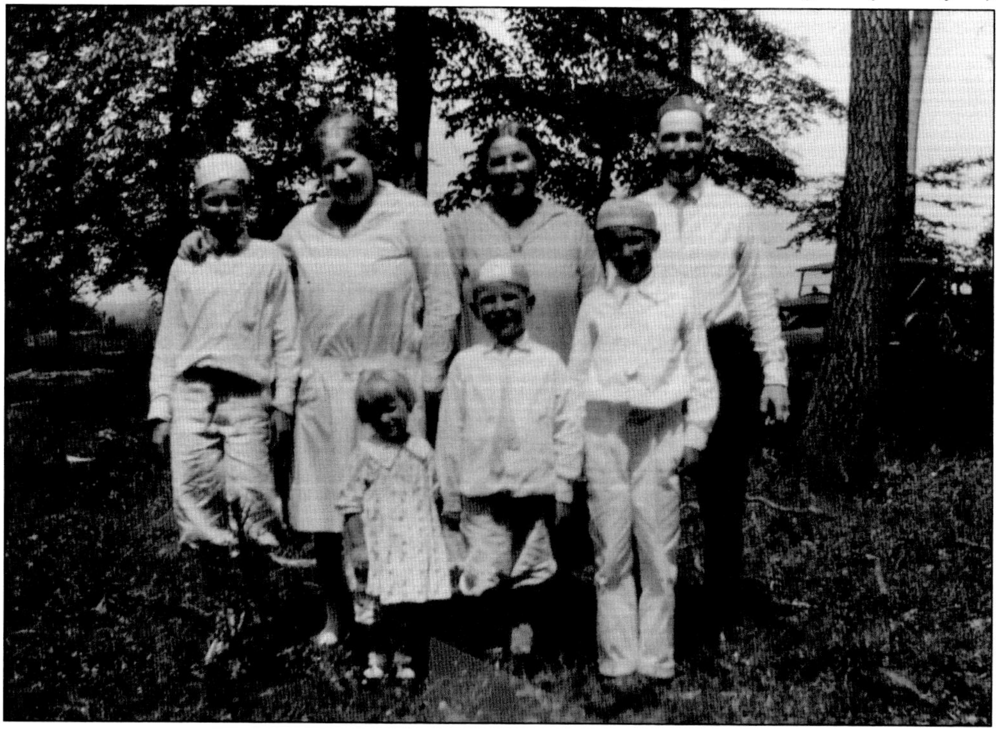

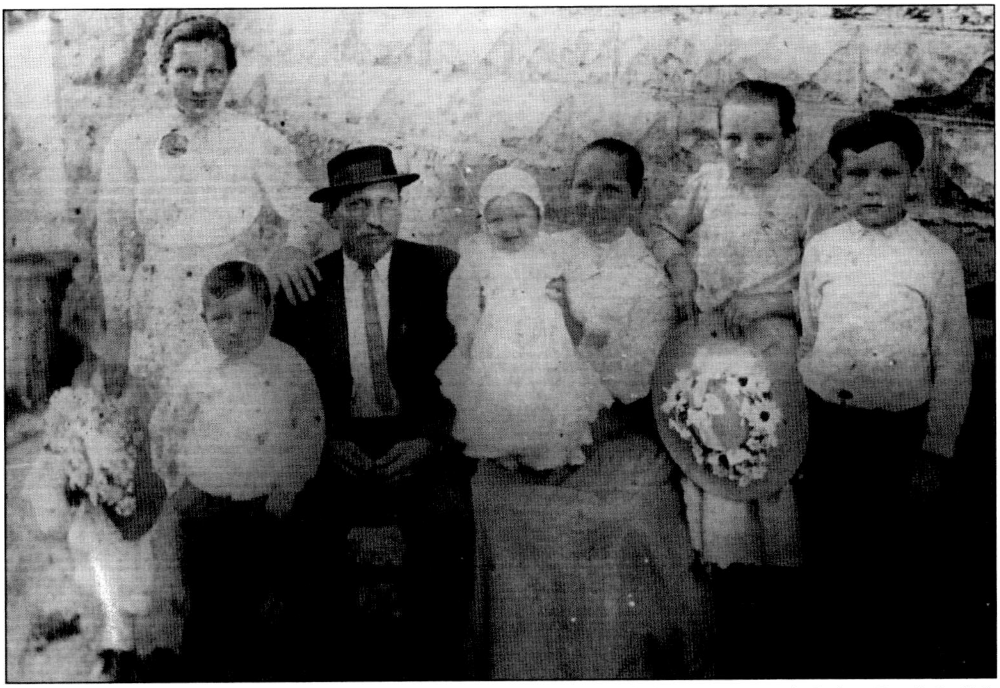

Pictured in about 1910, the Textoris family are, from left to right, Mary, Paul, father Paul, Judith Antolek Textoris holding Anna, Susan, and Andrew. Paul Textoris had a grocery store on Midland and Maryland Avenues on Youngstown's West Side. (Courtesy of Margaret Textoris Tomo.)

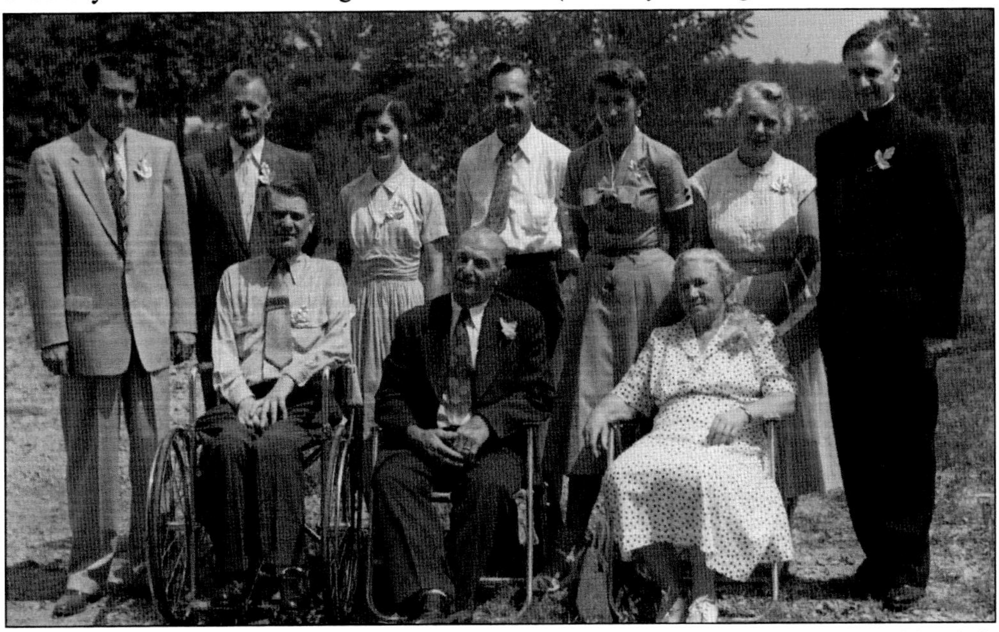

The 50th anniversary of John and Katherine Slanina Novotny saw them surrounded by their eight children. Shown from left to right are (first row) Stephen, John W., and Katherine; (second row) Albert, John, Kathryn, Michael ("Mitchell"), Johanna, Anna, and Father Cyril, OSB. John emigrated from Domaňovec, and Katherine was from Štvrtok in Spiš. (Courtesy of Kathryn Novotny Franko.)

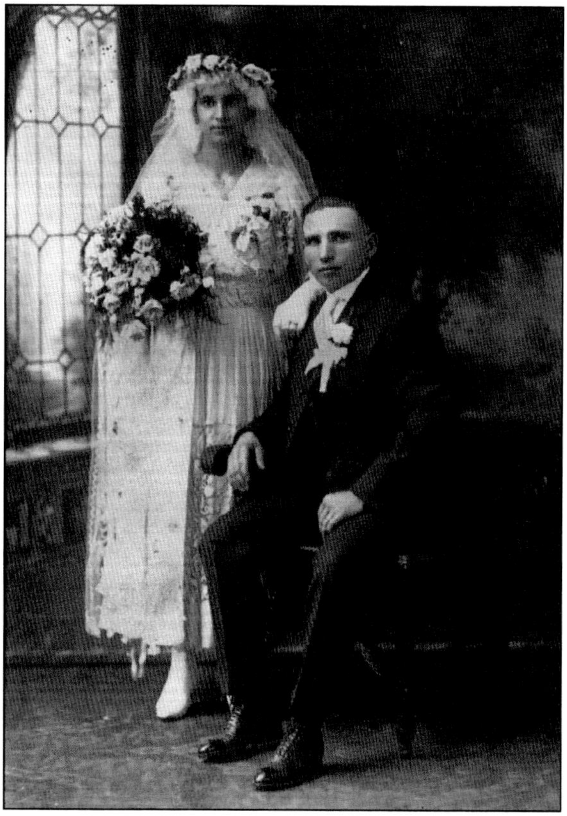

Helen Horvat, who emigrated from Spišská Nová Ves, and John Olenik from Teplička are pictured at their 1917 wedding, which took place at St. Matthias Church in Lansingville. They had three children: Helen, Cecilia, and Johnny. Helen was an organist at St. Matthias Church for many years and taught her son Johnny to play. He played the organ at St. Matthias Church for 32 years. (Courtesy of John Olenik.)

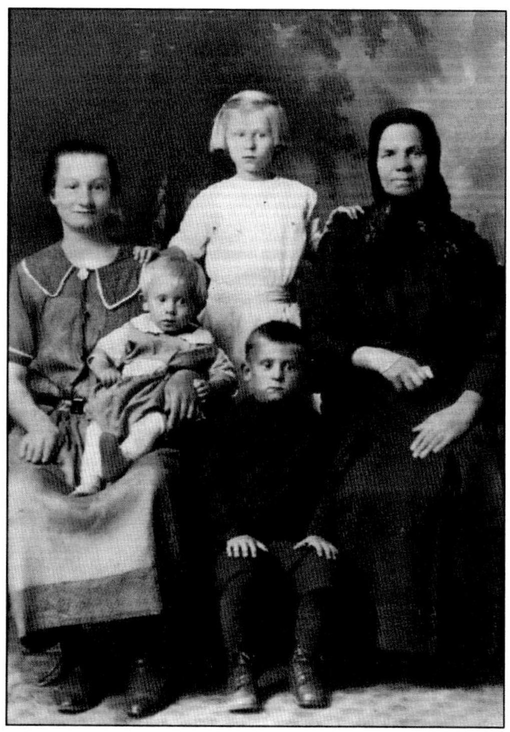

Veronika Hopko, wife of Jakob Stanek, is shown with her mother Anna Catherine Bača Hopko (far right) and her children Joseph (on her lap), Mary, and John in 1925. Veronika, born in Prešov, came to Pittsburgh, Pennsylvania, when she was 18. Jakob was born in Pennsylvania, returned to Slovakia, and came back at age 16. He and Veronika met in Pittsburgh and married in 1917 at St. Matthias Church in Youngstown, Ohio. Their other children were Helen, John (named after his older brother who died in an auto accident at age 6), and Dorothy. (Courtesy of Kurt Lesnansky.)

Andy Krainock and Mary Mikita were married at St. Nicholas Byzantine Church on Wilson Avenue on June 14, 1925. They had three children, Andy Jr. (who was a founder of Masters Tuxedo), Marion (Salopek), and Nancy (Daniels). (Courtesy of Lillian Bigley Johnson.)

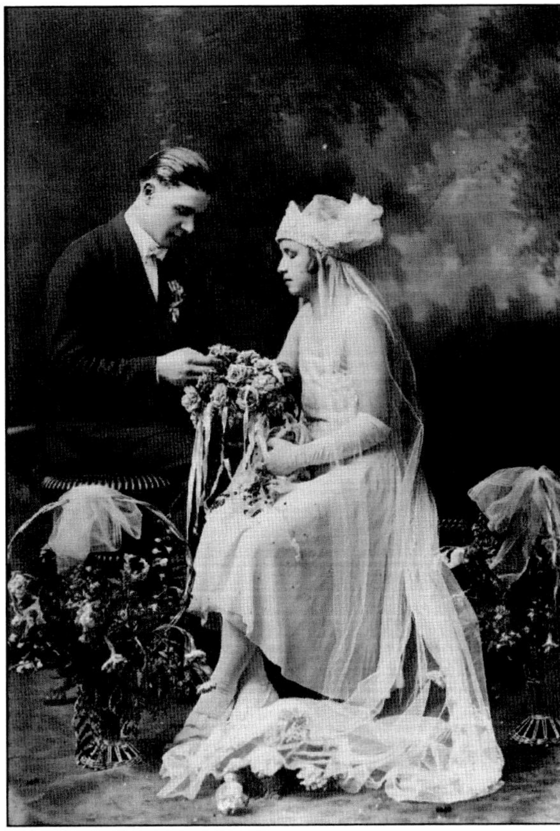

Joseph Horvat (third from left, first row) and Catherine Sova (fourth from left, first row), both from Spišská Nová Ves, were married at SS. Cyril and Methodius Church in Youngstown on October 22, 1907. Joseph Bacha (second from right, first row) was the best man, and Stephanie Skolo (second from left, first row) was the maid of honor. Fr. Joseph Novak officiated at the service. (Courtesy of Joseph J. Rakocy Jr.)

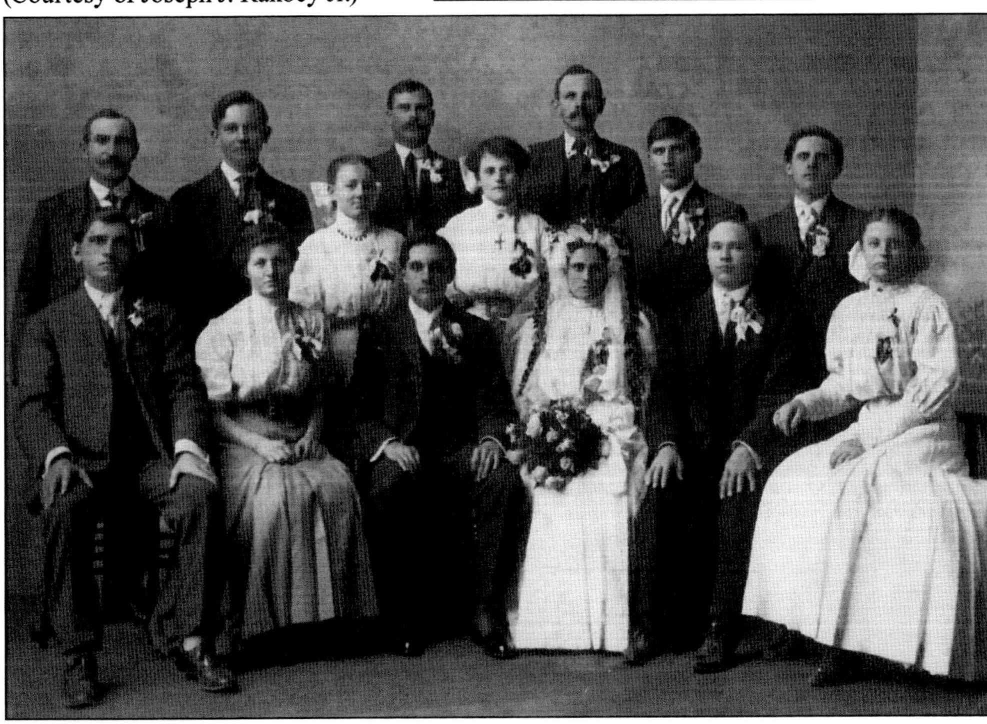

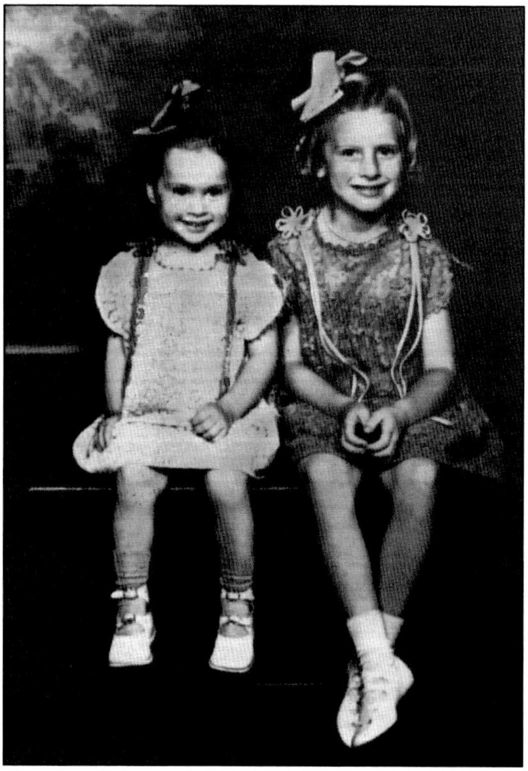

Like all parents, Slovaks were very proud of their children and would often go without to make sure their children did not lack anything. They loved having pictures, even at a time when personal cameras were not at all common. At Strouss Department Store in downtown Youngstown, the photography studio on the mezzanine was a popular place to have pictures taken. Shown here are Marie (left) and Eleanore Ekoniak in the early 1940s. (Courtesy of Loretta Hanuschak Ekoniak.)

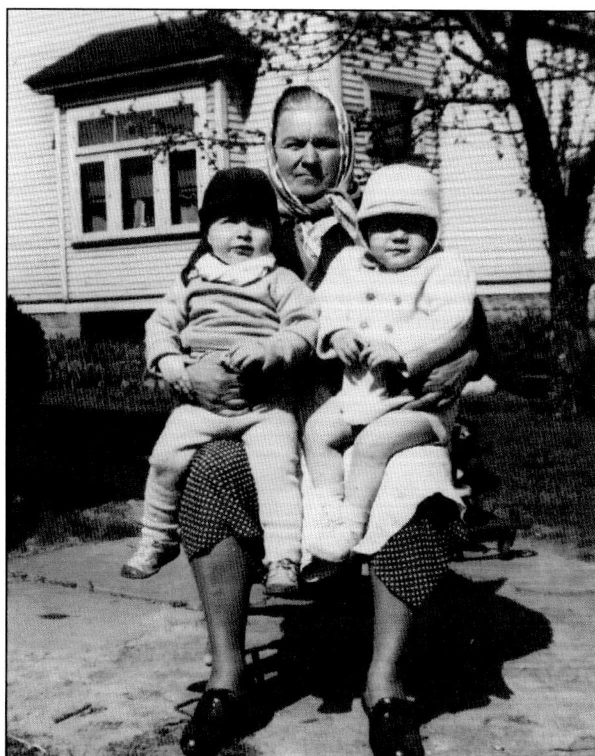

Baba ("grandma") especially loved having her grandchildren around and, just as today, loved to spoil them. Pictured on May 12, 1947, is Baba Anna Popovich with grandsons John Babik (in dark cap) and Joe Stanislaw. (Courtesy of Gene Babik.)

Another very popular event was when the "pony man" came around offering pictures on his pony and even providing the cowboy outfit for the children to wear. Many families have similar pictures in their collections. Here is Michael R. Ekoniak Jr. in about 1949. (Courtesy of Loretta Hanuschak Ekoniak.)

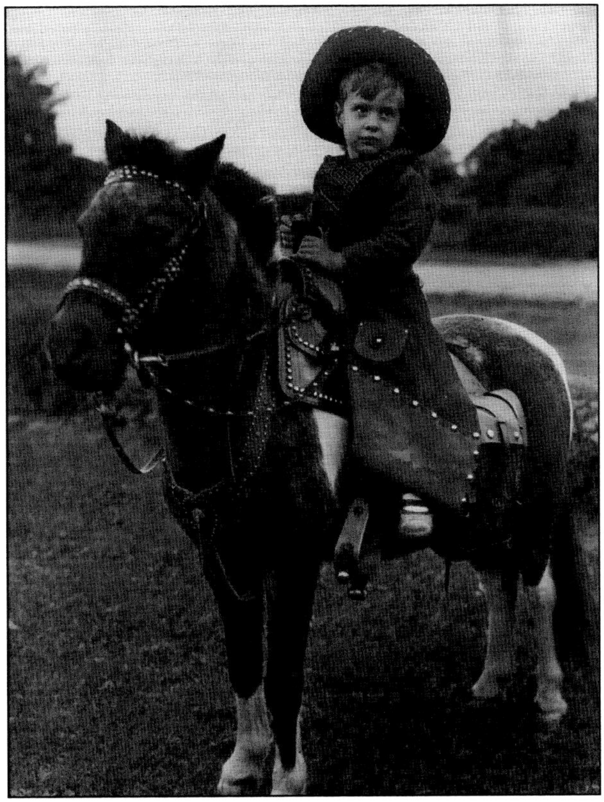

Pictured in their yard in Lansingville, the Smercansky family includes, from left to right, Mary, "Mama" Anna (Dostal), John, Frank, Joseph, "TaTa" John holding Ceil, and Ann. Only Robert is not present. John came from Malý Hnilčík and was a coal miner in Bitumen, Pennsylvania; Anna's father was a foreman at the mine where he worked. (Courtesy of Robert Smercansky.)

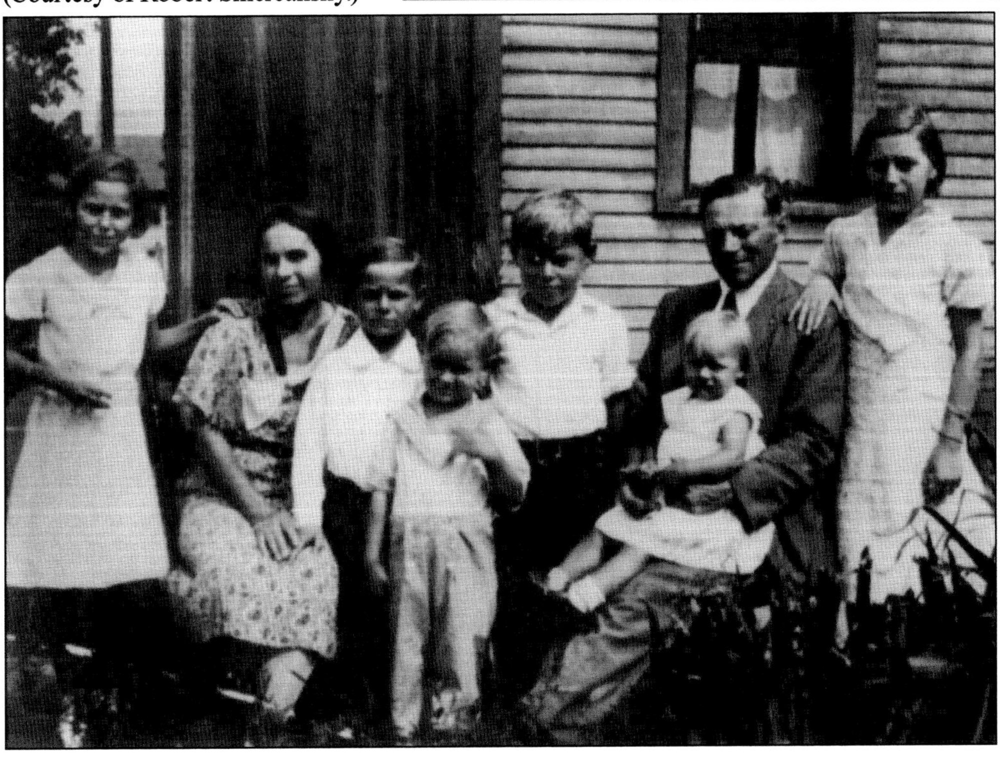

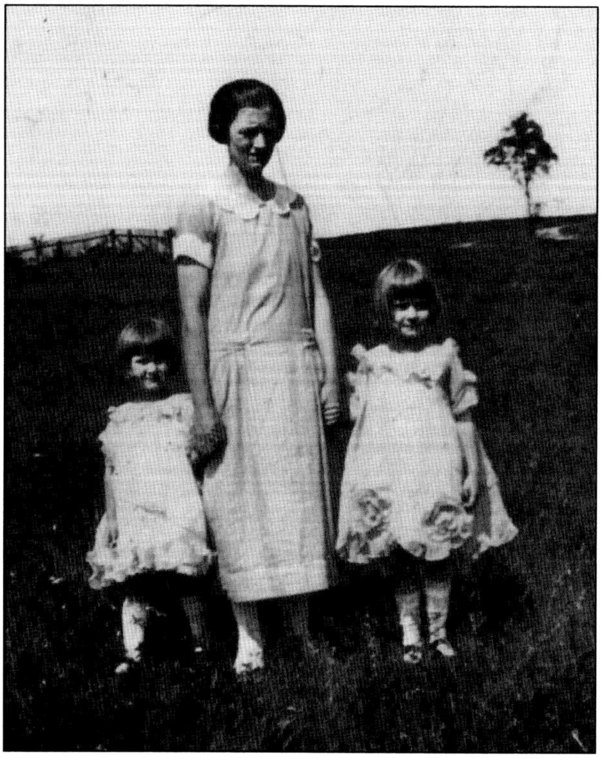

Mary Báka, wife of Charles Báka from Hanušovce, Spišská zupa, walks with her daughters Helen (left) and Ann through Gordon Park in Campbell. (Courtesy of Mary Lou Baka Macala.)

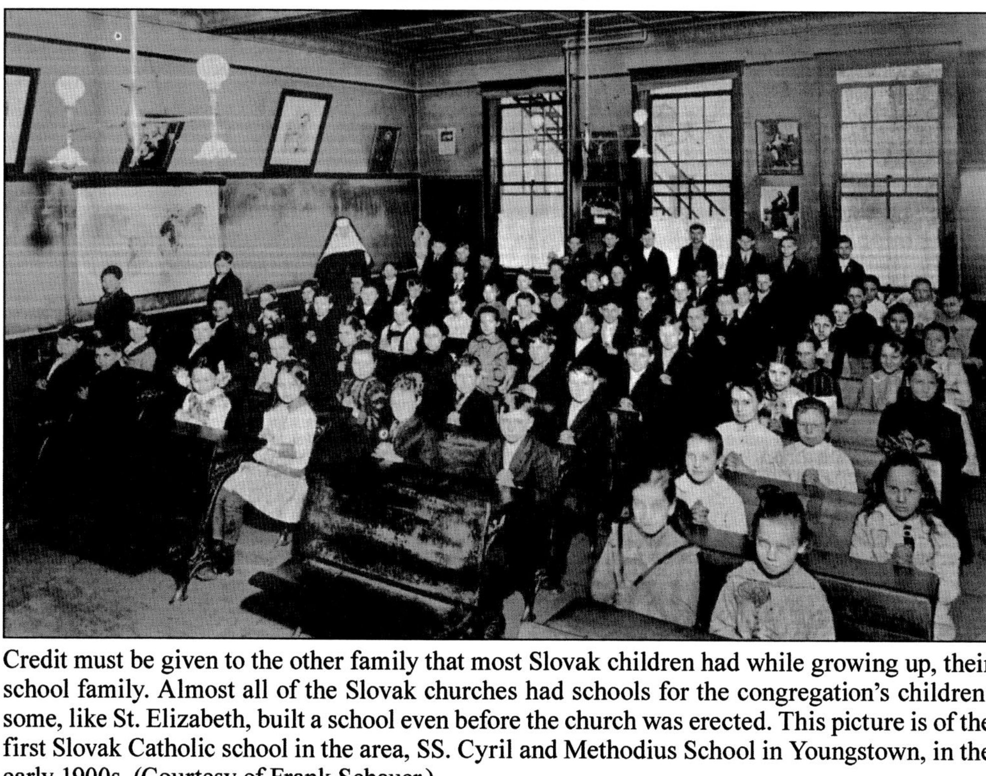

Credit must be given to the other family that most Slovak children had while growing up, their school family. Almost all of the Slovak churches had schools for the congregation's children; some, like St. Elizabeth, built a school even before the church was erected. This picture is of the first Slovak Catholic school in the area, SS. Cyril and Methodius School in Youngstown, in the early 1900s. (Courtesy of Frank Schauer.)

Four

For the Glory of God

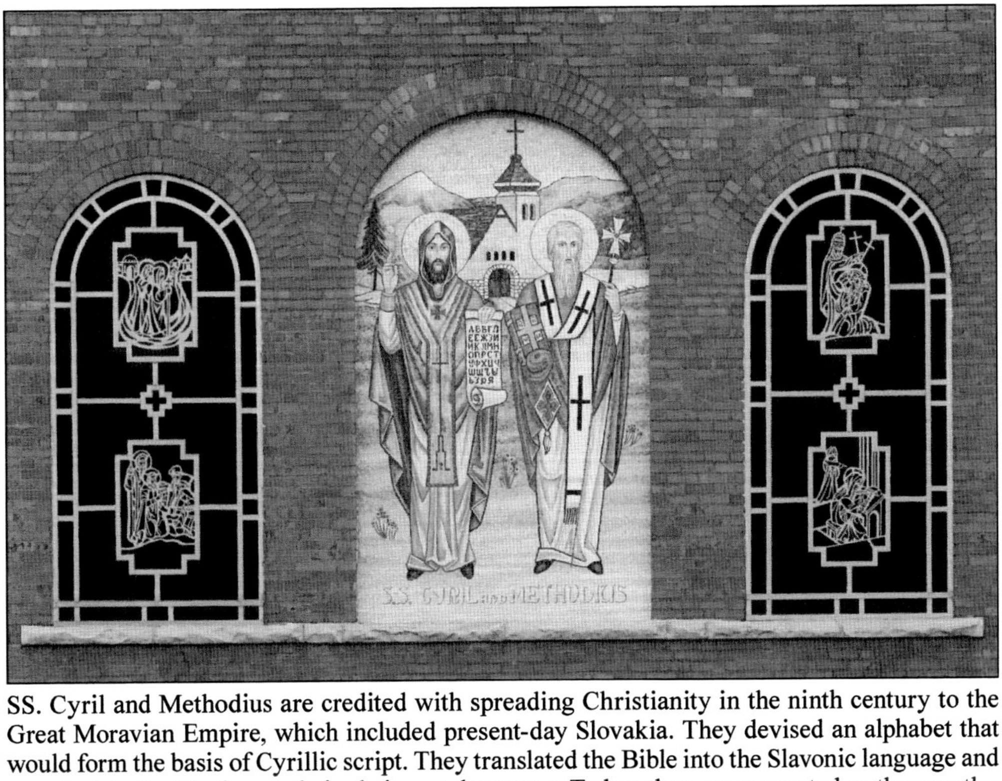

SS. Cyril and Methodius are credited with spreading Christianity in the ninth century to the Great Moravian Empire, which included present-day Slovakia. They devised an alphabet that would form the basis of Cyrillic script. They translated the Bible into the Slavonic language and preached to the Slavic people in their own language. Today, they are venerated as the apostles of the Slavs. (Courtesy of Robert England.)

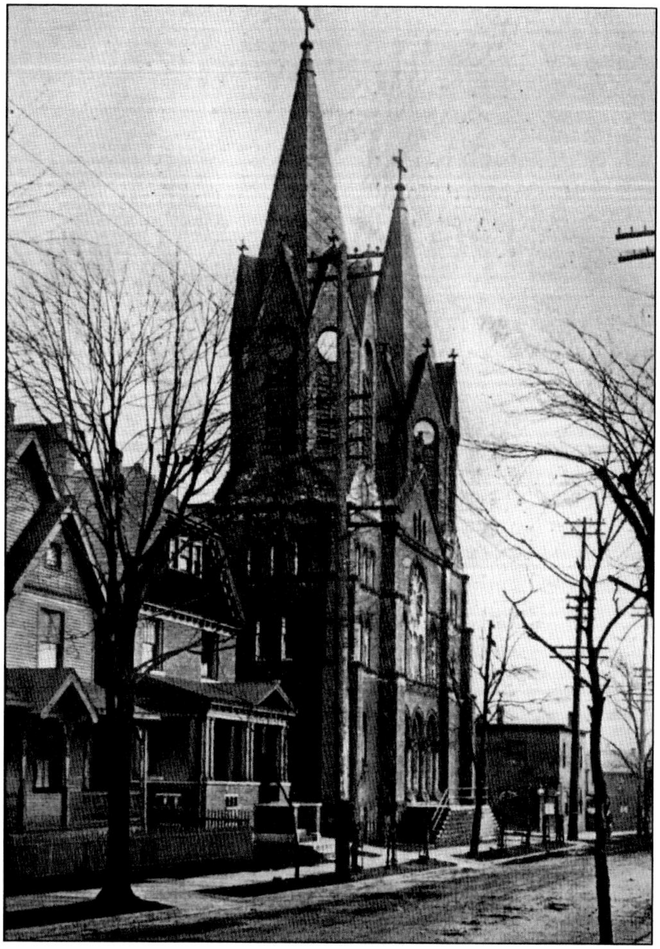

SS. Cyril and Methodius Church was the first Slovak parish in Mahoning and Trumbull Counties. It was founded in 1896 following the rapid increase of Slovak immigrants between 1880 and 1896. It received its first pastor, Fr. Aloysius Kollar, in 1898, and services were held in the newly finished basement of the present church until the building was completed in 1901. (Courtesy of Frank Schauer and Rev. Nicholas Mancini.)

Shown is the interior of SS. Cyril and Methodius Church as it presently appears. After the services of several pastors, during which time a school was established under the Ursuline Sisters, the Reverend Stephen W. Begalla became pastor in 1931 and remained until 1952. (Photograph by Frank Schauer.)

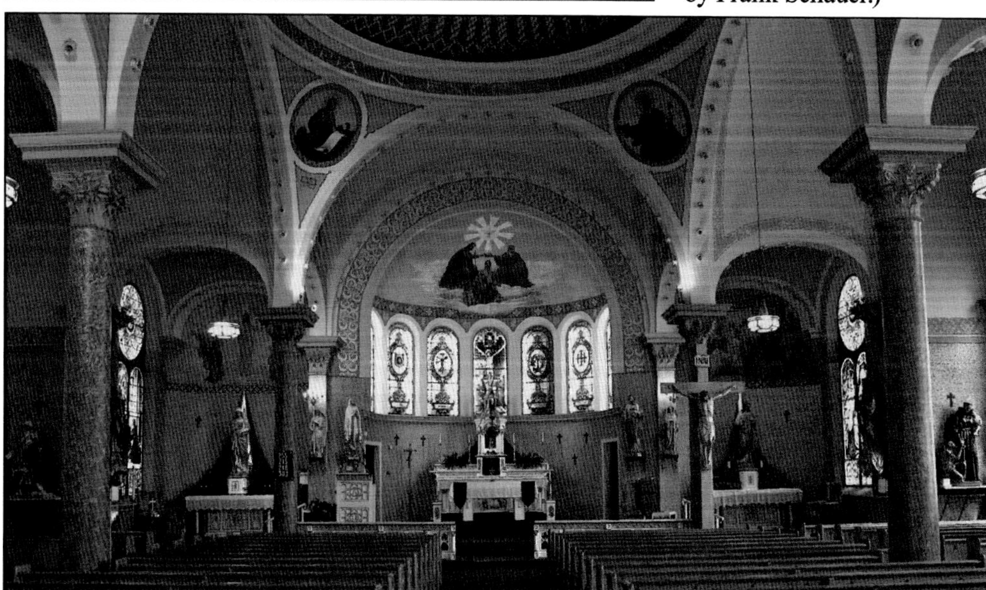

The Steelton area of Youngstown saw many Ruthenian Catholics emigrate from the foothills of the Carpathian Mountains in what is present-day Slovakia. In December 1899, they purchased property on Salt Springs Road and dedicated their new church, St. Mary Greek Catholic Church, on July 4, 1900, when the Reverend Anthony Mhley offered the first Mass. (Courtesy of George Chichak.)

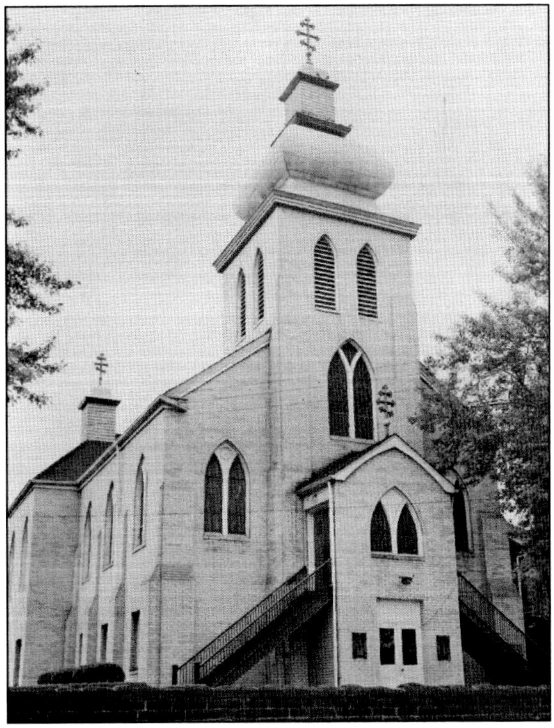

The beauty of the old St. Mary's Byzantine Church in Steelton is seen in this picture taken some time after 1916. St. Mary's became the mother church for all Byzantine-Slavonic Rite Catholics, including St. Michael's in Sharon, Holy Trinity Ukrainian, St. Nicholas Byzantine, and St. George Hungarian in Youngstown and SS. Peter and Paul in Struthers. (Courtesy of Linda Wibley.)

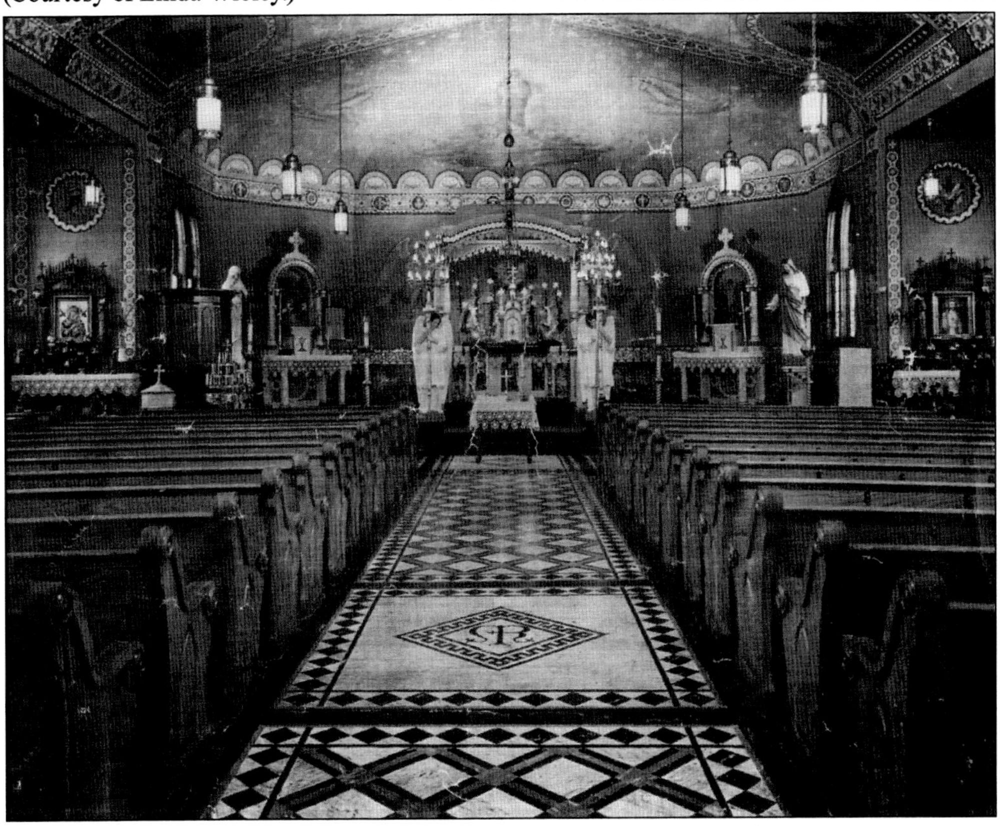

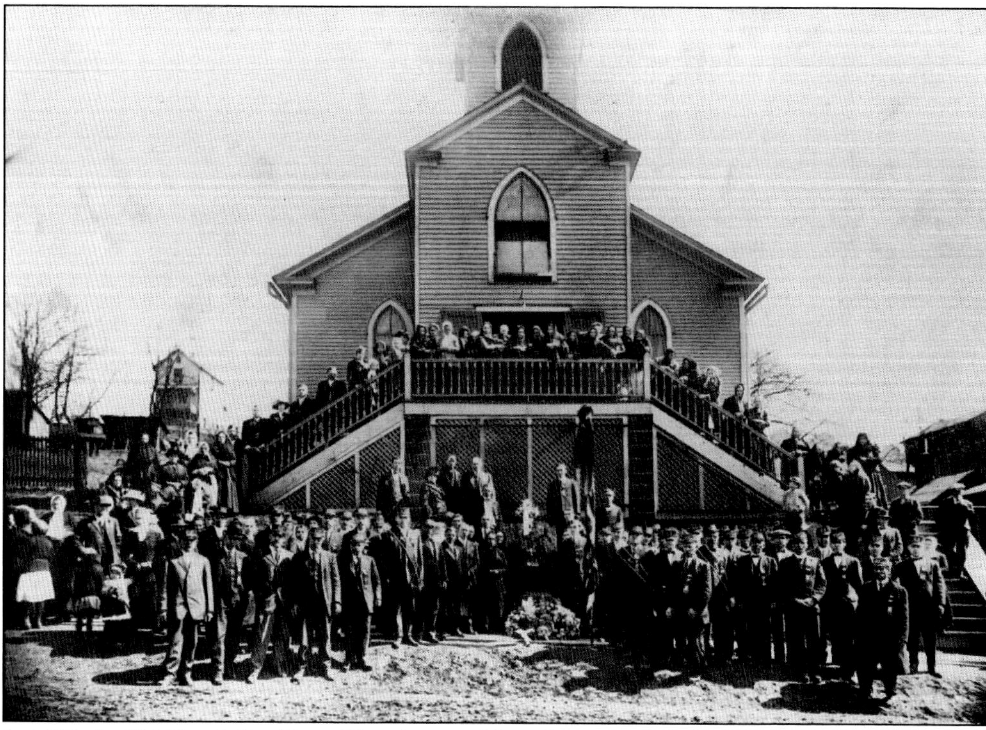

In 1902, the 103 Slovak families of Struthers petitioned for their own church, given the difficulty of the five-mile trip to attend SS. Cyril and Methodius Church, especially after a 72-hour workweek. Struthers's first Holy Trinity Church was not completed on West Washington Street until the end of 1910, although Masses were held in the basement during construction, beginning in December 1908. After its completion, school classes were held in the basement. Shown above is a funeral service at the church. Below, a happier occasion is a May crowning ceremony outside the old church. Rev. George Bobal (1939–1952) formed plans for the new church at the top of the hill on Bridge Street. Sadly, he died before seeing his dream come true. (Above, courtesy of Holy Trinity church; below, courtesy of Janet Repasky Morris.)

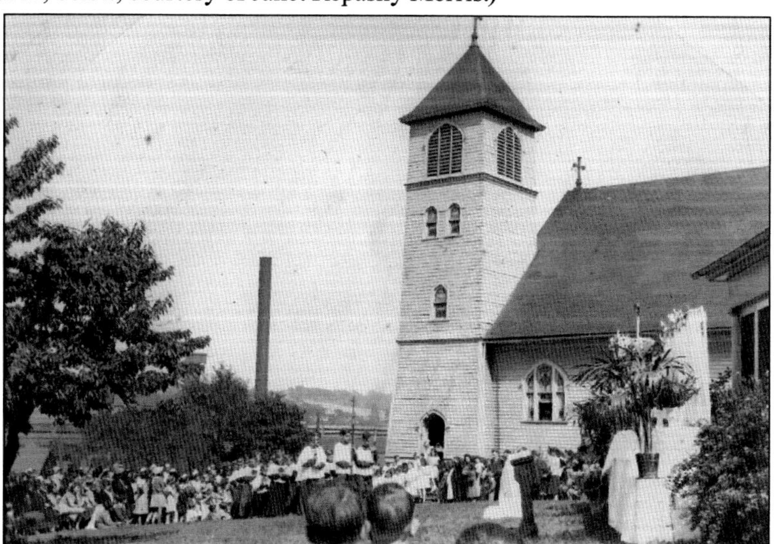

The Slovak Evangelical Lutheran Holy Trinity Church of South Sharon, Pennsylvania, was organized October 1, 1900. George Roskos, congregation president, was tasked with finding a place for the first church. It was built on Greenfield Street in what is now the town of Farrell, Pennsylvania. The women of the congregation made the altar dressings, and George Krajnak constructed the altar, pulpit, and pews. It was dedicated June 9, 1901. By 1918, the congregation, in need of a larger church, purchased the Croatian Catholic Church on Wallis Street. From 1921 until 1955, the pastor was Rev. John Zabadal, shown below with the 50th Jubilee committee. From left to right are (first row) Anna Hnida, Anna Zabadal, Rev. Zabadal, Elizabeth Zipaj, and Elizabeth Podolsky; (second row) John Svrček, George Ondič, John Pališin, and Jacob Yohman. (Both, courtesy of Rev. Jerrold Caughlin.)

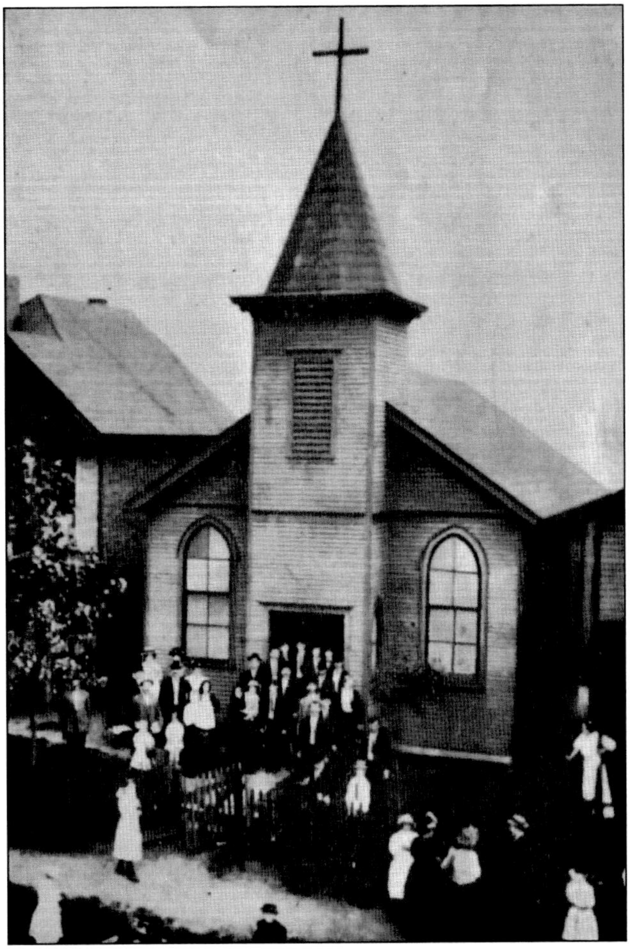

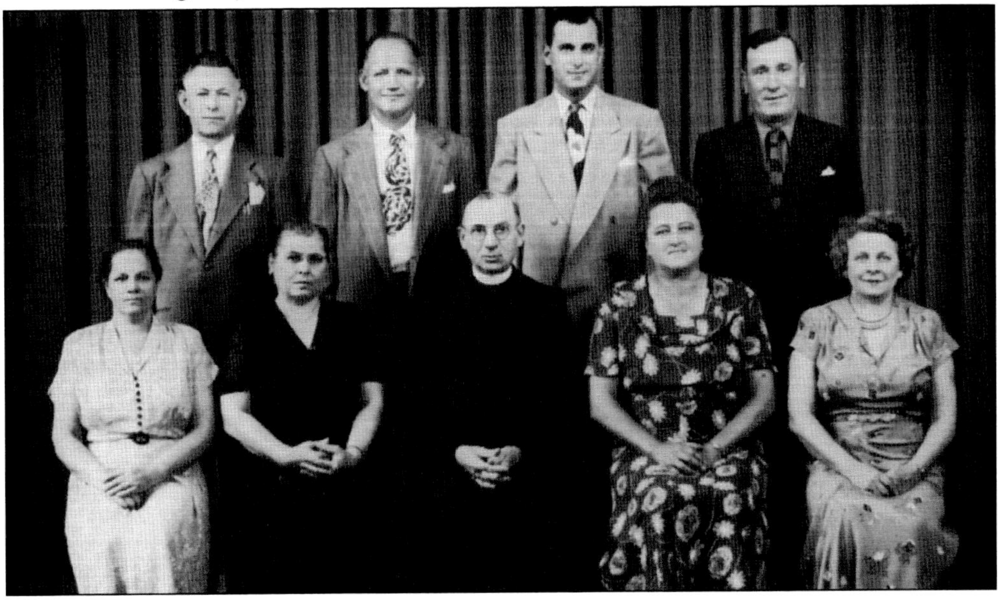

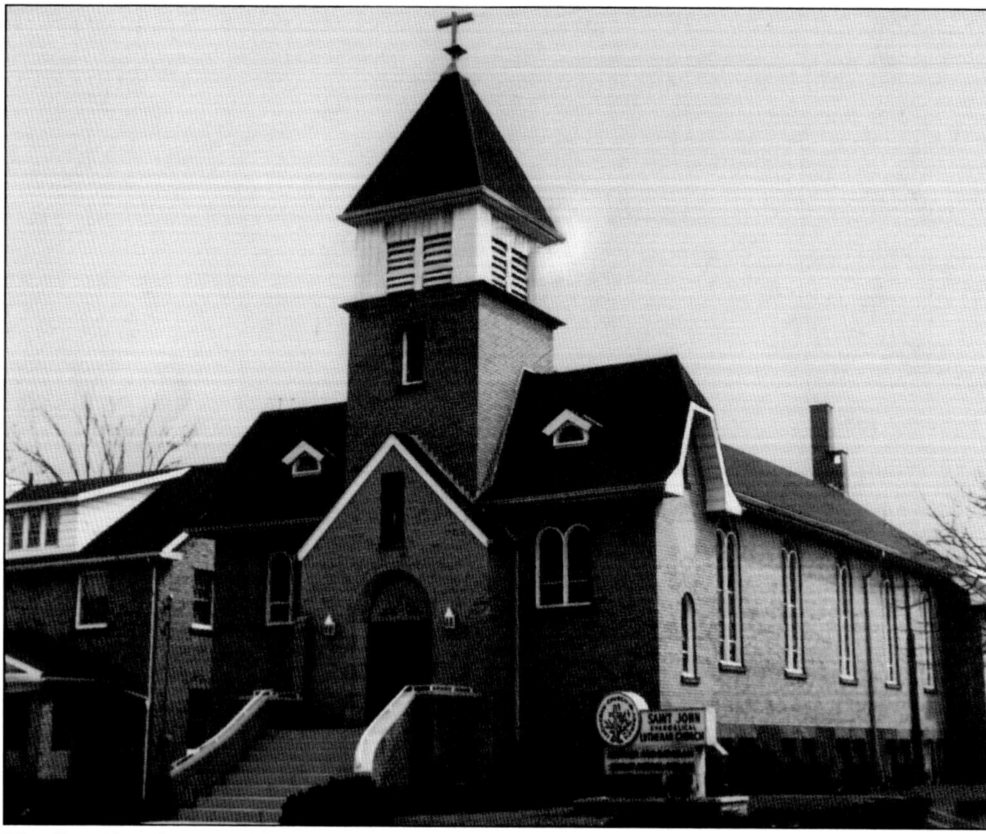

The first Slovak Evangelical Lutherans came to the valley before 1900. In 1903, they formally organized as the Ján Hus Evangelical Lutheran Church. By 1906, they had collected enough money to buy land on Mahoning Avenue, but hard economic times meant their church was not completed and dedicated until April 1911. The church was enlarged and remodeled under pastor George Roh, who served the congregation for 40 years. Shown below from left to right are the founding fathers of Jan Hus Evangelical: (first row) Ján Jurco, Pavel Pallo, Samuel Bradač, and Ján Kulišek; (second row) Andrej Balint and Matej Pallo. (Both, courtesy of Margaret Textoris Tomo.)

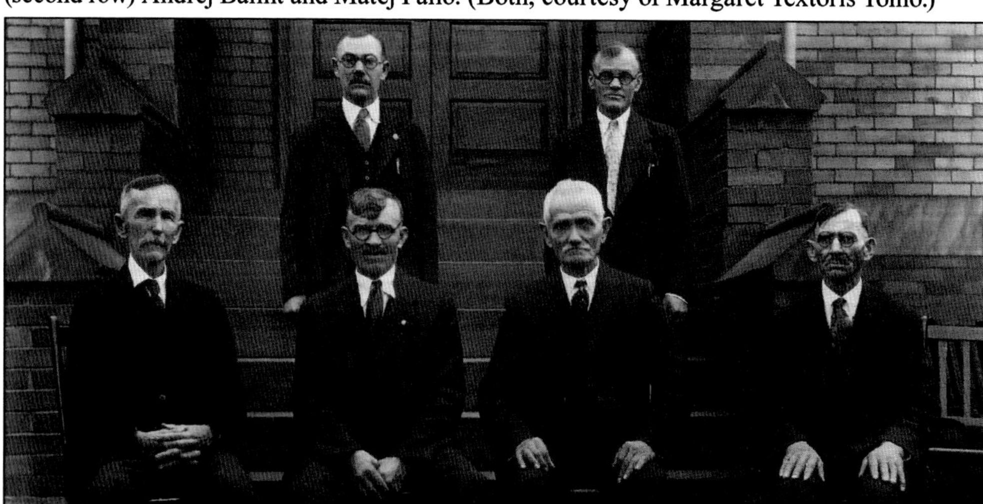

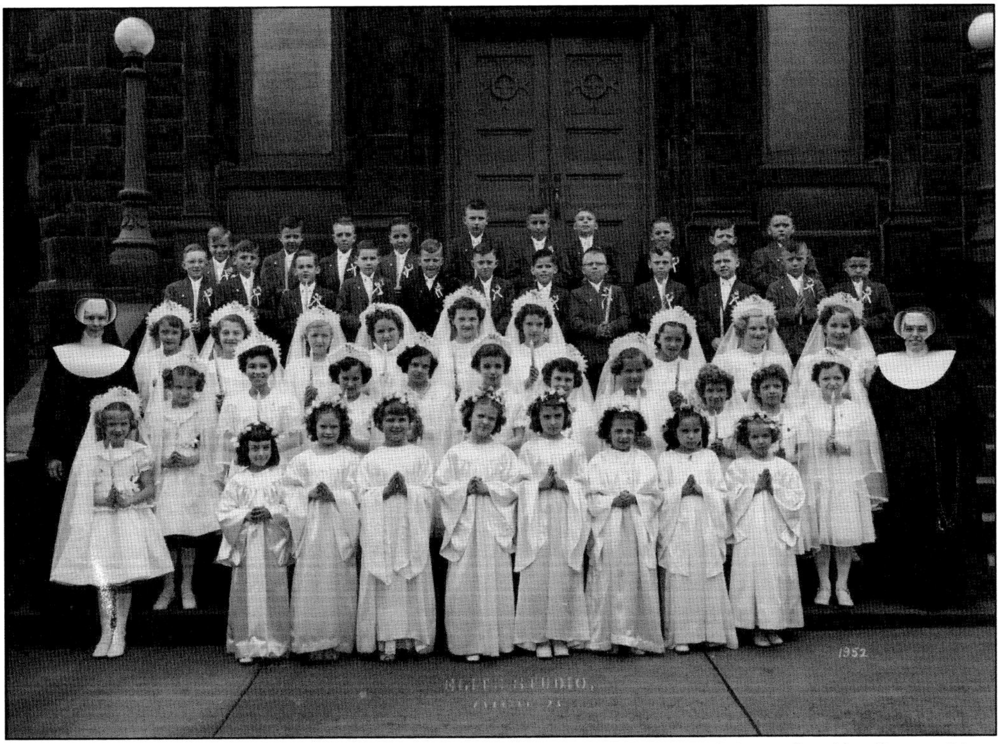

St. Ann's parish in Farrell was organized in 1902. In May 1903, the parish received its first resident pastor, Rev. Francis Cherny, who acquired the first rectory. It was under the fifth pastor, Rev. Simon Miškovčik, when additional lots were purchased, and a new brick church was built and dedicated in 1919. A new school was dedicated in October 1929. Father Miškovčik served until 1944. When his health deteriorated, Miškovčik was succeeded by the Reverend John S. Chizmar. He soon undertook complete renovation of the church and its grounds, along with expanding the church cemetery. Above is the 1952 communion class, and below is an image of the church interior before its remodeling, which was sent to all parishioners as a Christmas card from the pastor. (Both, courtesy of Sophia Richnavsky.)

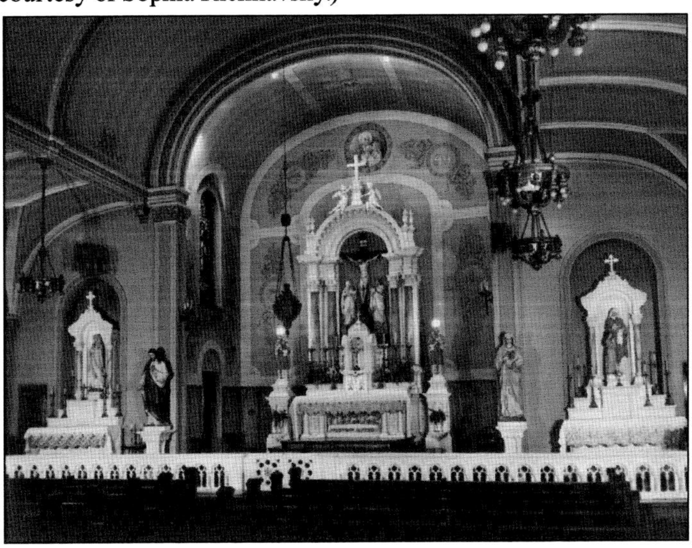

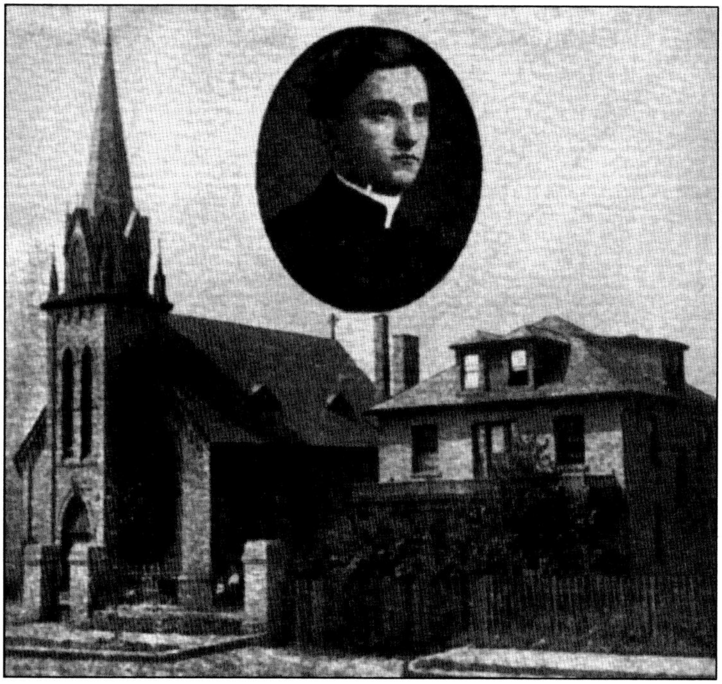

In 1905, parishioners from St. Mary's Byzantine in Youngstown, Ohio, organized St. Michael the Archangel parish closer to their homes in Farrell, Pennsylvania. Fr. Alexander Dudinsky purchased land in Farrell on Spearman Avenue, and a new church was completed and dedicated July 4, 1906. From 1910 to 1923, Fr. John Danilovich served the parish, working to free it of debt and establish a school next to the church. (Courtesy of Marilyn Bross Mickholtzick.)

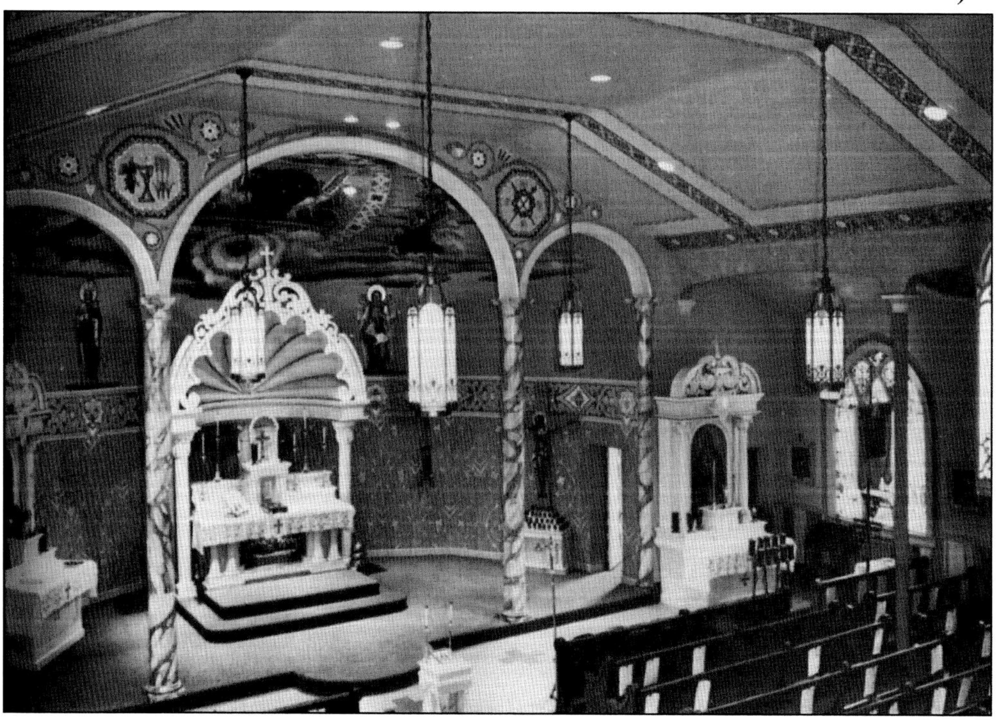

Under Fr. Elias Gojdics, the church was expanded, and the interior was remodeled in the beautiful style seen here. The parish flourished, and in 1931, Fr. Aurelius A. Petrick was appointed, serving the congregation for 32 years. In 1959, he purchased property on Highland Road for future needs. In 1963, a parish center was completed, and in 1971, ground was broken for the present church. (Courtesy of Marilyn Bross Mickholtzick.)

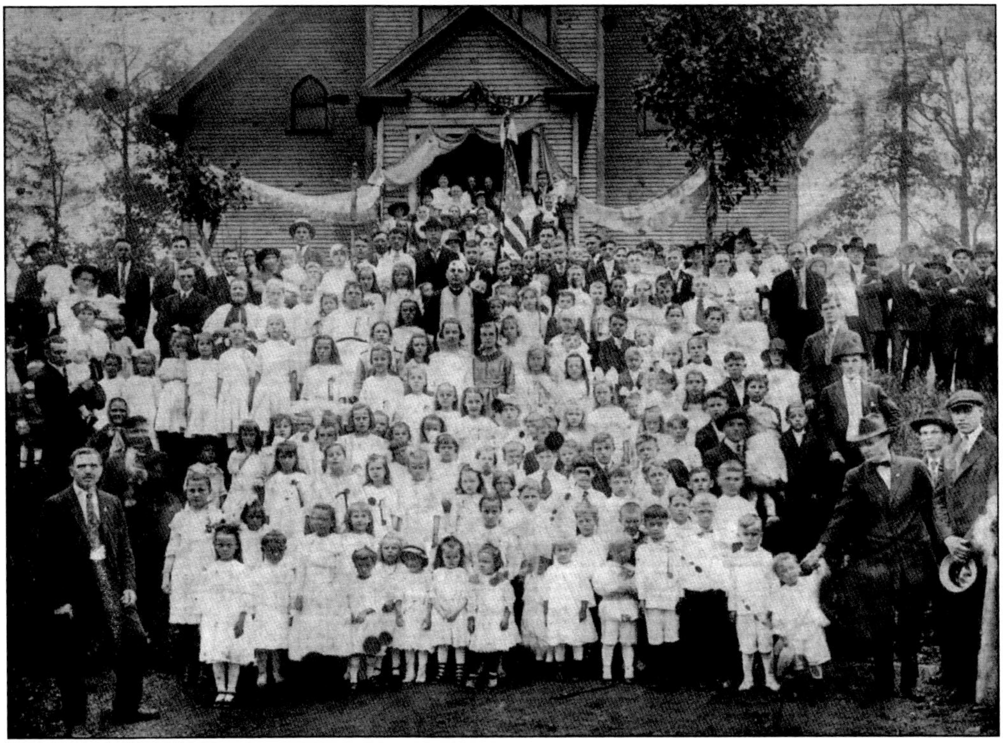

In 1907, a group of Ruthenian (Rusyn) immigrants who belonged to St. Mary's in Youngstown purchased property in Struthers, Ohio, to build their own church on Frank Street. Thanks to their hard work, the church seen here was dedicated as SS. Peter and Paul Greek Catholic Church in 1917. The pastor in the center is either Anthony Mhley or Peter Racz. (Courtesy of Joanne Basista Lewis.)

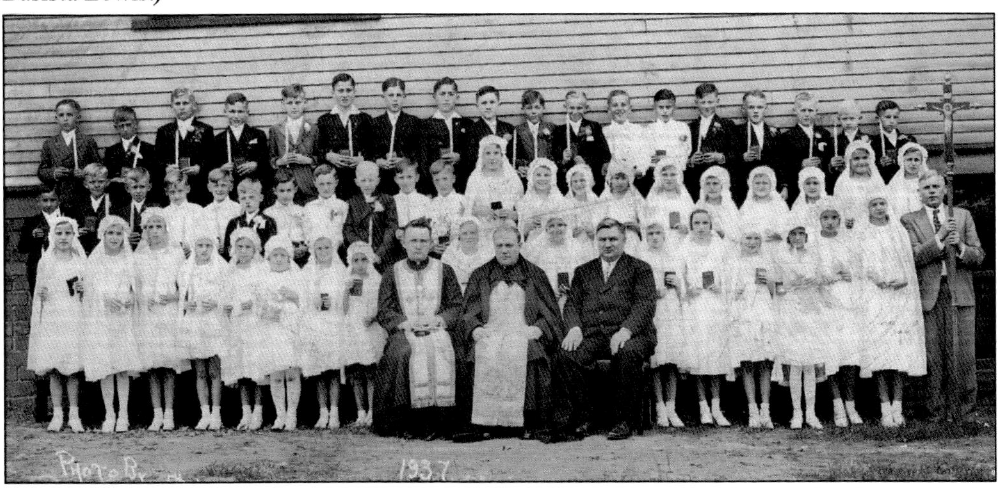

The First Communion class of 1937 is shown with pastor John Gaspar (center, front), Mr. Chasko to his right, and an unidentified clergyman on his left. Children from the Busonik, Blasko, Shevetz, Pavlik, Vasilchek, Democko, Gaspar, Kovach, Basista, Flak, Tovtin, Silchek, Ondrey, Fogarish, Stanko, Suhey, Meek, Tabak, Novotny, and Jonda families were present. In 1970, a new church was built in Boardman, Ohio, and dedicated as Infant Jesus of Prague. (Courtesy of Joanne Basista Lewis.)

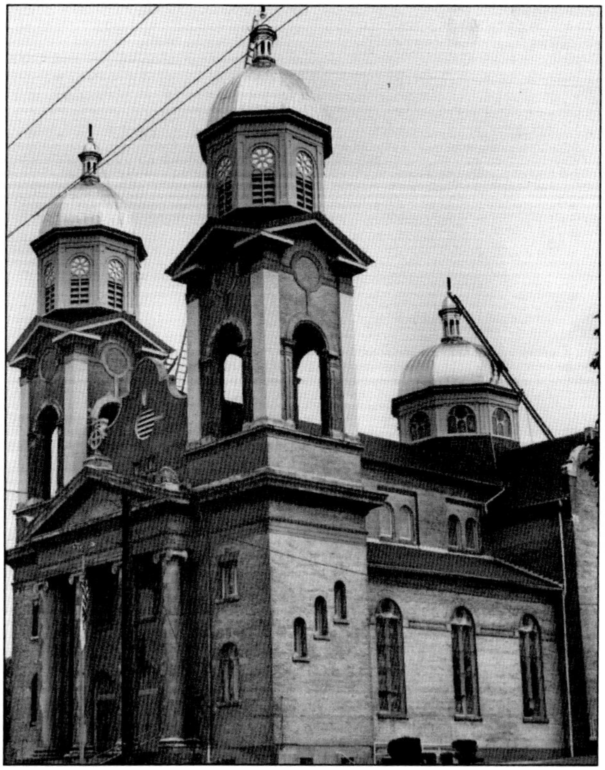

The second Byzantine parish in the Youngstown area was organized in January 1912 under the patronage of St. Nicholas. The first building, a former Swedish church, was soon outgrown, and in 1914, pastor Alexander Papp made plans for a magnificent church designed after the Cathedral Church of the Holy Cross in Užhorod, Subcarpathian-Rus'. Until 1932, all church services were conducted in the Rusin language. (Courtesy of Campbell Historical Society, Florence Katula Galida.)

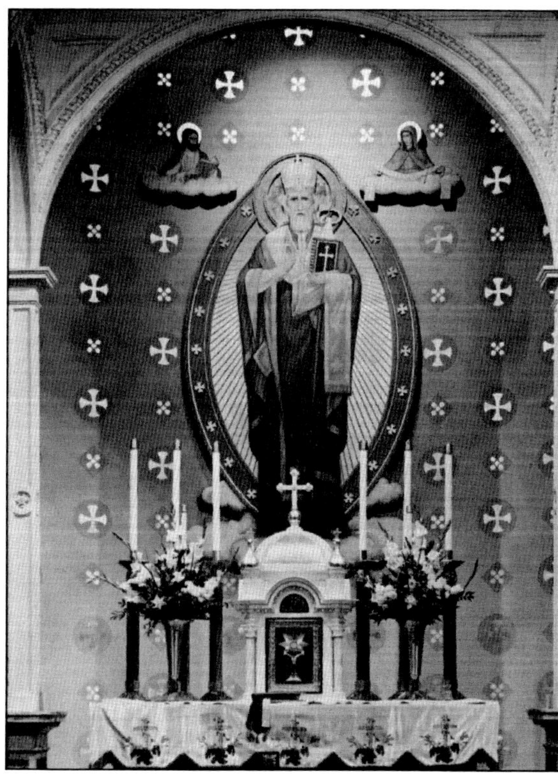

Byzantine Rite churches place great importance on the use of icons as a link between the human and the divine. This photograph shows the icon mural of St. Nicholas behind the main altar. Over St. Nicholas's left shoulder, Christ is depicted holding out a book of the Gospels, and over St. Nicholas's right shoulder, Mary, the God Bearer, holds out his liturgical stole. (Courtesy of Loretta Hanuschak Ekoniak.)

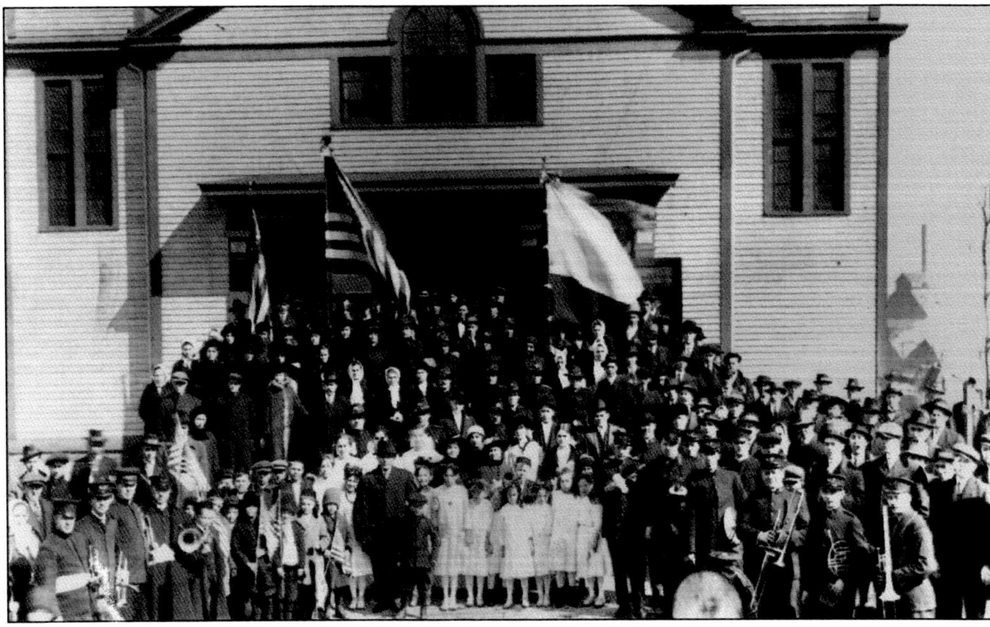

In 1913, Slovaks in the Youngstown neighborhood of Lansingville petitioned for their own parish. Their request was granted, and in 1914, work began on St. Matthias Church on the corner of Homewood and Harmon Avenues. Above, the church is shown at its dedication on July 4, 1915, with Fr. John Gerenda as pastor. Shown below is the inside of the first St. Matthias Church. Father Gerenda stands at the left side of the Holy Sepulcher, which is displayed during the Lenten season. Men from the Knights of Columbus and altar boys from the parish guard the sepulcher. In 1925, Fr. Francis Kozelek began construction of a larger church for the growing congregation. The former church was converted into classrooms where the Vincentian Sisters of Charity conducted classes. (Above, courtesy of Joseph J. Rakocy Jr.; below, courtesy of Lucille Martinko Kramer.)

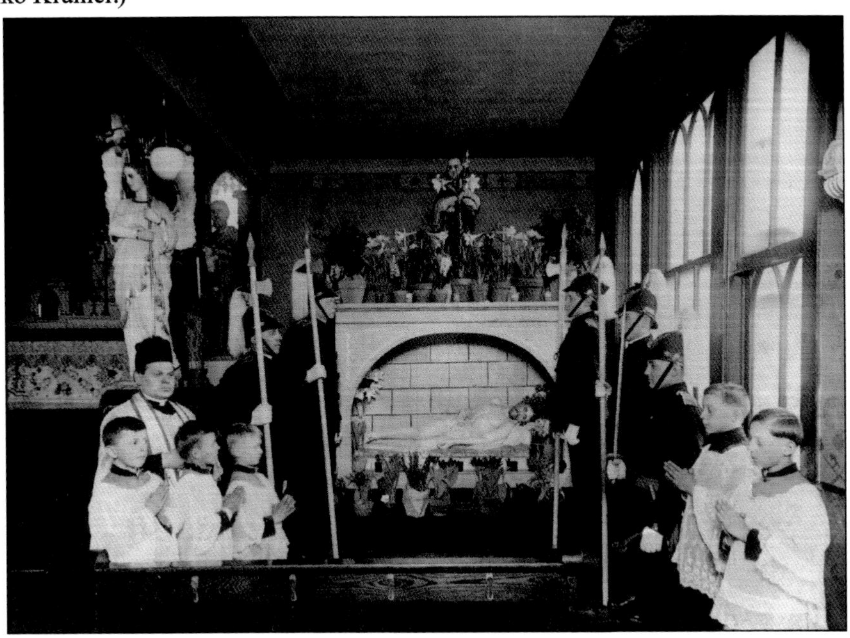

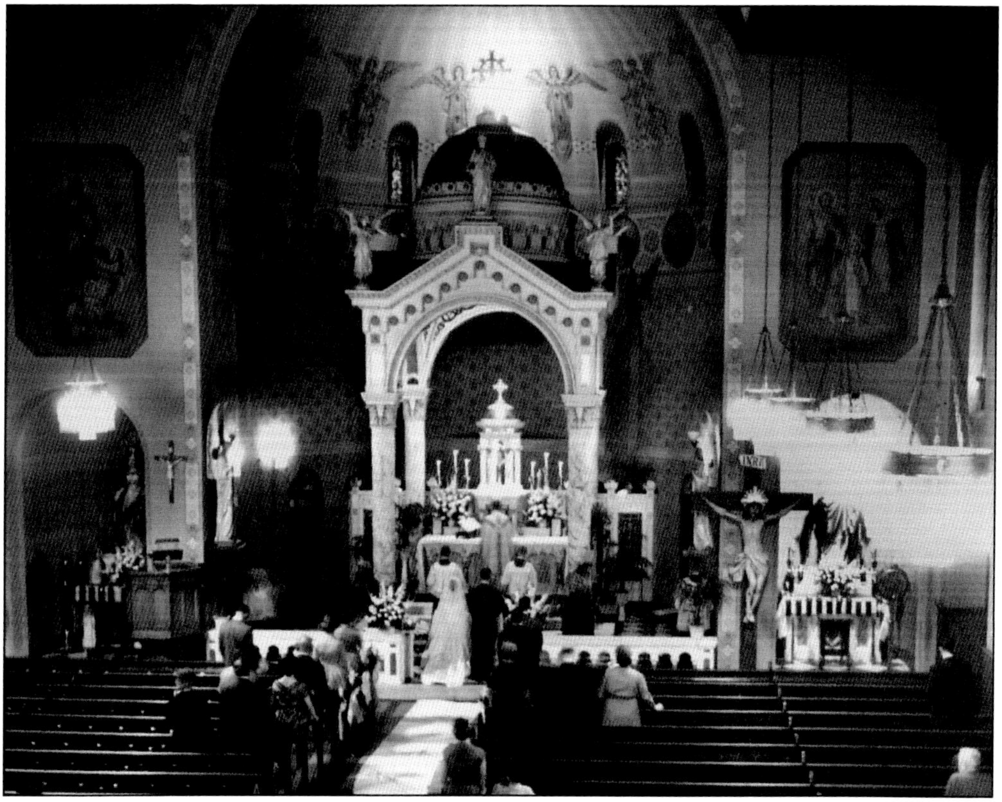

The second St. Matthias Church, built on Indianola and Homewood Avenues, was dedicated in 1926, and the interior is shown at the wedding of Kathryn Novotny and John Franko. The third pastor, Msgr. John Hamrak, was responsible for the construction of a new school and convent on property purchased on Shady Run Road. Under Rev. George Winca, a new church was dedicated on that site in 1973. (Courtesy of Kathryn Novotny Franko.)

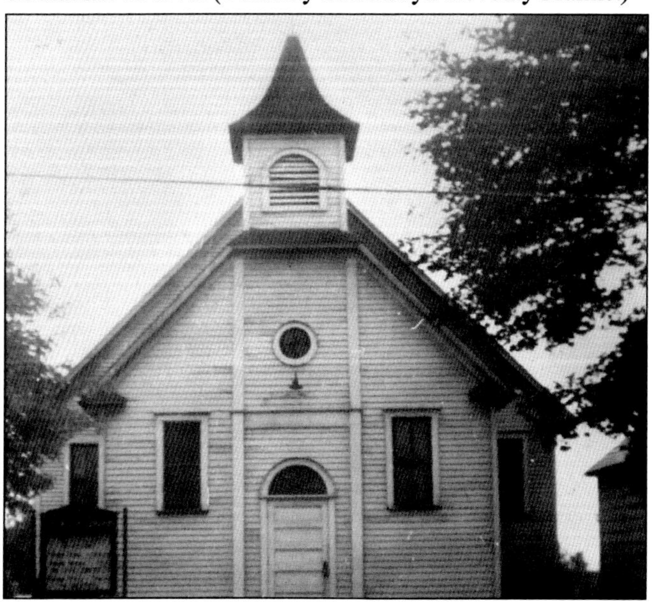

The First Slovak Baptist Church in Campbell was organized as a mission in 1906 by Rev. R. Hughes of Youngstown. The first members were John Kana and Daniel Shramo, and a frame church was dedicated in 1912. The first ordained minister to serve the church was Rev. Michael Kuznik, who served from 1919 to 1922. The Reverend Karel Dushek and the Reverend Michael Hiben followed. (Courtesy of the Campbell Historic Society, Florence Katula Galida.)

Before World War I, many Slovak emigrants settled in the Steelton area of west Youngstown. In 1914, they proposed a Catholic parish dedicated to the Holy Name of Jesus. Property was purchased on Midland Avenue, and under the guidance of the first pastor, Rev. John Stipanovic, ground was broken in late 1916. Under Fr. Francis Dubosh, the church was dedicated on June 2, 1918. Fr. Stephan Kocis was named the third pastor in 1922 and served until his death in 1952. Under his direction, a school was built, and the rectory and church were extensively remodeled and expanded. The beautiful mosaic of Christ as teacher can be seen below in this photograph of Msgr. Peter Polando conducting the Blessing of Baskets, a Slovak Easter tradition. (Both photographs by Michael J. Kopanic Jr.)

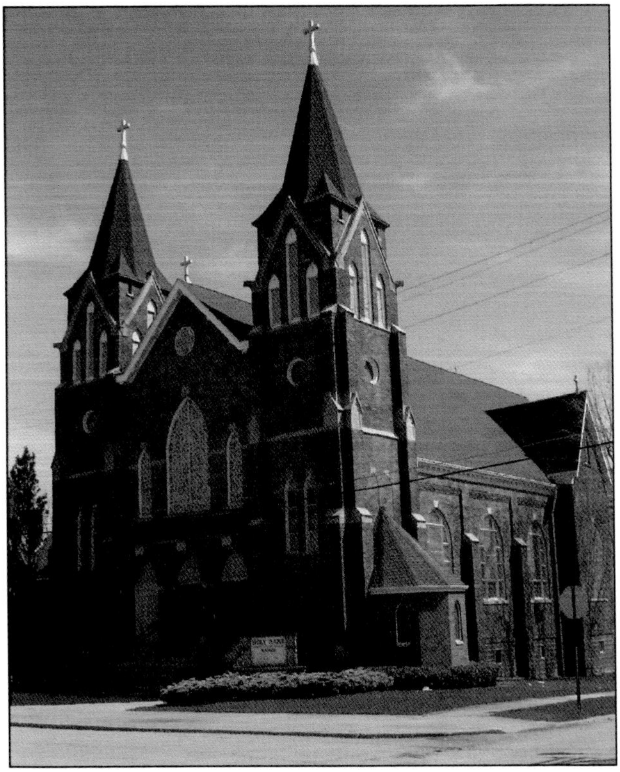

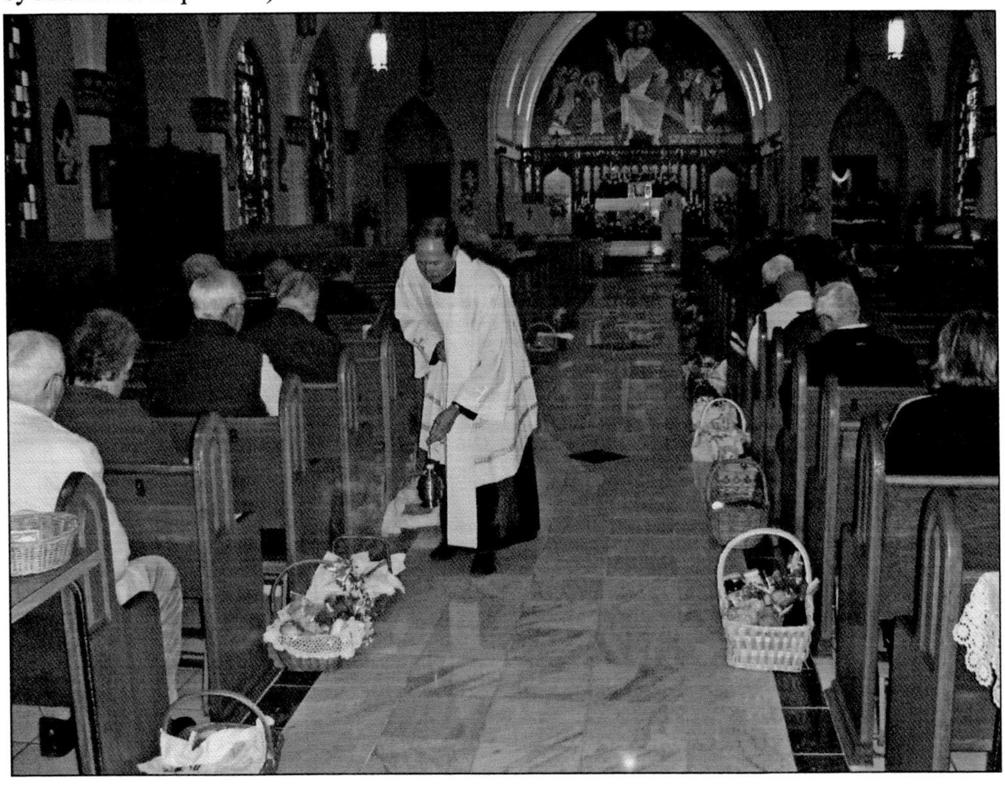

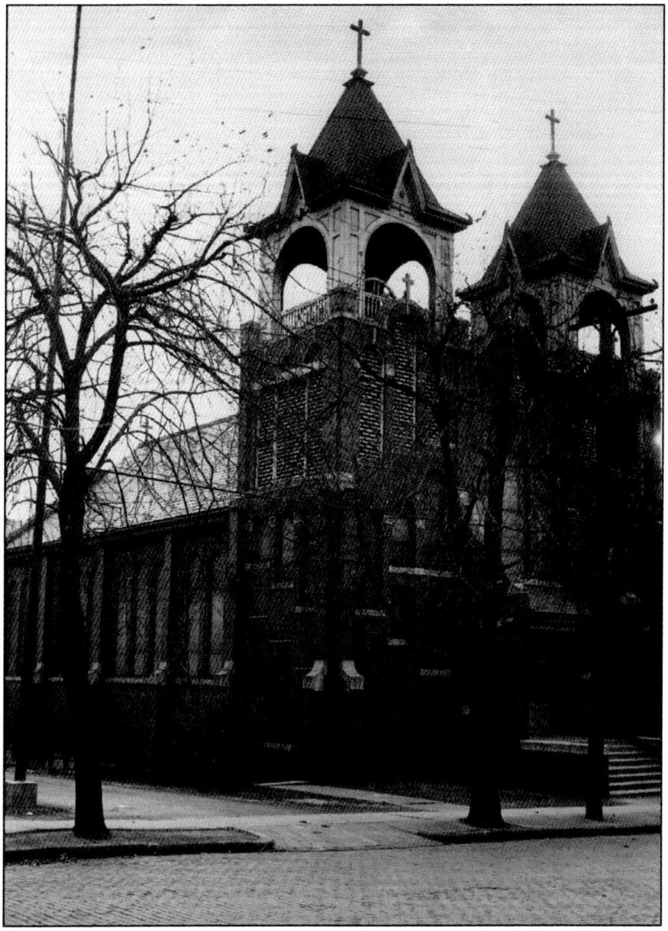

In 1914, the Slovaks of East Youngstown (Campbell) who had been attending services in Struthers petitioned Bishop Farrelly for their own parish. Because of a shortage of priests, their request could not be granted immediately. In 1916, ground was broken, and St. John the Baptist was established under the Slovak National Catholic Church. In 1920, it was reorganized as a Roman Catholic Church, and Fr. Joseph Krispinsky became its pastor. He established a school under the Ursuline Sisters in 1926. The church was noted for the beauty of its decorations, as seen in the photograph below. When the floor started to give way under the weight of the midnight Mass congregation on Christmas Eve 1951, a new church was quickly planned. It was dedicated in June 1952. (Both, courtesy of Susan Gubany Summers.)

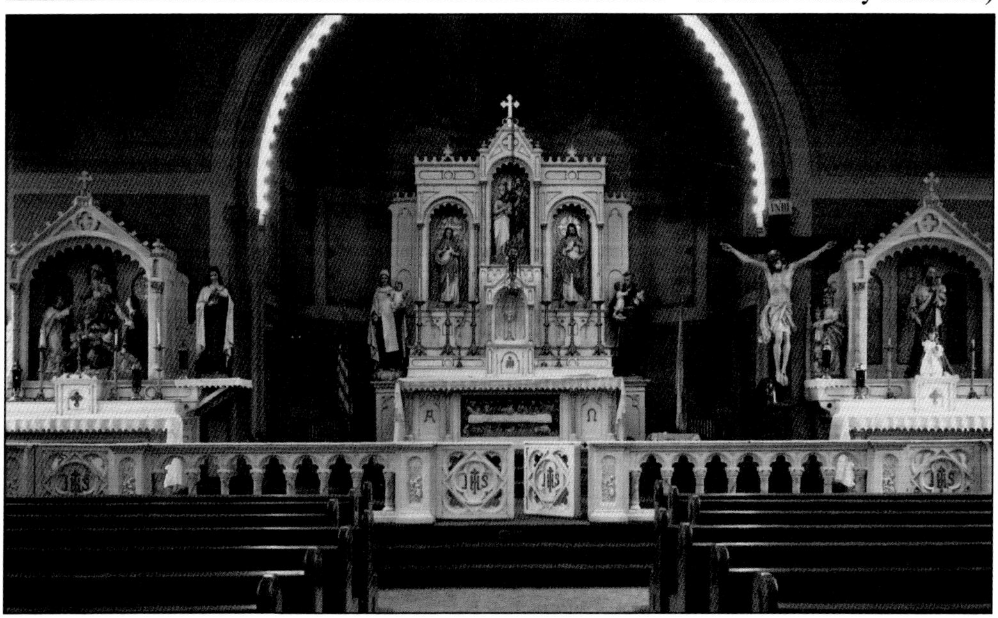

In 1917, a charter was granted to emigrants from the Carpathian Mountain area to form the St. John's Congregation of East Youngstown. In 1918, Reverend Kulchitsky was assigned as pastor. The congregation was first under the influence of the Uhro Russian Greek Catholic Church. The church founders built their first St. John Greek Catholic Church with their own hands on Fourteenth Street in Campbell. In 1919, the congregation embraced orthodoxy and was known as St. John the Baptist Russian Orthodox Greek Catholic Church. Shown below is the Carpathian custom of the Blessing of Baskets at Easter. With the building of the new church on Struthers-Liberty Road, the church is now known as St. John the Baptist Russian Orthodox Church. (Both, courtesy of Campbell Historic Society, Florence Katula Galida.)

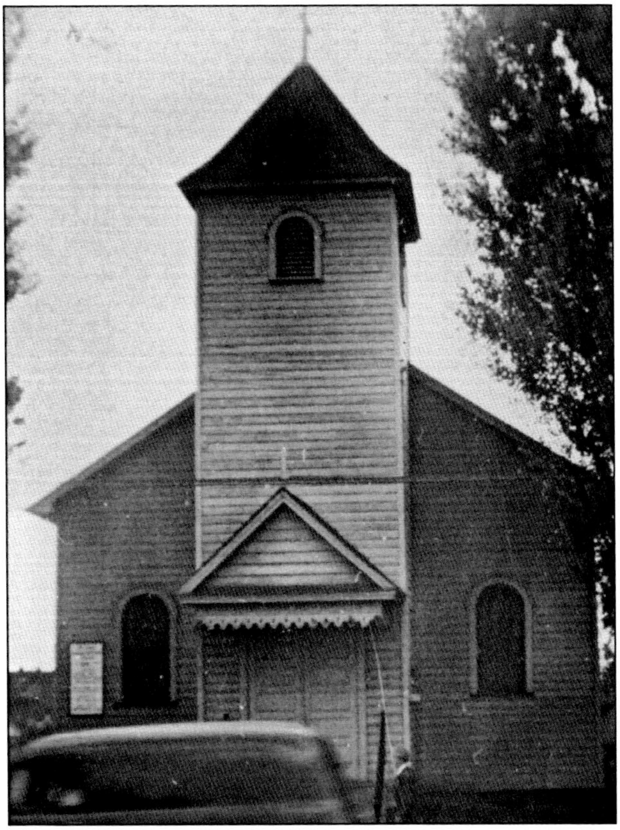

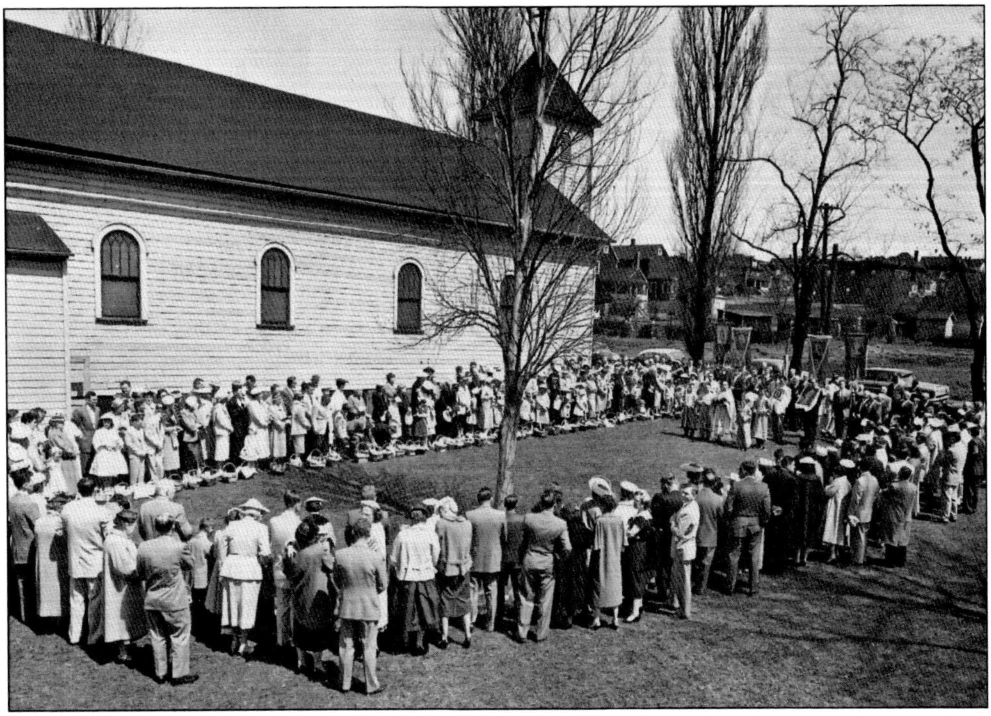

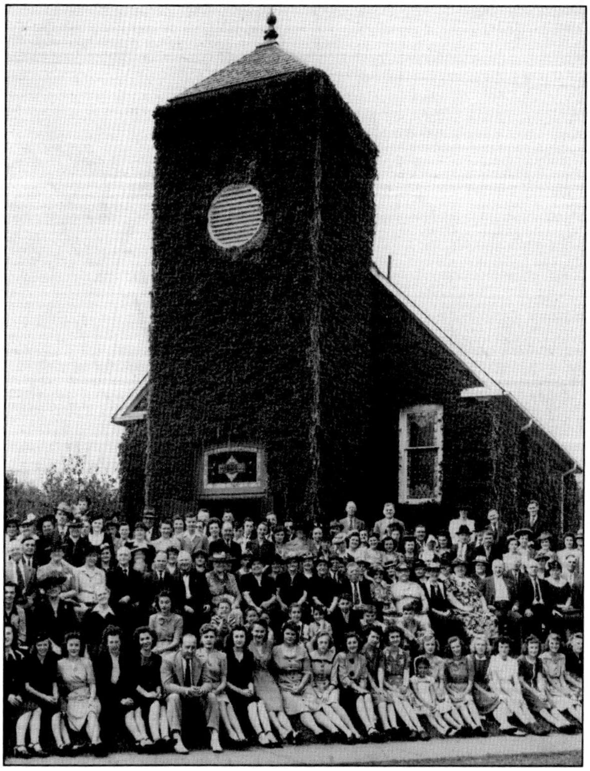

Slovaks of the Calvinist Presbyterian faith began to settle in the Youngstown area in about 1912. They worshipped in the Hungarian Reformed Church until they organized as the First Slovak Presbyterian Church in May 1917. Joseph Nádeniček was installed as the first pastor in 1917. In 1920, the first church was dedicated on the corner of Shirley Road and Taylor Street in Lansingville. From left to right, the members of the 1930 confirmation class of First Slovak Presbyterian below are (first row) Pauline Sič, Dorothy Yosay, Helen Valinsky, Dr. M. Filipi, Emily Bari, Mary Yosay, and Mary Bednarik; (second row) Edward Hudak, Paul Tomašula, George Kruppa, John Sič, George Semyan, David Sopko, and Michael Valo; (third row) Paul Kolesar, Michael Kasony, Michael Varkonda, Pavel Nádeniček, and Joseph Sabo. (Both, courtesy of Judy Semyan Bayus.)

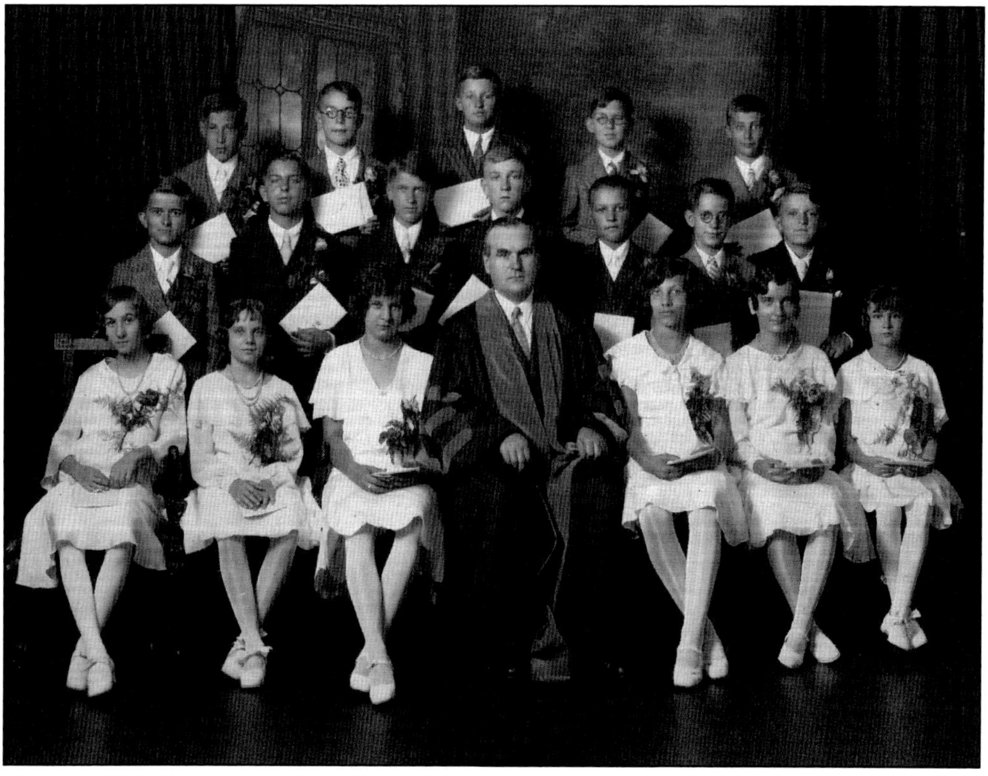

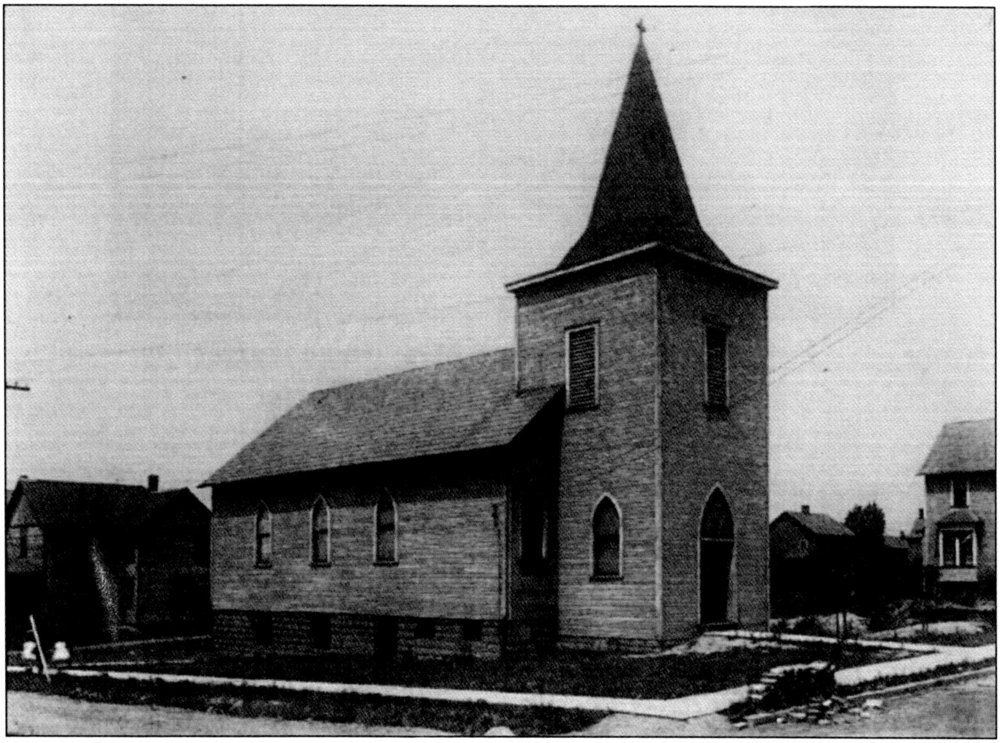

In 1914, a group of Slovak Lutherans from the Sharon and Farrell area split from the congregation of Holy Trinity Lutheran to organize their own congregation. In June 1917, the Slovak Evangelical Lutheran Church of SS. Peter and Paul was formally founded. The congregation was accepted into the Slovak Evangelical Lutheran Synod of the United States. In December 1918, their newly built church was dedicated. From October 1917, the Reverend Andrew Hvizdak from John Hus Church in Youngstown became the vacancy pastor until he became the first permanent pastor in 1922. Shown below in front of the new church (built after a tornado destroyed the old one) are some of the founding fathers. From left to right are Ján Stiavnicky, Ján Petro, Pavel Krivoš, John Drobny (not a founder), Michael Tomko, and Michael Sulek. (Both, courtesy of Holy Trinity Lutheran Church.)

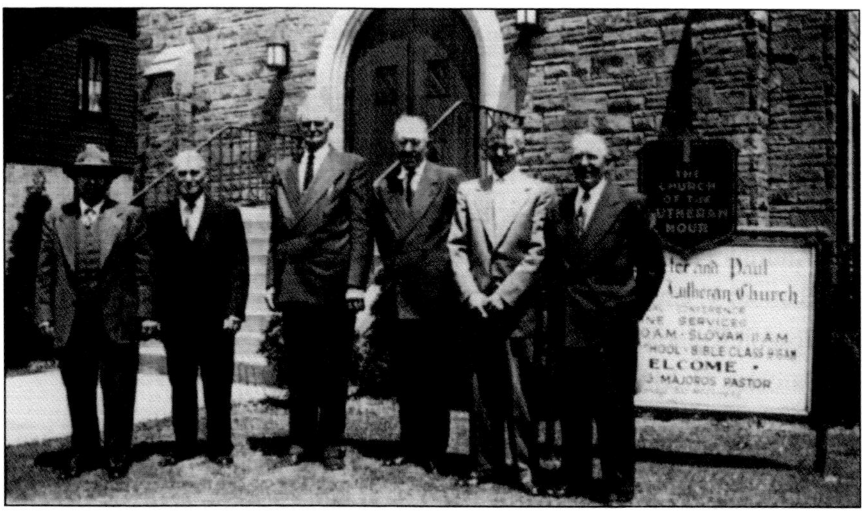

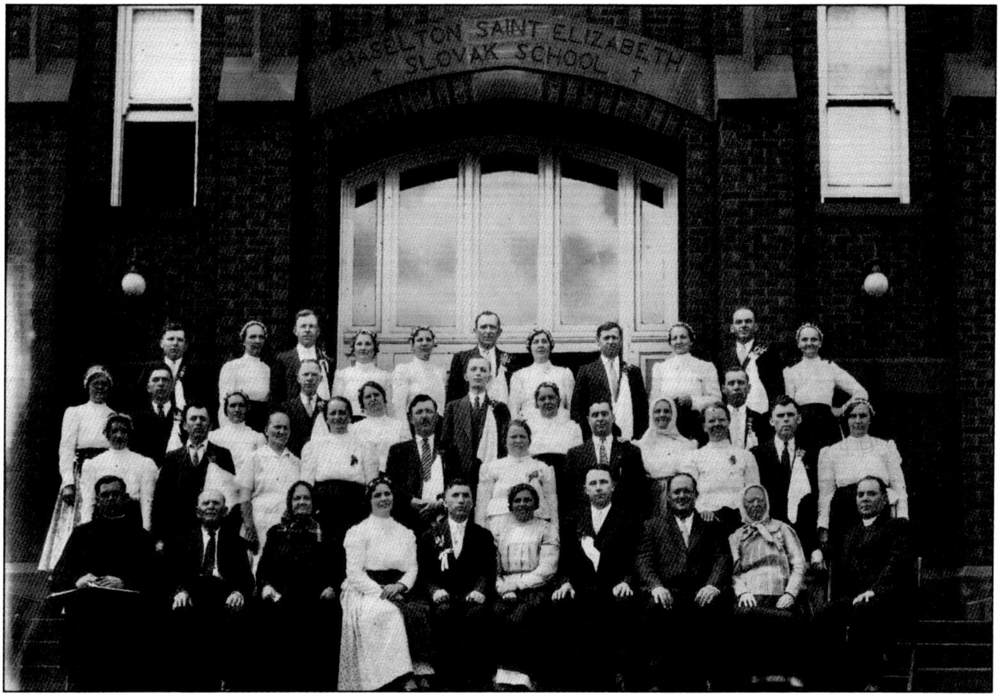

The Slovaks in the Haselton area wanted their own parish, but because of a shortage of priests, they built a school instead; it was located on Haseltine Avenue. In 1922, their wish for their own parish was granted, and the first Mass was celebrated on Easter Sunday in the school building, which would serve as their church until 1956, when a new church was dedicated. The 1933 Drama Club is shown here. (Courtesy of Robert Beck.)

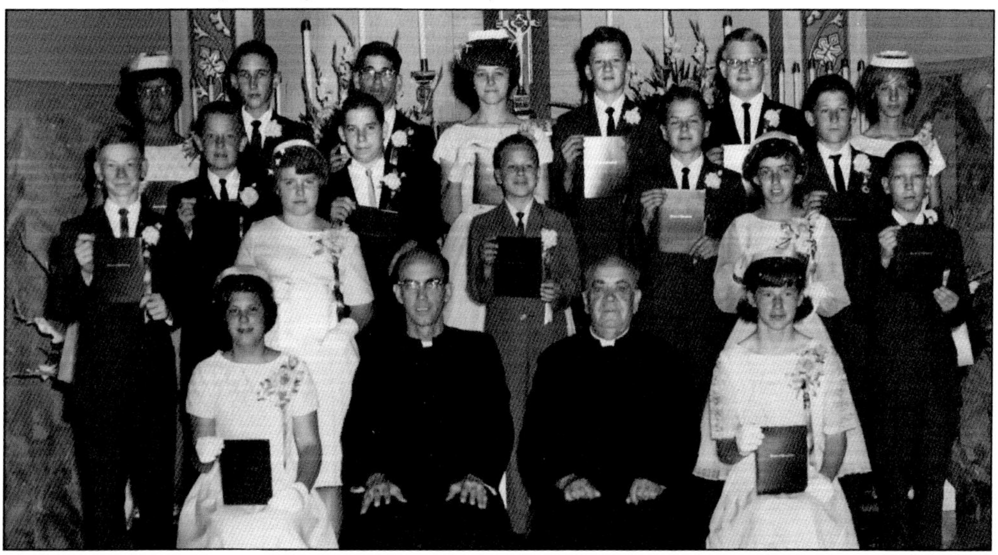

The 1965 graduating class appears inside the new St. Elizabeth Slovak Church on Campbell's Keystone Street. With them are the first two pastors of St. Elizabeth Church, Fr. Joseph L. Kostik (seated center right), who faithfully served St. Elizabeth parish for an amazing 45 years from 1922 until his retirement in 1967, and Fr. Cyril A. Adamko (seated center left), a parish son, who served the parish for 24 years until 1991. (Courtesy of Helen Hrehovcik Seman.)

Ruthenian immigrants from eastern Slovakia first attended St. Mary or St. Nicholas Byzantine Churches, but with strong support from the Greek Catholic Union, they established St. Michael the Archangel Byzantine Catholic Church in August 1922. Located in Campbell, the church was temporarily under Fr. John Krusko, and Fr. Nestor Rakovsky became the first resident pastor in 1926. Msgr. Victor Romza has served the parish at the new church on Robinson Road since 1963. Shown below is the first communion class of 1924. They are, from left to right, (first row) Fr. John Krusko, ? Geletka, Betty Kovach, Helen Vansuch, Veronica Cebula, Ann Vasko, and cantor Mr. Horvath; (second row) Steve Kalitich, ? Hostal, Dan Cebula, and Dan Kovalchick; (third row) George Jevesok, Frank Galida, and John Timcisko; (fourth row) Paul Vansuch, Joe Galida, and ? Perhach; (fifth row) Mike Dudick, John Kovach, and John Orjavsky. (Both, courtesy of the Campbell Historic Society, Florence Katula Galida.)

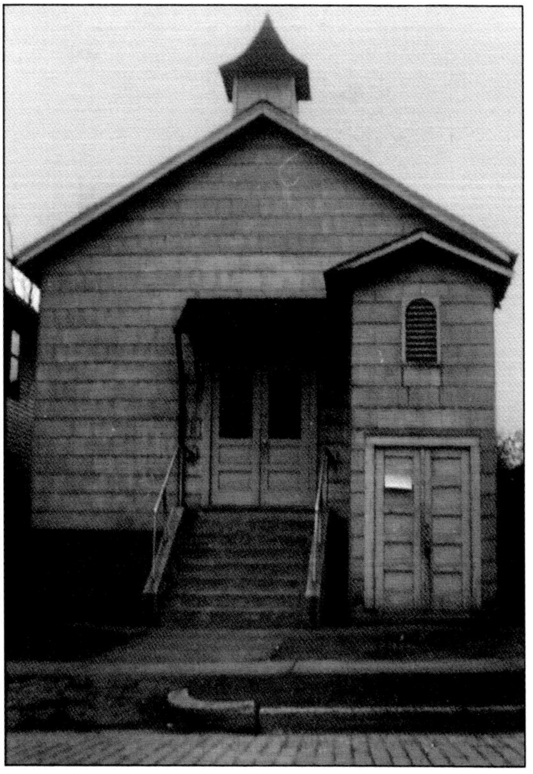

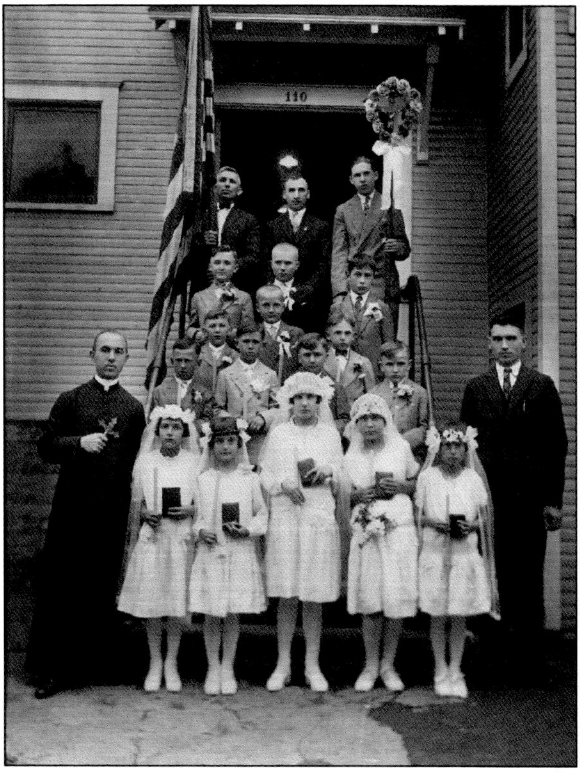

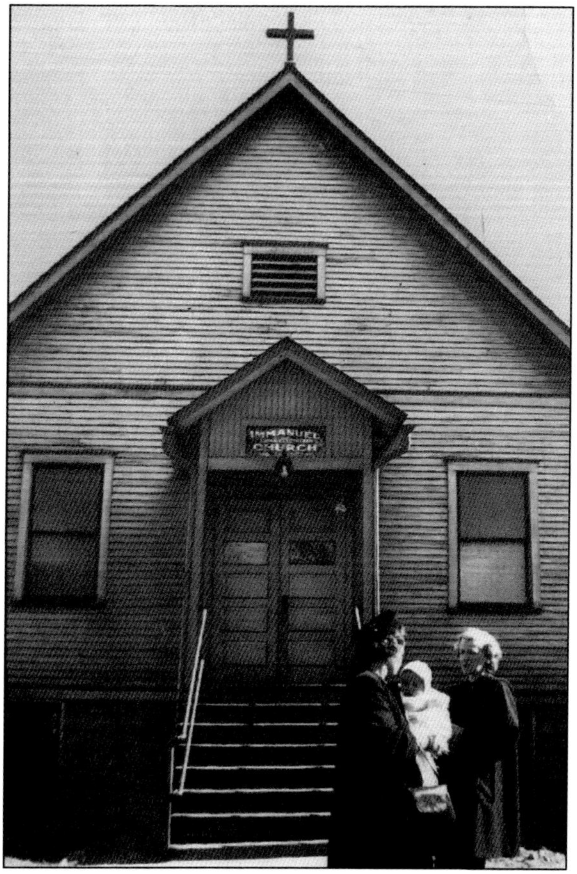

In June 1922, Ján Hus Lutheran members who wished to form a Lutheran congregation associated with the Slovak Evangelical Lutheran Church organized as Immanuel Slovak Lutheran Church. They asked Rev. Andrew Hvizdak to be their pastor. In 1925, they purchased property on North Brockway Avenue in Youngstown's West Side, bought the old United Methodist Church, lifted it onto rollers, and moved it one and a half blocks to its current site. Between 1926 and 1936, 14 vicars served Immanuel until John Zornan was appointed the first regular pastor. In 1942, the Reverend M. Dusan Marcis became pastor and would serve for 30 years. During his pastorate, the simple frame church was transformed into a brick Gothic structure. Fortunately, the beautiful wooden altar seen below was left intact. (Both, courtesy of Mark Miller, Concordia Lutheran Church.)

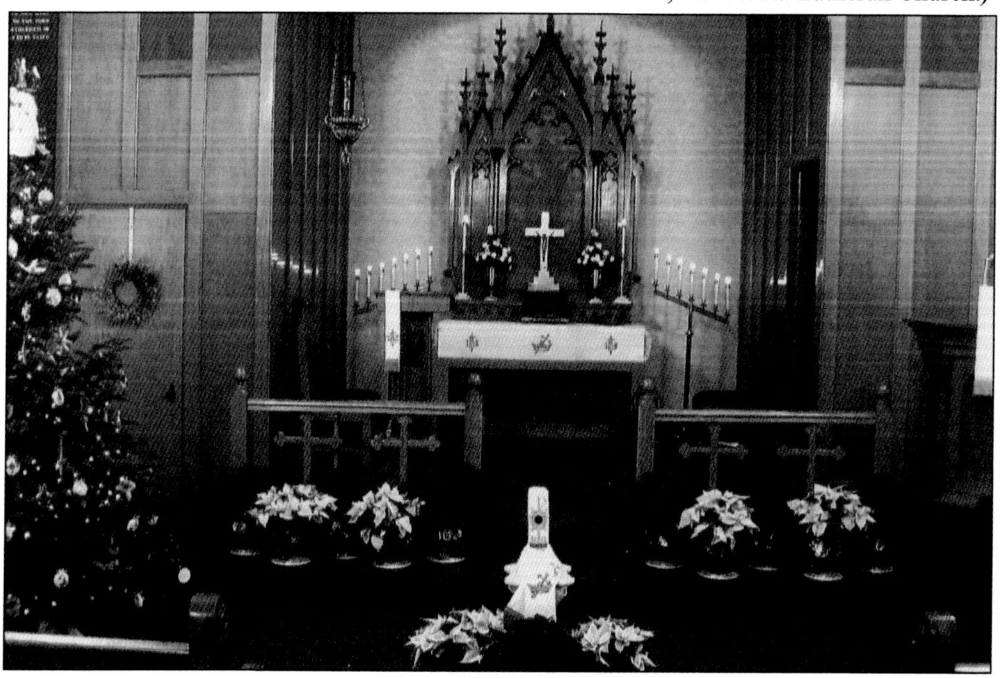

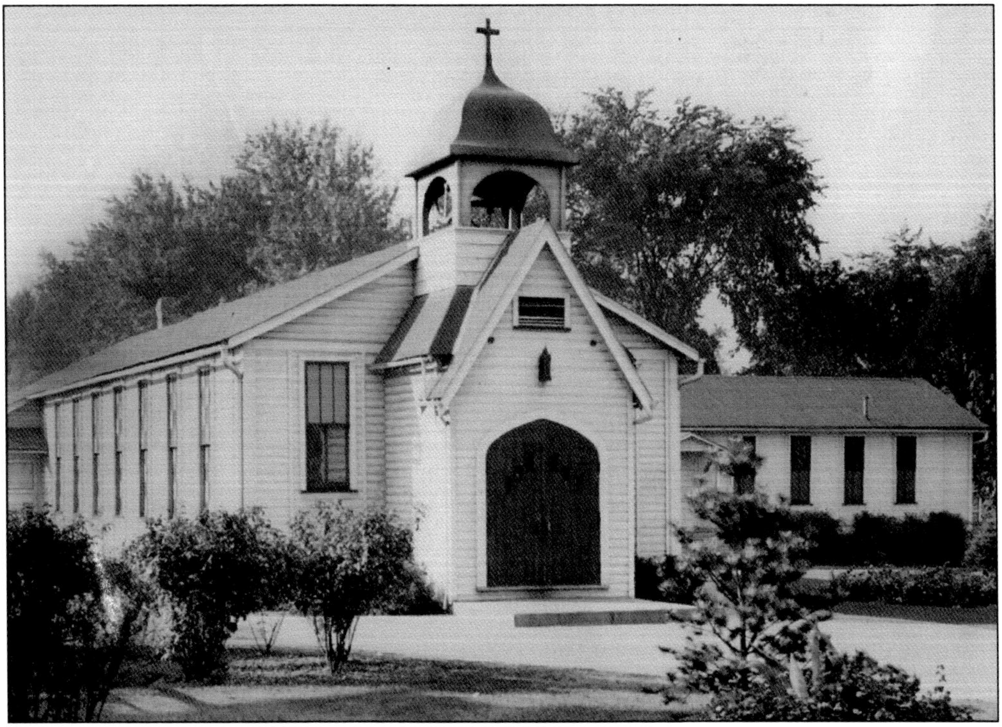

With the help of the local branch of the First Catholic Slovak Union in 1928, the Slovaks of Warren, Ohio, were able to organize SS. Cyril and Methodius Church, the only Roman Catholic Slovak parish in Trumbull County. For its first five years, the congregation worshipped at the Ruthenian Church of SS. Peter and Paul. The first pastor was the Reverend George R. Bobal, shown below with the First Communion class of the new parish in May 1929. Bobal was followed by Rev. John M. Kandrac. In September 1933, he constructed the first church (above) on High Street. In 1941, Rev. Joseph Krispinsky became the next pastor. As the congregation grew, he oversaw construction of the present church in 1949. (Both, courtesy of Sandra Saluga.)

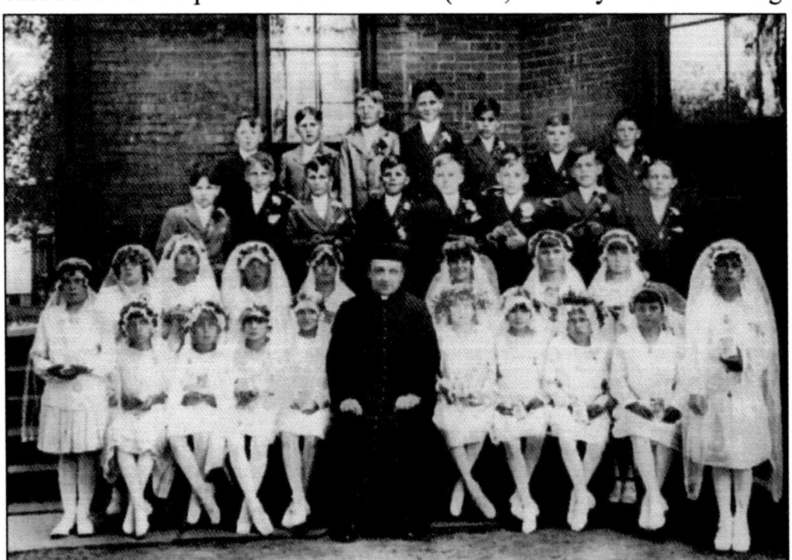

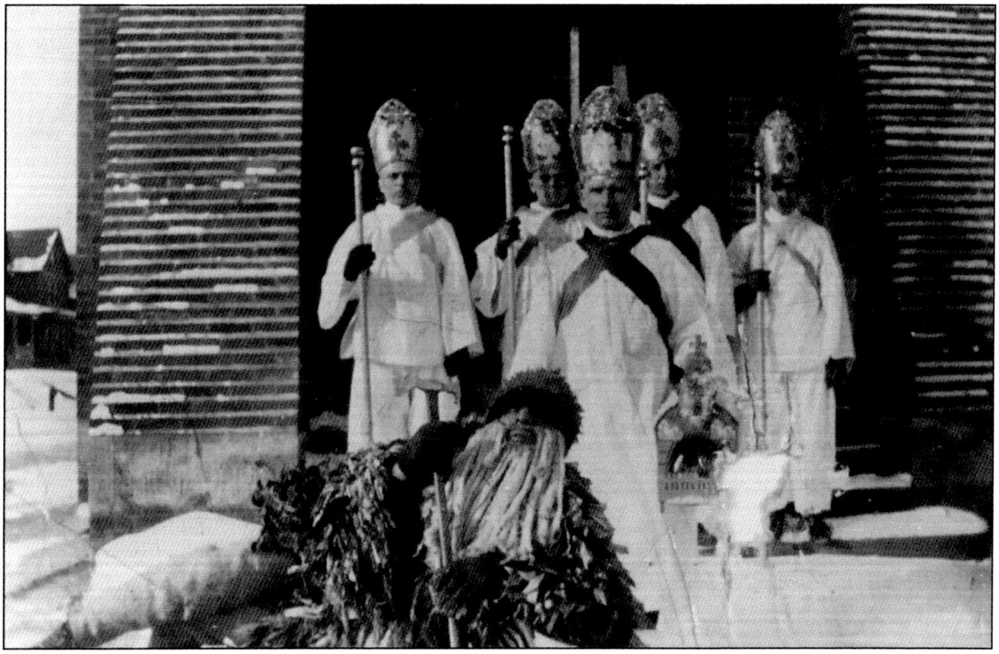

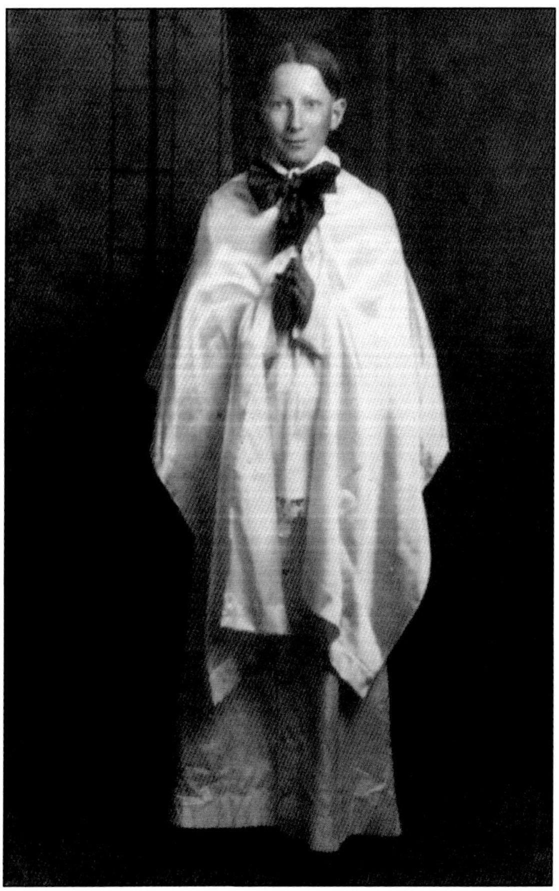

The Jasličkare, or Bethlehem Carolers, are a long tradition in many Slovak churches. Traditionally, this group went from house to house on Christmas Eve, telling the Bethlehem story. The costumes varied from church to church, and the skit could be serious or comical, but the theme was the same: the Christ Child is coming—get ready. John Olenik Sr. stands in front of the group. (Courtesy of St. Matthias Church.)

John Macalla was the son of Michael Macala from Poráč, Spiš, and Mary LaBuda-Gonda from Spišská Nová Ves. John attended Holy Trinity School in Struthers, seen here about 1925, when he served as an altar boy at the church, an honor and responsibility for the boys of Slovak families. (Courtesy of Barbara Macalla Jennings.)

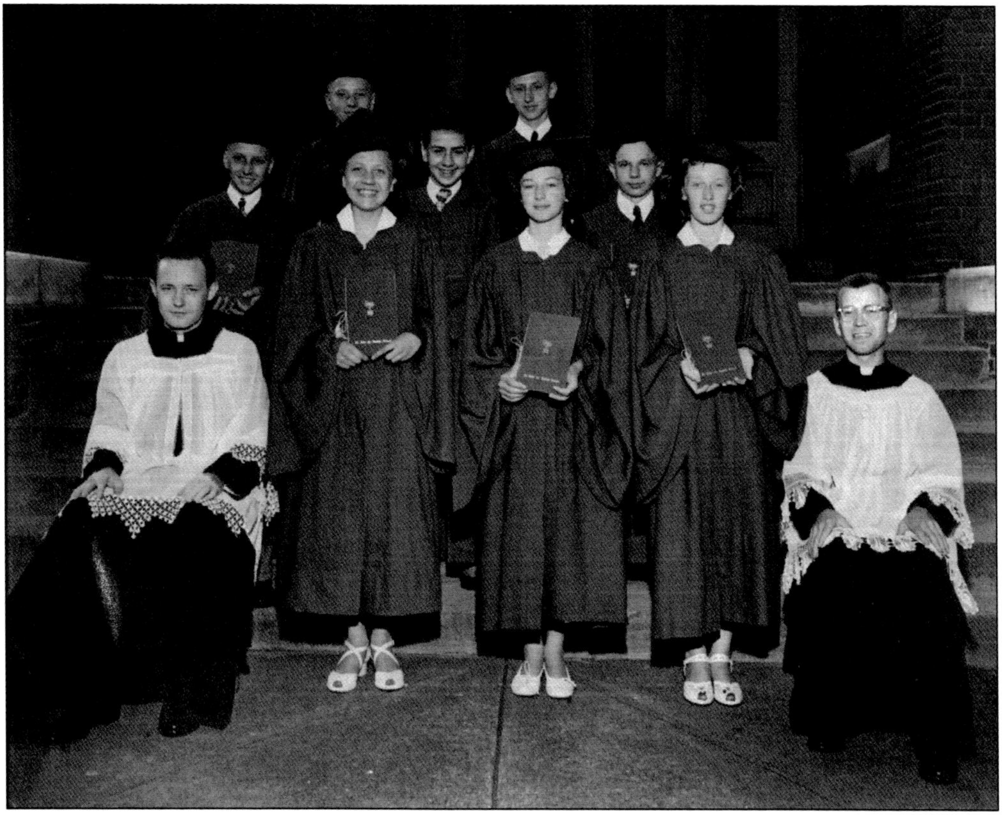

The 1950 eighth-grade graduating class of St. John the Baptist School is shown in front of the church. From left to right are (first row) Fr. George Franko, Theresa Duboj, Regina Rusnak, Patricia Hudak, and Fr. Michael Chonko; (second row), Joseph Hudak, James Surak, and Joseph Matvey; (third row) John Siva and Cyril Elias. (Courtesy of Regina Yurick Rusnak and Joseph Matvey.)

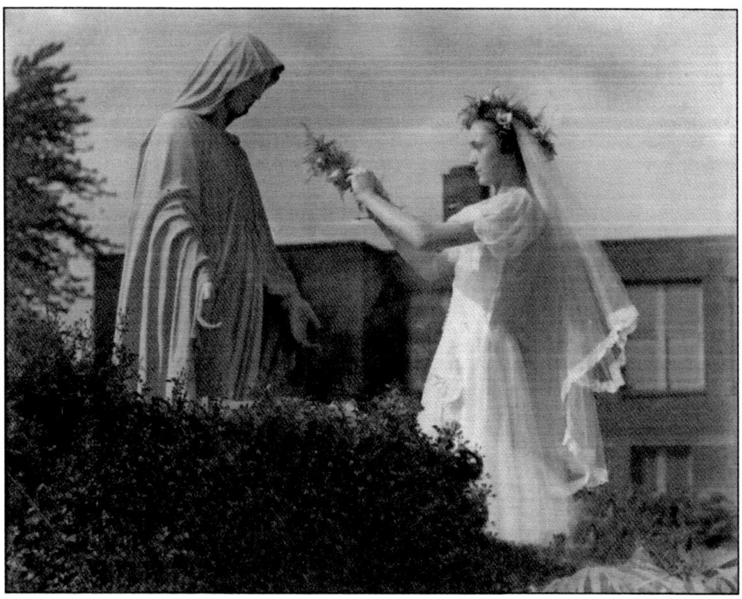

The parishioners of St. Elizabeth have a great devotion to Mary, patroness of both the United States and Slovakia, and the May crowning ceremony has always held a special place in their hearts. Shown in 1942 is Theresa Rudy crowning Mary in the outdoor garden at the Keystone Street property, where the new church would be built in 1954. (Courtesy of Alexia Sepesy Magazine.)

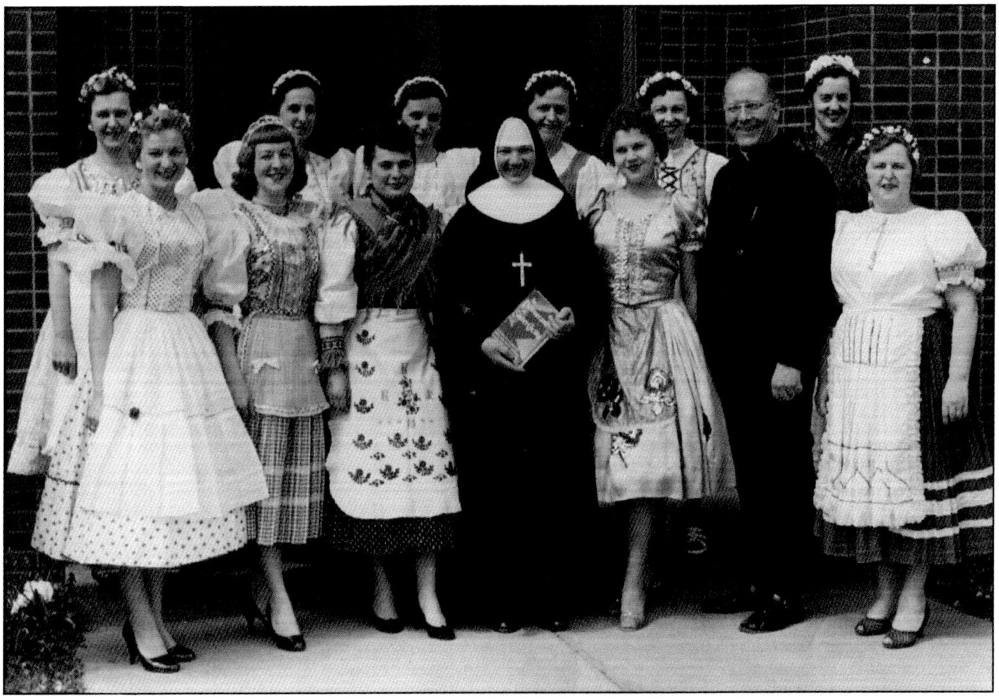

Sr. Cecelia Kondrc fled Czechoslovakia, fearing for her safety after helping many people escape the Communist regime. Seen here in 1957 at St. Matthias school are, from left to right, (first row) Dorothy Dulovic, two unidentified women, Sister Cecelia holding her book *The Deliverance of Sr. Cecelia*, unidentified, Father ?, and Julia Tomaskovich; (second row) Helen Krajnak, Helen Torica, Marguerite Doyel, Mary Novotny, Mary Sofranec Pavlina, and ? Hrishus. (Courtesy of Mary Sofranec Pavlina.)

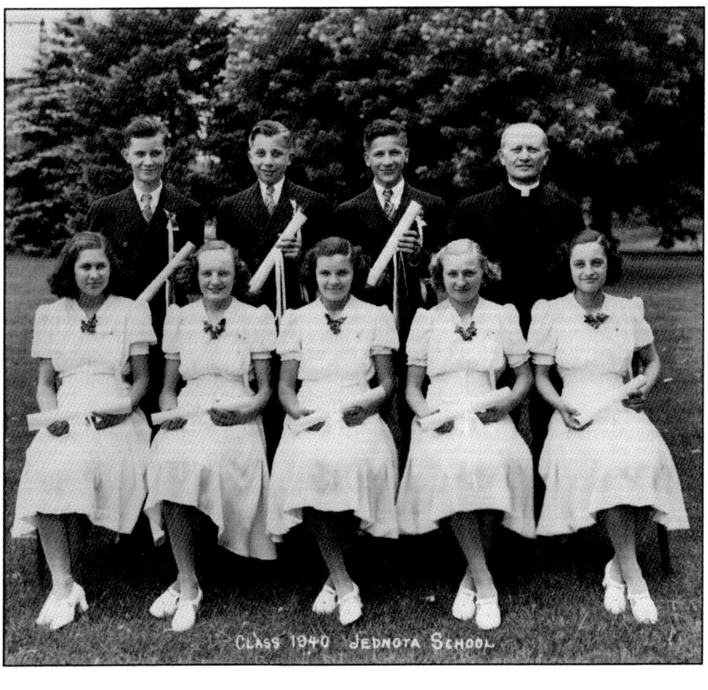

The early Slovak emigrants led hard lives, and often, children were left orphaned. Many were sent to the Jednota School run by the Sisters of SS. Cyril and Methodius in Middleton, Pennsylvania. Shown in this graduation picture from 1940 are, from left to right, (first row) Helen Hrehovčik, Irene Puškar, Katie Sarisky, Susie Smatlik, and Eleanor Dutko; (second row) John Kučinsky, unidentified, Billy Cuprik, and Fr. Michael Koško. (Courtesy of Helen Hrehovčik Seman.)

Five

For Love of this New Country

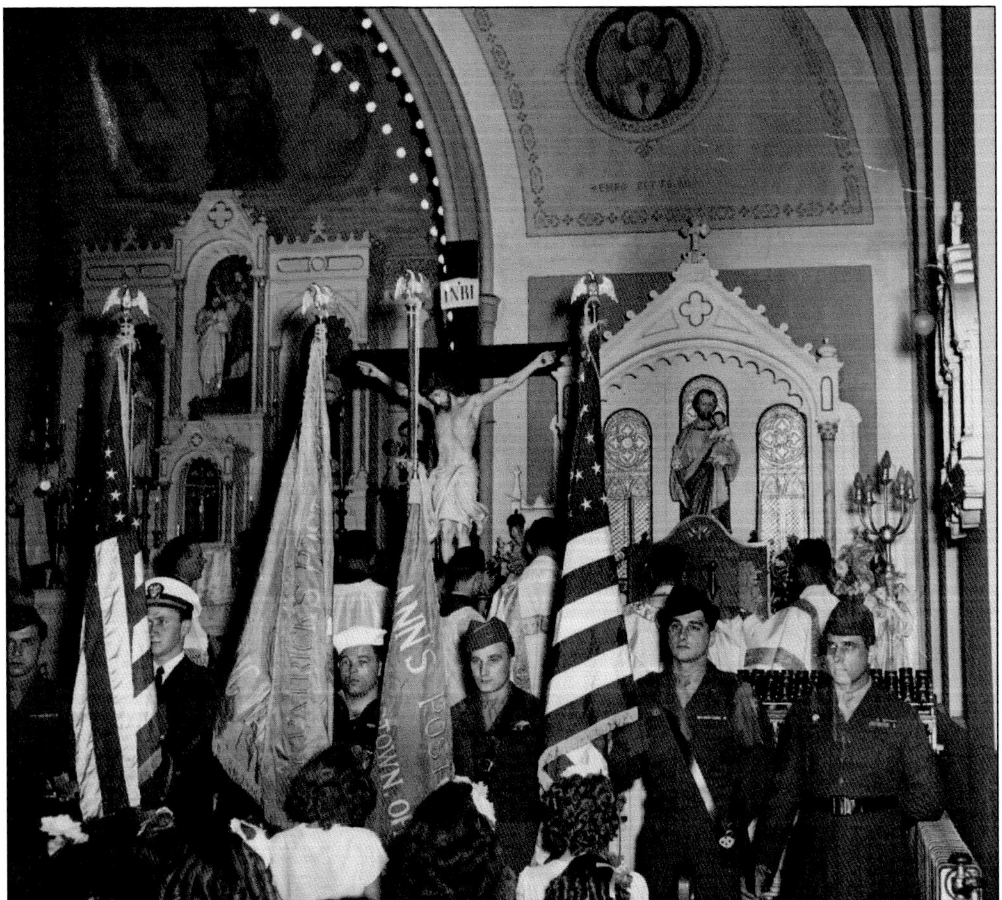

The Slovaks of the Greater Mahoning Valley were very proud of their sons who went to war for their new country. Many men (and women) served in the armed forces, and their families prayed for their safe return. Not all of them returned. This ceremony took place in St. John Slovak Church in Campbell, Ohio, honoring the soldiers who served during World War II. (Courtesy of Susan Gubany Summers.)

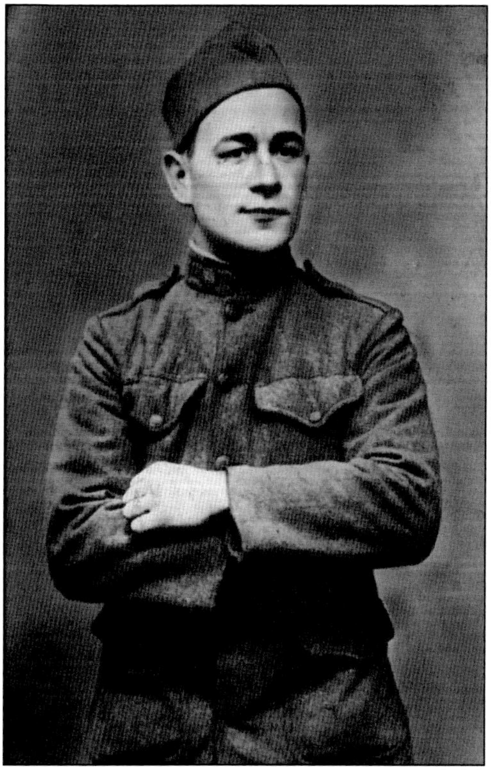

John Kramer served in the Army during World War I with Company B, 52nd Engineers Regiment. In 1918, he was assigned to Camp Upton in Long Island, New York. He also served in France. He married Mary Beck and made his home in Youngstown after the war. (Courtesy of Lucille Martinko Kramer.)

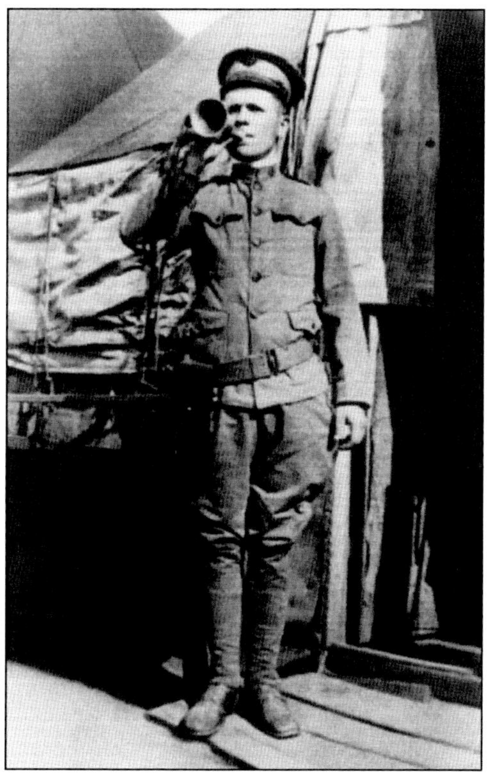

Sandor Sepesy emigrated from Austria-Hungary in 1914. Just three years after arriving in America, he enlisted in the US Army and served as the bugler in Company C, 29th Infantry, from September 1917 to July 1919. His wife was Anna Petrek Sepesy, who immigrated in the early 1900s. (Courtesy of Alexia Sepesy Magazine.)

Bernard Kramer, son of John and Mary Beck Kramer, was a US Army staff sergeant in the 15th Field Artillery Observation Battalion, APO 512. He served in Africa and the Italian Campaign. When he returned to Youngstown, Bernard married Lucille Martinko, whom he had met before the war. They had two sons, Kenneth and Glen. Bernard was the cutting floor foreman for Sydney Moyer Tailors. (Courtesy of Lucille Martinko Kramer.)

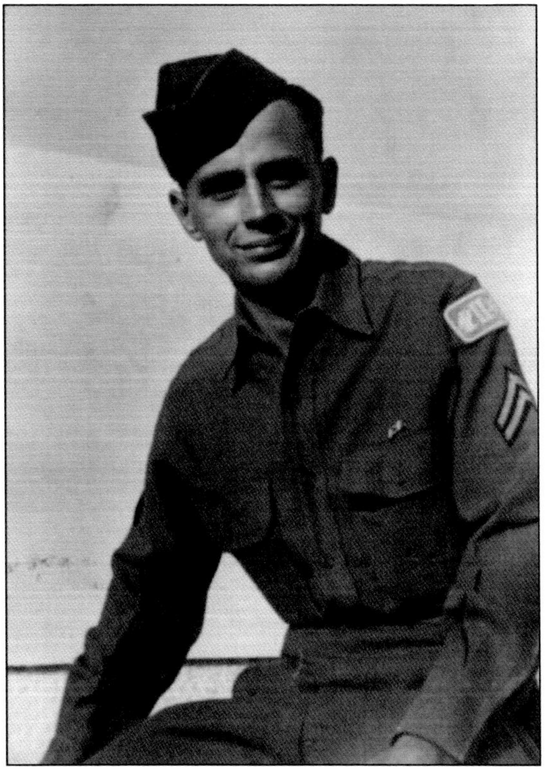

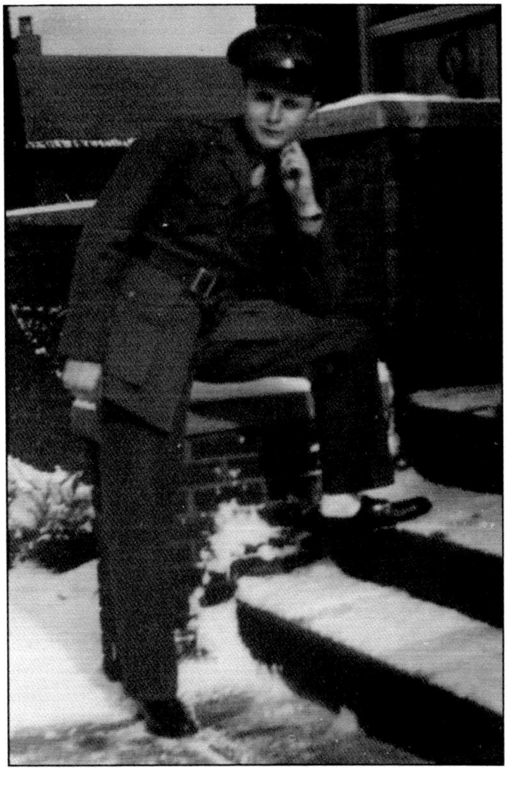

Alexander Sepesy, son of Sandor and Anna Petrek Sepesy, was drafted into the Marine Corps in 1945. After basic training, he was shipped out to China, where he served with the 1st Marine Division, 7th Marine Regiment. He actually received his high school diploma in 1946 while serving in China. After the war, he married Theresa Rudy. Alexander's brother Frank served in the US Navy. (Courtesy of Alexia Sepesy Magazine.)

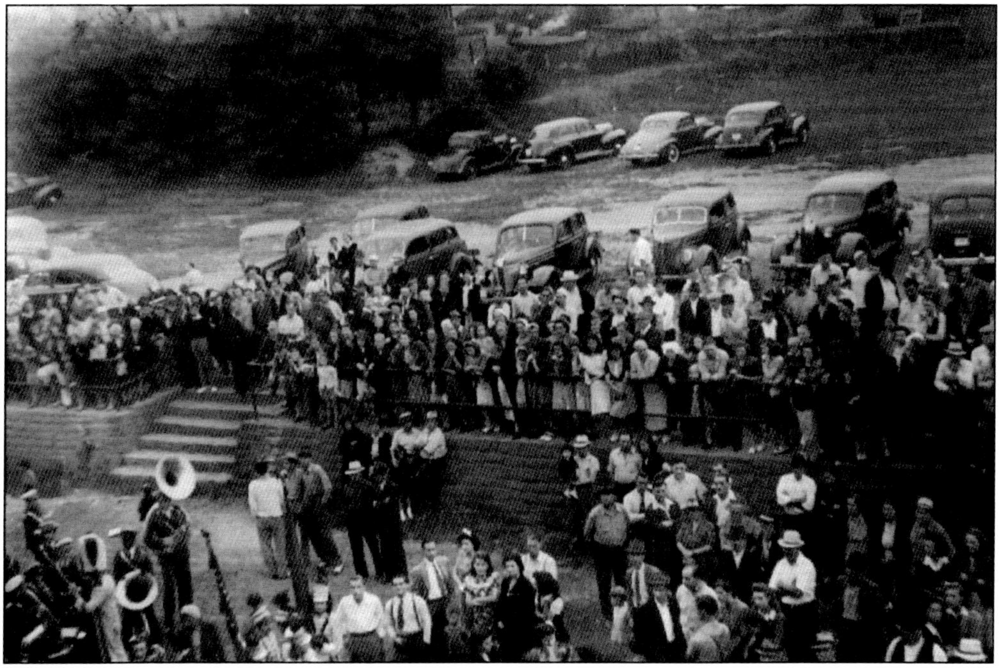

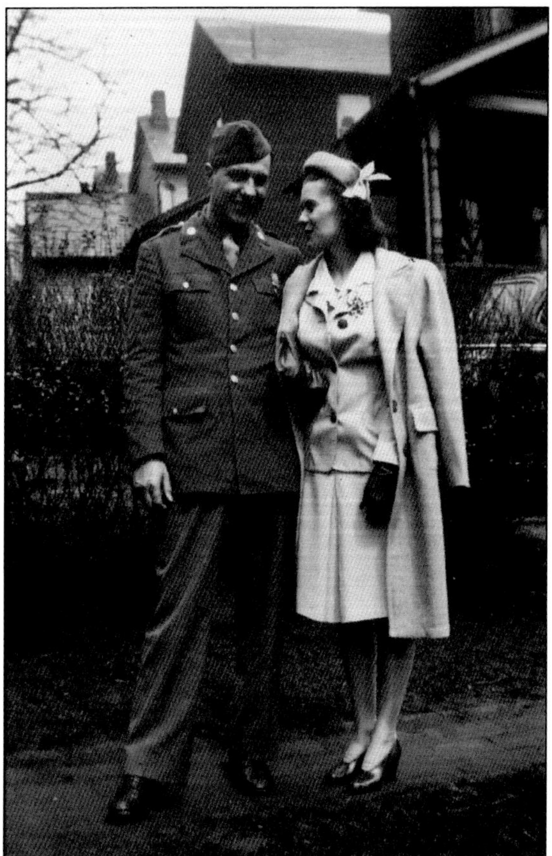

Families gathered at Gordon School in Campbell, Ohio, to send off the first group of draftees into service at the beginning of World War II. The men boarded buses to Cleveland, Ohio, for their physicals and were then sent directly to their bases throughout the United States. As the buses pulled away, the tears began to fall. (Courtesy of the Campbell Historical Society, Florence Katula Galida.)

Michael Hanuschak—shown with his wife, Margaret Baker Hanuschak, on Campbell's Morley Avenue—served in the 106th Division of the US Army as a combat MP (military police). He fought in the Battle of the Bulge and was stationed in Belgium. After his discharge, he worked at Jones and Laughlin Steel. He and his wife had two children, Delbert and Loretta. (Courtesy of Loretta Hanuschak Ekoniak.)

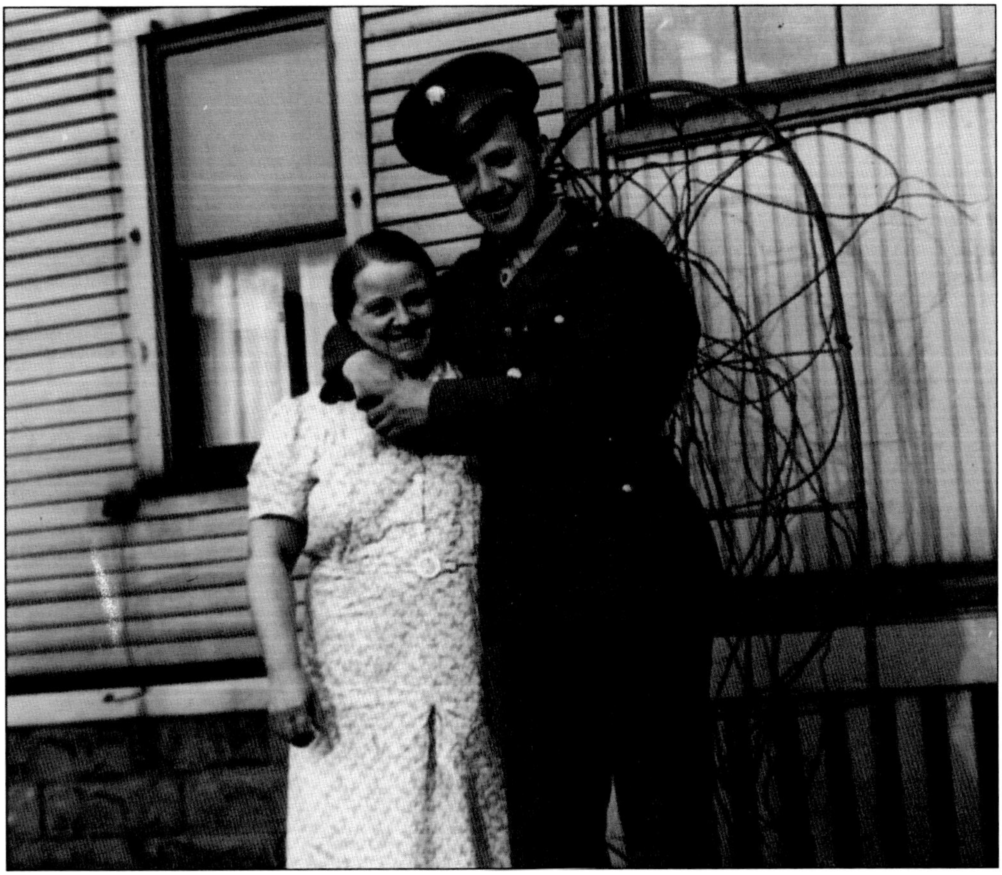

Paul Sedzmak is shown with his mother, Katarina, outside their Bruce Street home while on leave during Easter 1942. Shortly after returning to duty, he was taken prisoner of war and spent December 1942 to May 1945 at the notorious German prison camp, Stalag IIB. (Courtesy of Joseph Sedzmak.)

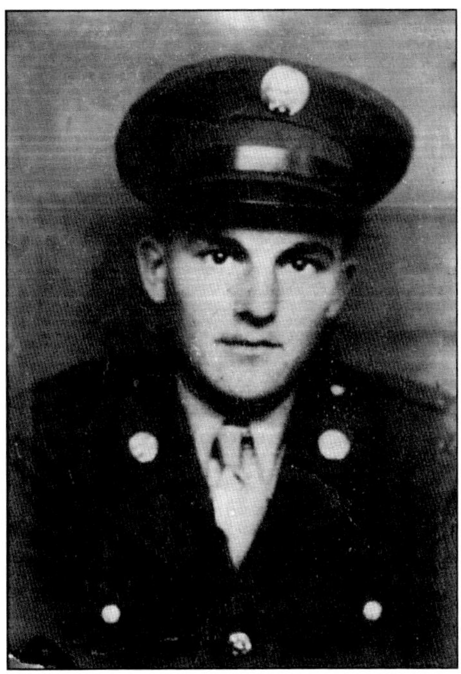

Paul Spisak was born July 12, 1924, in Youngstown, Ohio, the son of Michael and Anna (Segeda) Spisak, and attended Chaney High School. On December 21, 1942, at the age of 18, he enlisted in the US Army, serving in the Pacific theater, mainly in New Guinea. Upon returning home, he was employed at US Steel until retiring and moving to Florida. On May 9, 1950, he married Patricia Hann, and they had four children: James, Carol, Mary, and Kathleen. (Courtesy of Patricia Hann Spisak.)

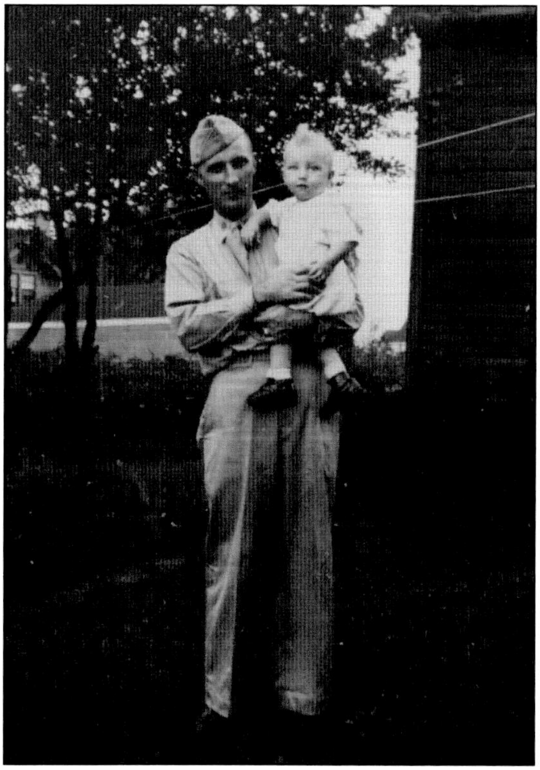

John Zajac Adams, while serving as a sergeant in the Ohio National Guard, is shown at his Cambridge Avenue home in Youngstown with his new son David. He served as a cook in the Guard until 1947. (Courtesy of David Adams.)

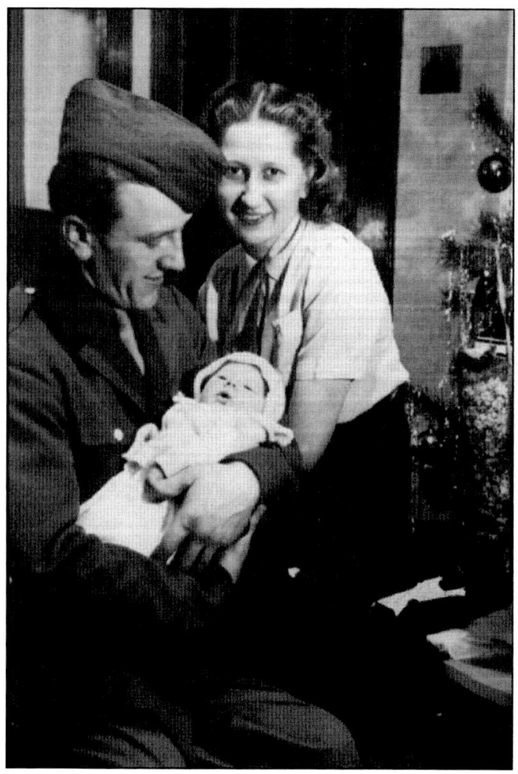

On December 27, 1942, Michael Repasky was home on leave from the Army for the Christmas holiday season. There to welcome him was his wife, Mary, and his newborn son, Michael Raymond, born on December 1, 1942. (Courtesy of Janet Repasky Morris.)

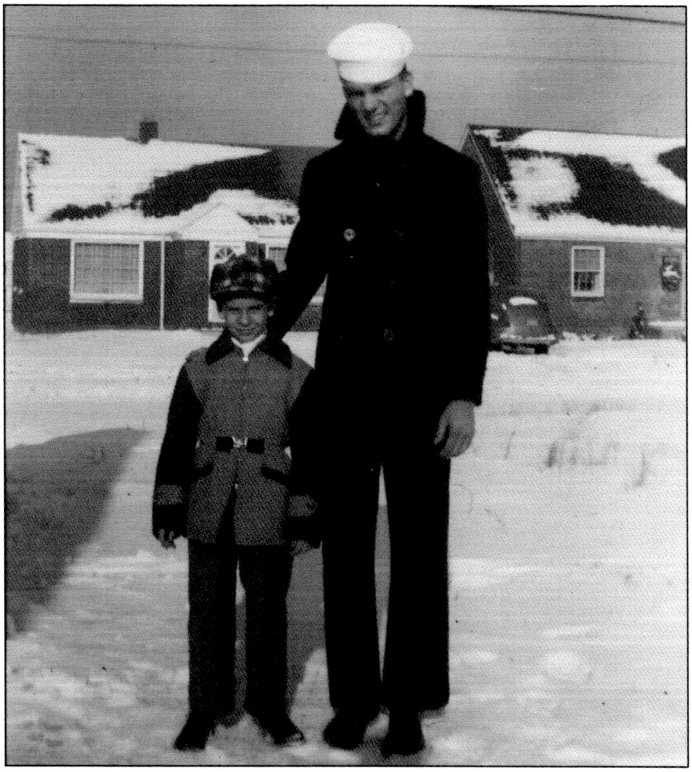

Raymond Baker, son of Michael and Anna Baker, is shown with nephew John Melvin Pachuta. Raymond enlisted in the Navy after graduation, serving on the USS *Toledo* during the Korean Conflict. He saw action during the Invasion at Inchon, receiving three Battle Stars. He married Audrey Ruane and had three sons: Mark, David, and Michael. He was an engineer at US Steel for 35 years. (Courtesy of Loretta Hanuschak Ekoniak.)

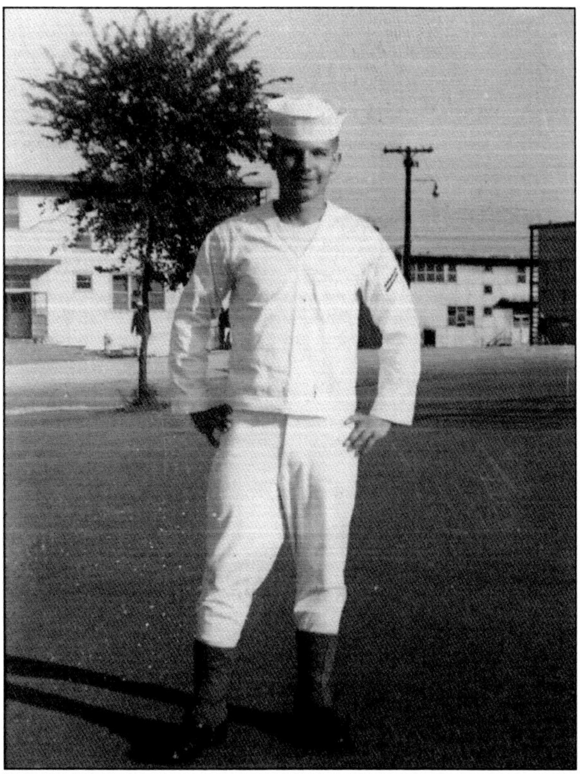

Joseph Matvey, shown in August 1954 at boot camp in Bainbridge, Maryland, served in the US Navy from 1954 to 1958. He served aboard the carrier USS *Bainbridge* and was in the Submarine Service with a rating of YN2 (SS). He spent most of those four enlisted years at sea. (Courtesy of Joseph Matvey.)

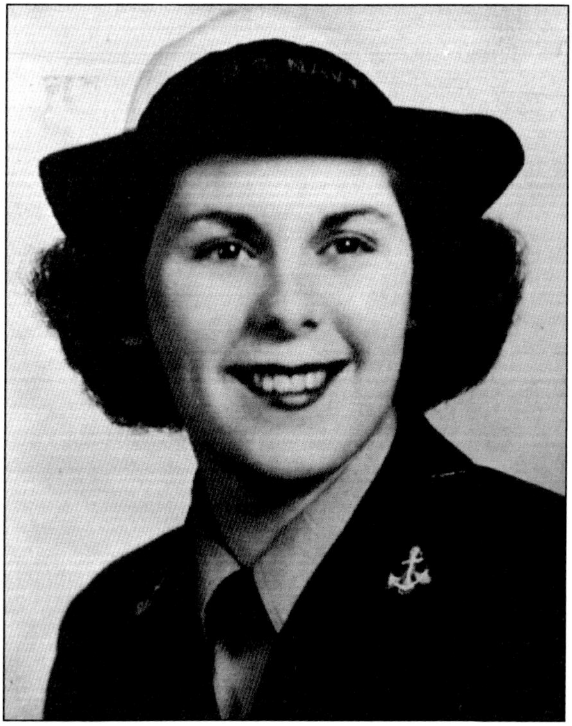

Mildred Kracko was a US Navy WAVE (Women Accepted for Volunteer Emergency Service) and served in Corpus Christi, Texas, and Memphis, Tennessee, with the Navy Air Corps during World War II. After her discharge from the service, she settled in Campbell, Ohio, with her husband, Joseph, who also was a Navy veteran. (Courtesy of Campbell Historical Society, Florence Katula Galida.)

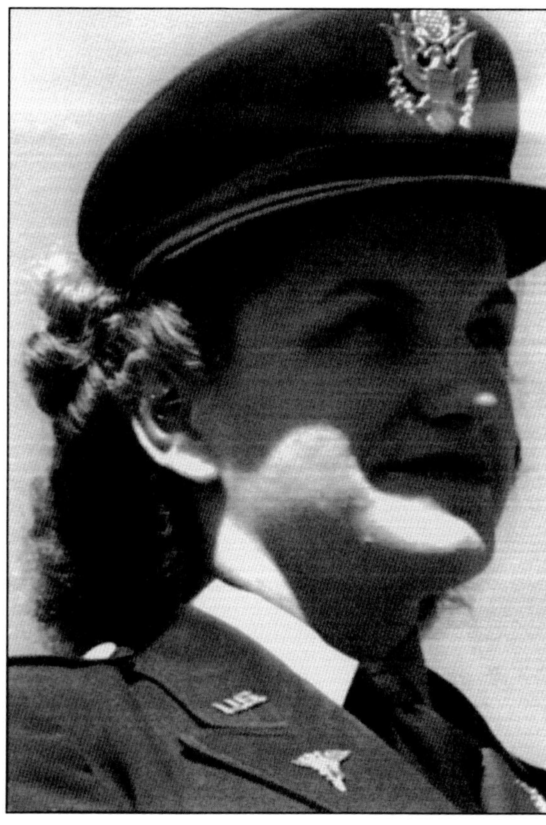

Mary Babnic, daughter of Steven and Julia Kvoriak Babnic from Závadka, Slovakia, served in the US Army Air Corps of Nurses from 1946 to 1953 during both World War II and the Korean Conflict. She was a nurse anesthetist for the Youngstown Hospital Association for 38 years. She was cohost of the *Slovak Hour* on WKTL radio in Struthers and president of the American Slovak Cultural Association for more than 20 years. (Courtesy of Diana Babnich Coliani.)

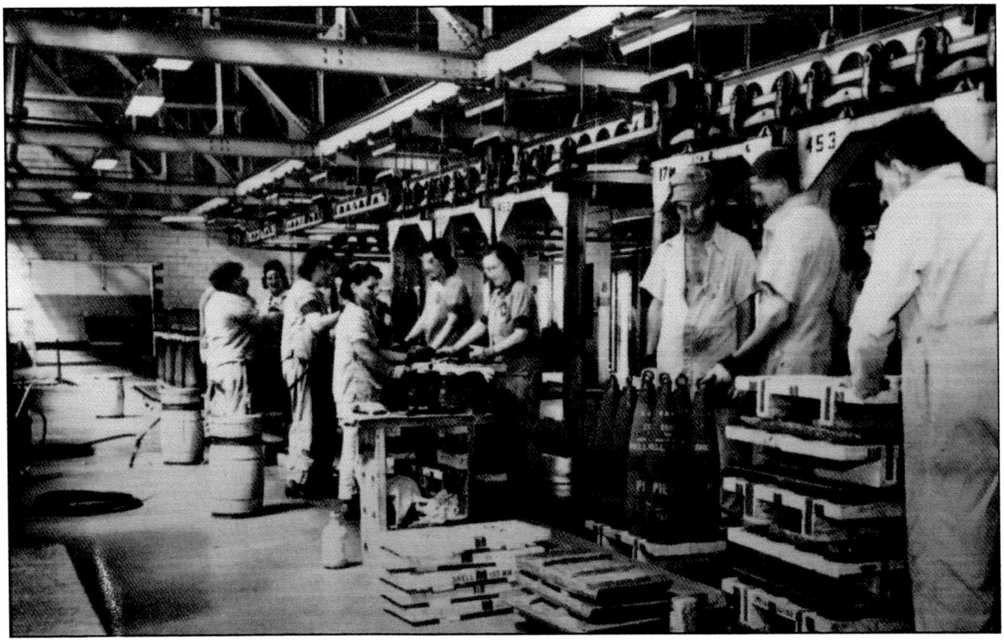

Not all women served their country in the military. Many served on the home front, filling jobs that the men were not there to do. The Ravenna Arsenal operated 12 production lines, manufacturing bombs, shells, and other munitions for the war effort. Women, as seen in this photograph from August 1945, filled many of those lines. (Courtesy of the *Cleveland Press* Collection, Cleveland State University Library.)

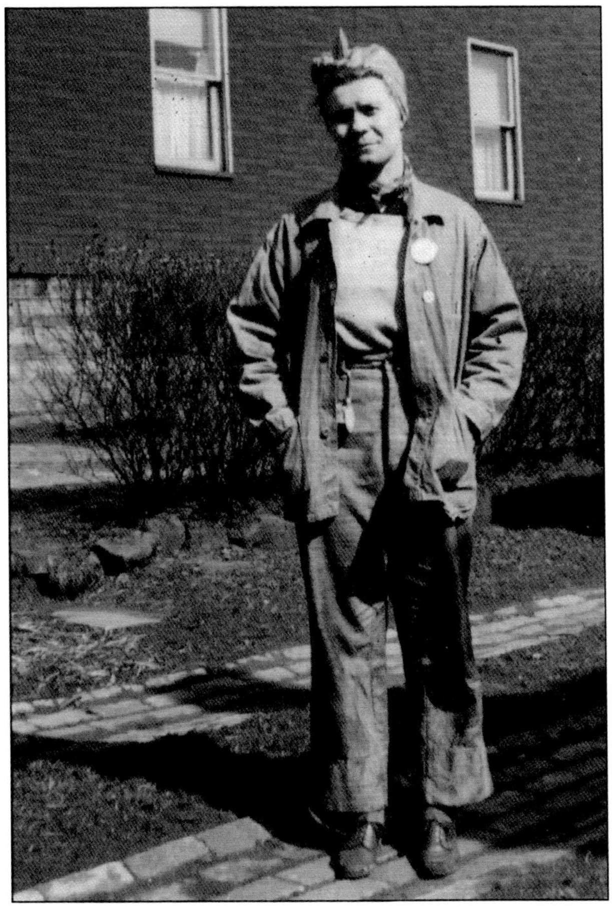

Other women took jobs in the mills to make sure that the production of steel vital to the war effort was not interrupted. Here, Margaret Baker Hanuschak gets ready to leave for her job operating the overhead crane at the Campbell Works of Republic Steel. Before this job, she and her sister Helen both worked at the Ravenna Arsenal. (Courtesy of Loretta Hanuschak Ekoniak.)

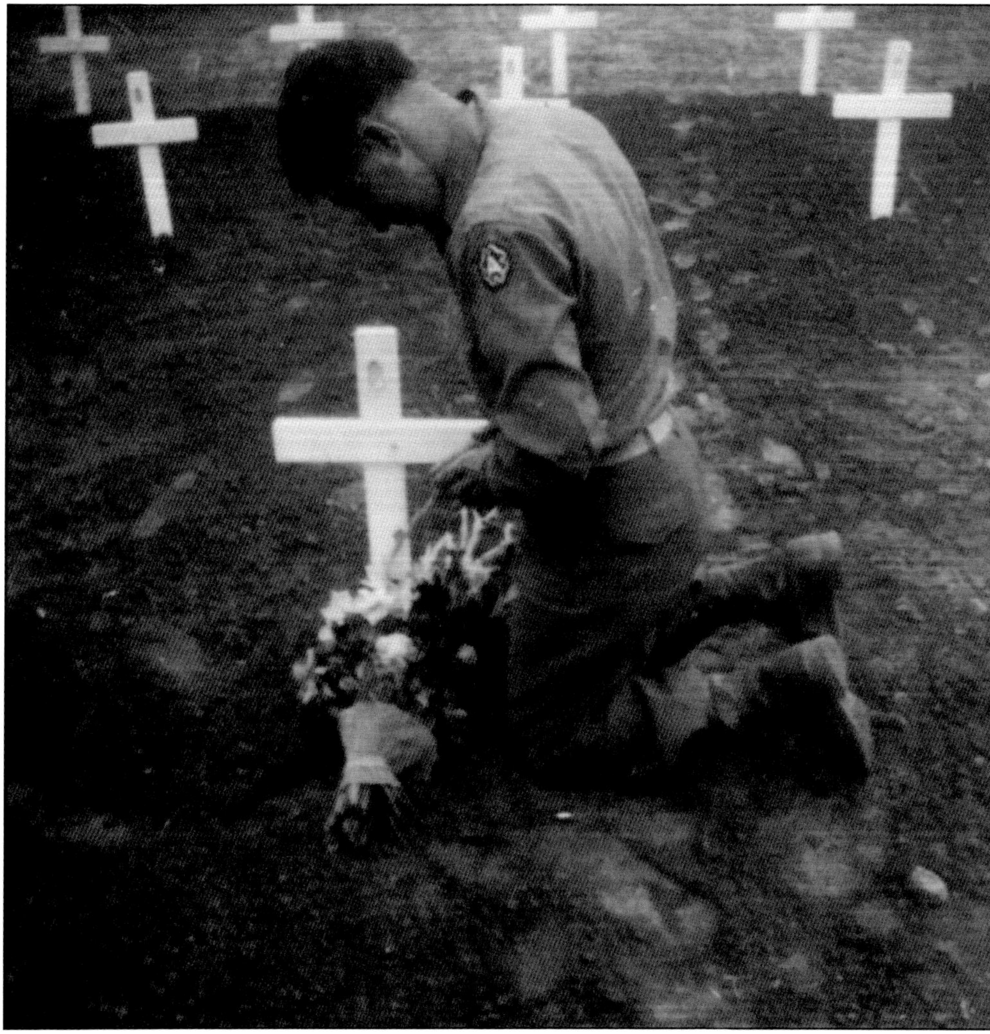

Sadly, many of the soldiers from Slovak families did not come back from the war. In 1945, as the war ended, Paul Garčar visited the grave of his brother T.Sgt. Andrew Garčar, 95th Division, 379th Infantry, who was killed on New Year's Eve 1944. He is buried in a cemetery in Hamm, Luxenbourg. (Courtesy of Ronald Garchar.)

VEČNÝ ODPOČINOK † VIČNAJA PAMJAT
"Eternal Rest † Eternal Memory"

Six

For Love of the Game

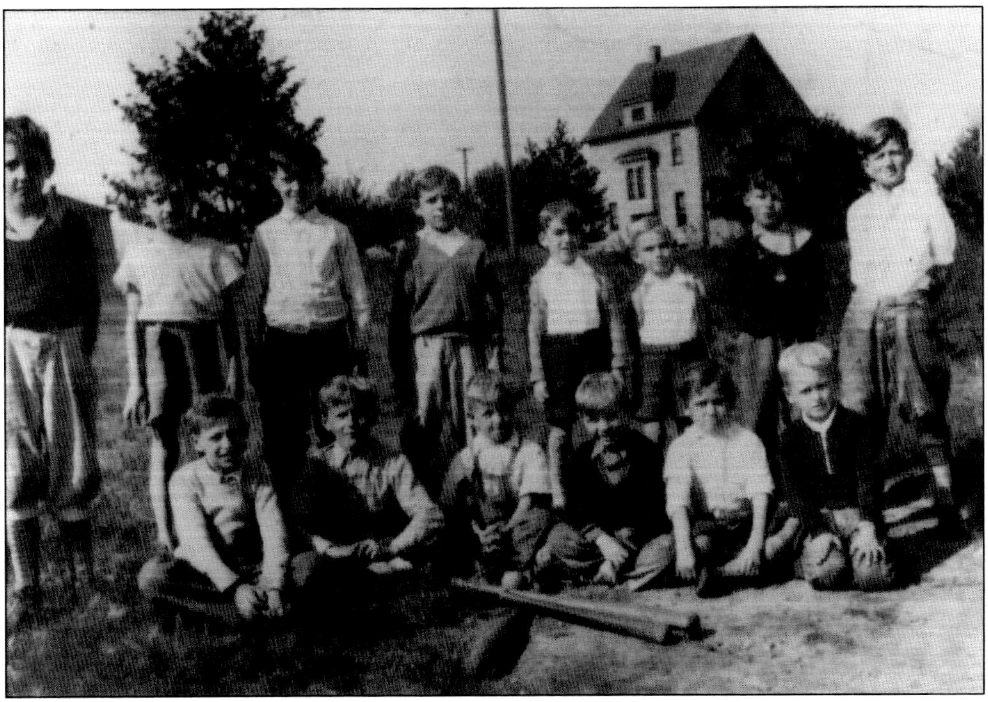

Sports were always important in the Slovak community. Slovaks worked hard but took time to play. Shown in October 1935 is the first Little League team in Lansingville. From left to right are (first row) Paul Rabovsky, Bern Repasky, Ray Staron, William Hoza, Joe Sobinovsky, and Jerry Novotny; (second row) Bill Repasky, Al Kotasek, Paul Petro, John Smercansky, Richard Berry, Jim Berry, Ben Balkan, and John Kuropchak. (Courtesy of Robert Smercansky.)

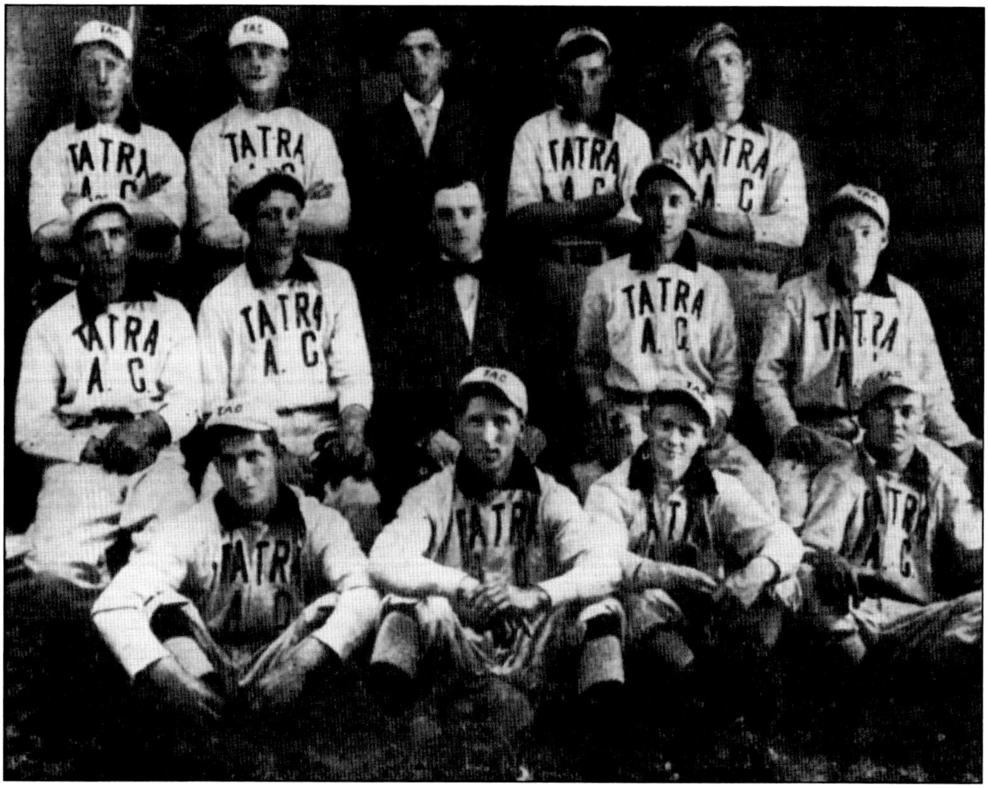

Started in 1908, the Tatra Club was the first organized Slovak baseball team. Players are, from left to right, (first row) George Masuer, Andrew Sekerek, Michael Chuey, and Joseph Vopersall; (second row) John Mauser, Michael Mauser, Joseph Vascak, manager Steven Hannis, and Andrew Hamrock; (third row) Joe Rakocy, John Chuey, Steven Almer, Joseph Almer, and Steven Slifka. (Courtesy of Michael Kupec and John Gingery.)

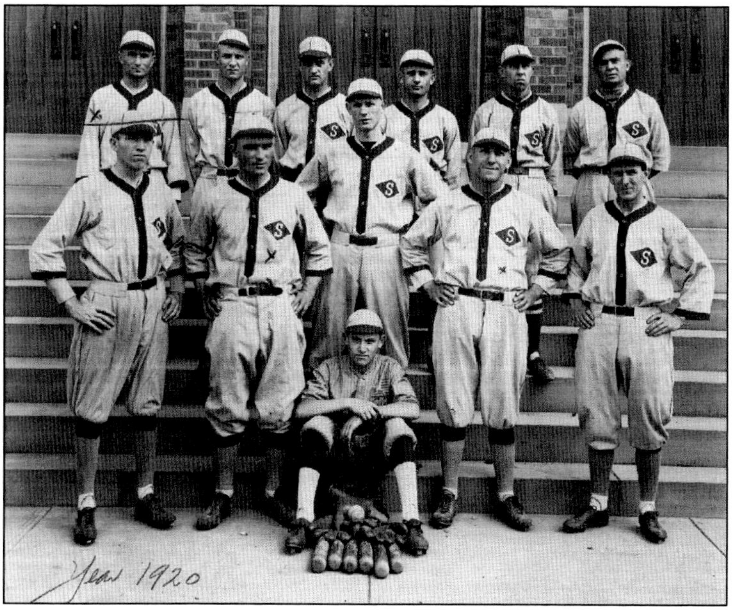

The 1920 Sokol baseball team is shown here. From left to right are (front row) ? Morrisey, Joe Kramer, Mike Obruba, George Prokop, Curly Blount; (second row) manager Joe Hura, Steve Vidis, Steve Hura, Mike Orenic, Tom Gundry, and Andy Johnson. The batboy in front is unidentified. (Courtesy of Ann Hruska.)

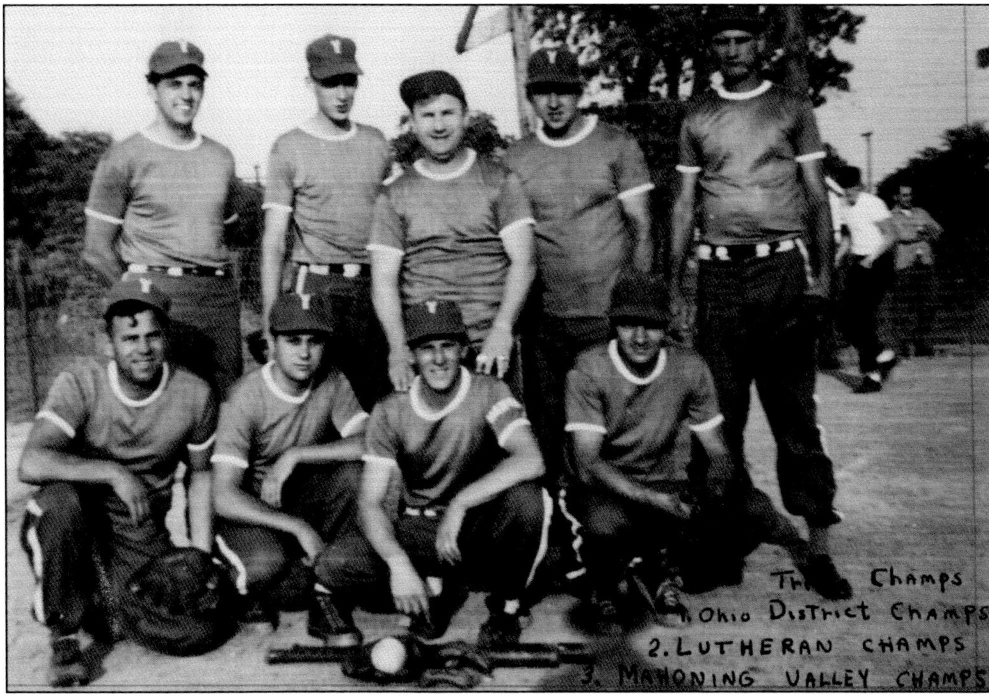

The John Hus 1954 Ohio District Lutheran and Mahoning Valley Champions are shown, from left to right, as follows: (first row) P. Barto, D. Balint, manager M. Barto, and P. Jakubec; (second row) J. Hlavec, J. Kaminsky, G. Barto, E. Dovala, and F. Antal. (Courtesy of Margaret Textoris Tomo.)

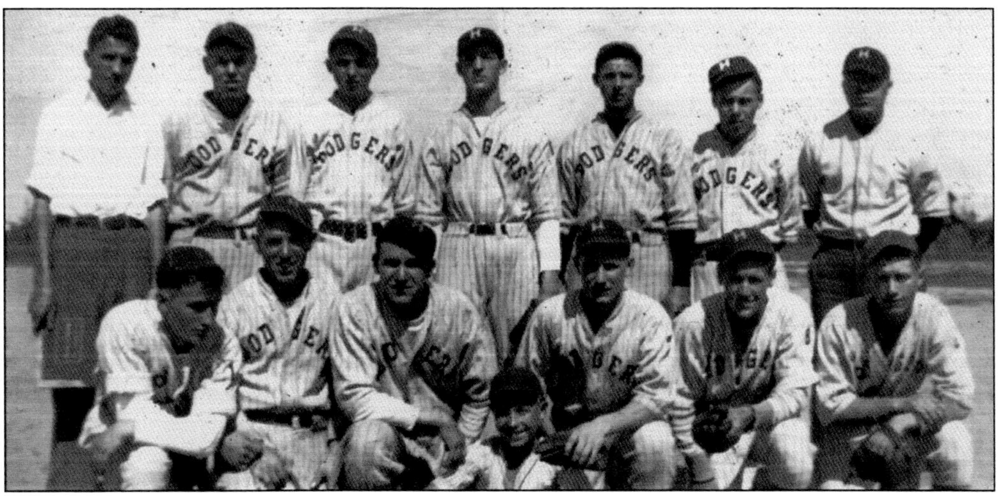

Sandlot baseball is senior baseball played by teams unaffiliated with Major League Baseball (MLB) teams, although many MLB players got their start playing sandlot ball. The Haseltine Dodgers belonged to the Slovak League, a powerful interstate league organized in 1920. In 1934, there were 22 teams in the league. The Haselton Dodgers team members in 1934 were Paul Chuey, John Elosh, Nick Galida, brothers Andy and John Garchar, Mike Hamrock, Eddie Hetmanski, brothers Mike and Nick Hanuschak, John Kacenga, John Krachko, Steve Macek, Andy Maretich, George Novak, Ernest Oblock, Steve Repasky, Martin Simchak, Frank Vitoskie, and Joe Zifchak. (Courtesy of Loretta Hanuschak Ekoniak.)

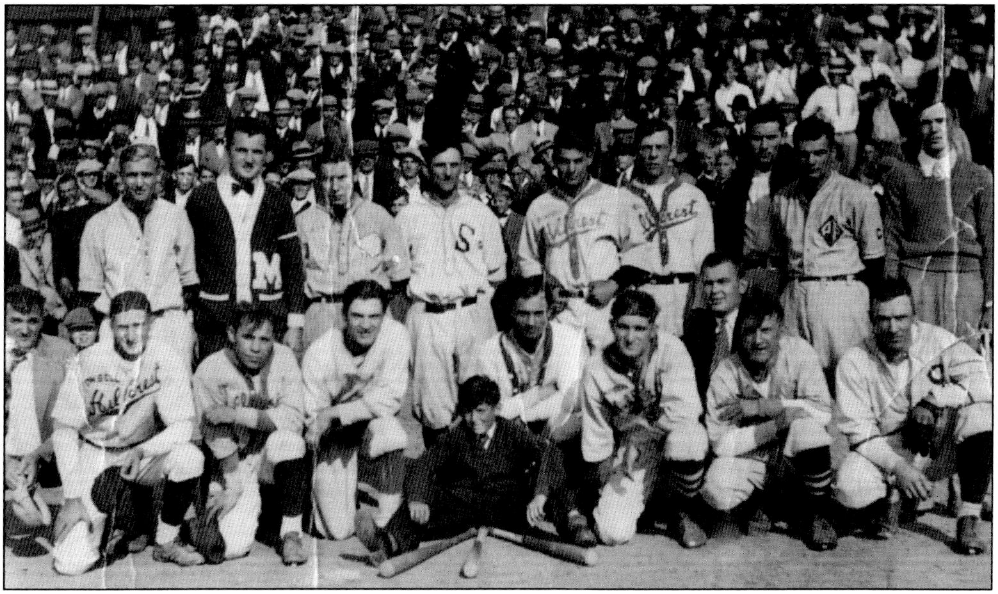

This Holy Trinity field shows the Campbell Hillcrest team in 1931. Players are, from left to right, (first row) Matthew Wansack Sr., Matthew Wansack Jr., Paul Hura, Matthew Yurak, Joseph Zetts, Michael Jumbar, John Komarc, Michael Guidos, and Frank Leskey; (second row) Michael Voytilla, Teamus Cernoch, Cyril McKula, Al Leskey, Michael Katula, Andrew Greene, Paul Minnick, Theodore Katula, and Joseph Vargo. The young boy in the center is unidentified. (Courtesy of the Campbell Historical Society, Florence Katula Galida.)

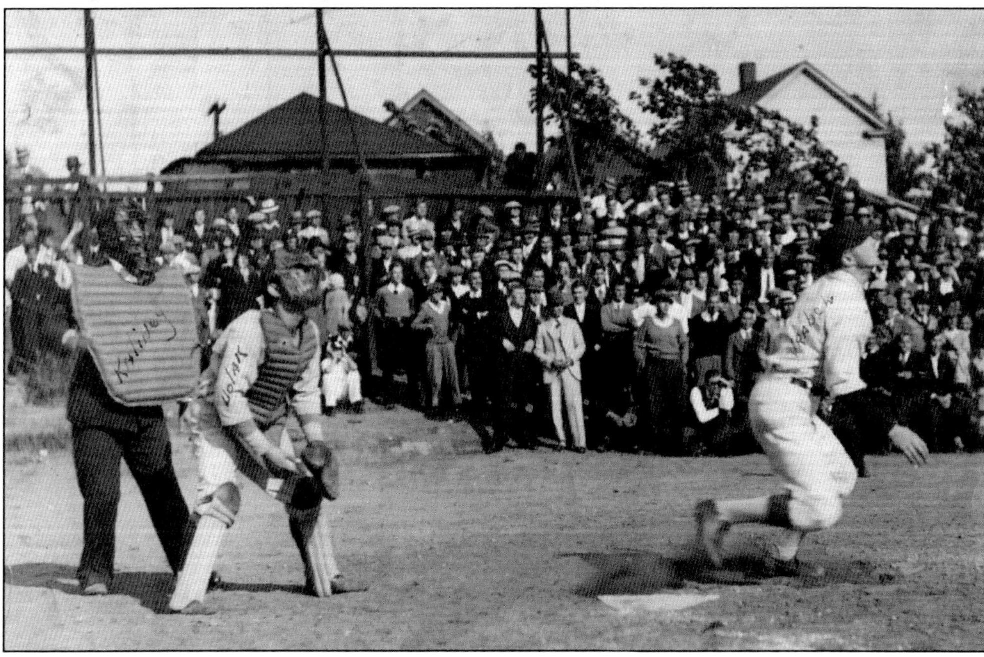

There were no stadiums or bleachers in the 1920s, so the fans stood or sat on the ground and cheered for their favorite team. Umpiring this game at Gordon Park in East Youngstown is Joe Kaliney, the catcher is Paul Dolak, and Joseph Vrabel has just hit the ball. (Courtesy of the Campbell Historical Society, Florence Katula Galida.)

One of the best-known Slovaks from the Mahoning Valley, who enjoyed a very successful career in Major League Baseball, is George "Shotgun" Shuba from Youngstown, Ohio. He played for the Brooklyn Dodgers, including three World Series games. He is known for shaking hands with Jackie Robinson as Jackie rounded the bases for a home run in 1946. He is shown at George Shuba Day in Pittsburgh with nephews Tommy (left) and Jimmy Shuba. (Courtesy of James Shuba.)

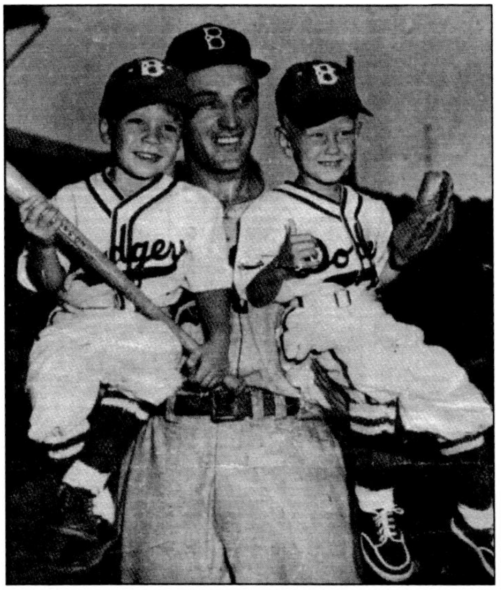

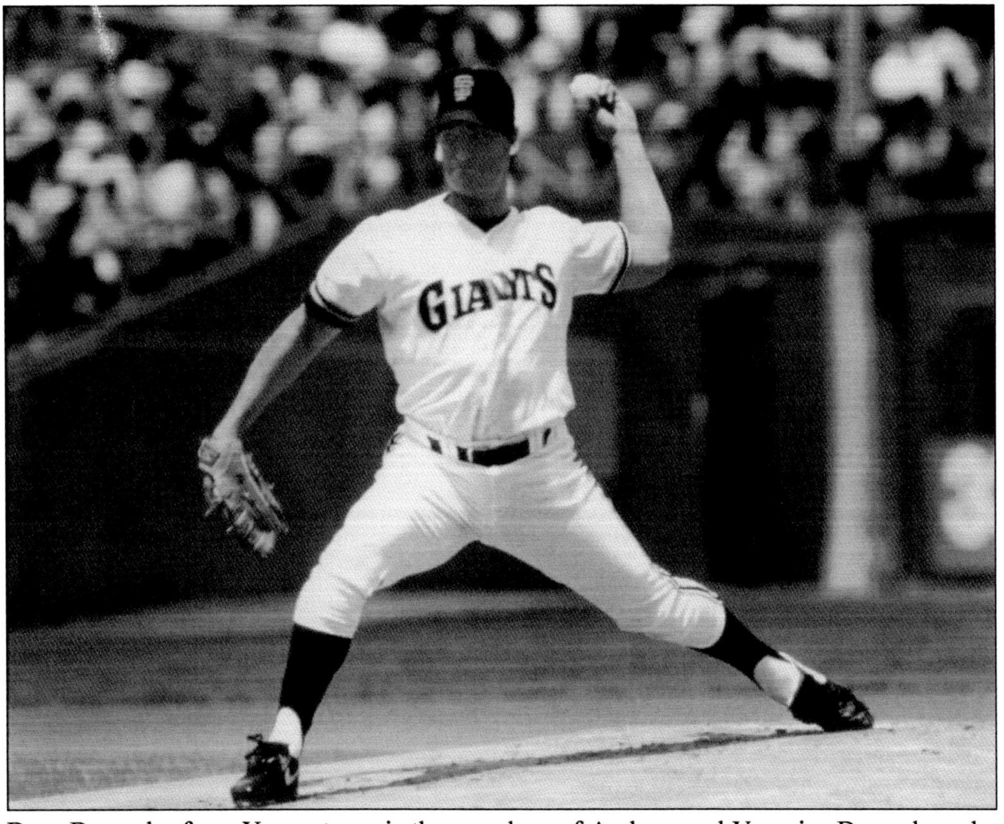

Dave Dravecky from Youngstown is the grandson of Andrew and Veronica Dravecky, who immigrated to America in 1920 from Dvorce, Slovakia. Dave pitched for the San Diego Padres and the San Francisco Giants in the 1980s until cancer ended his career and resulted in the amputation of his arm. He and his wife cofounded the organization known as Endurance, which offers provision to those suffering through serious illness, loss, or depression. (Courtesy of David Dravecky, www.endurance.org.)

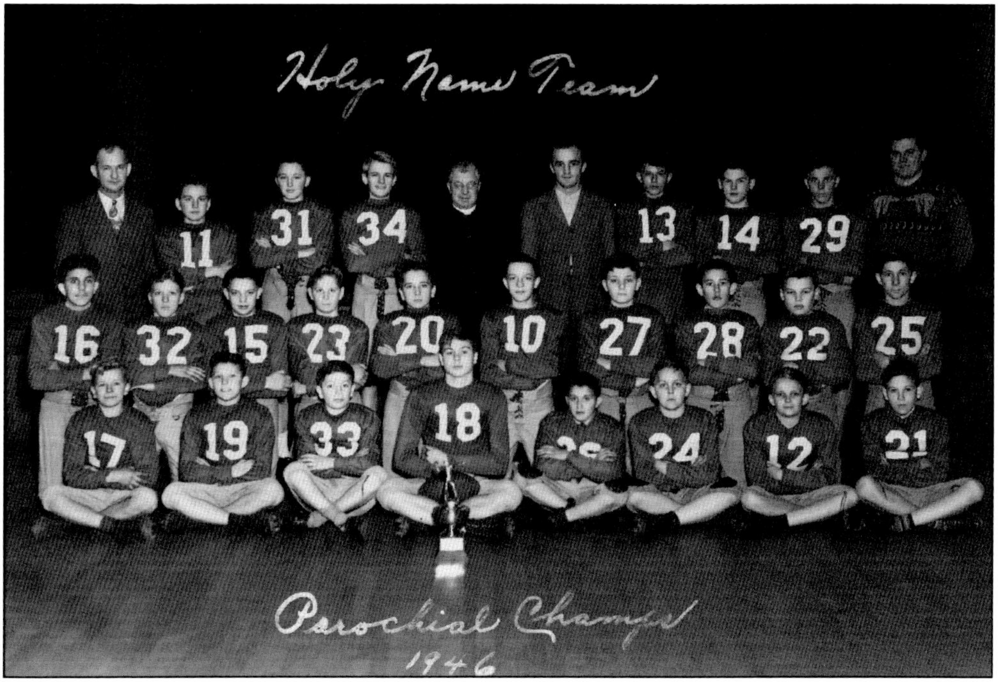

The 1946 Parochial Champion Holy Name team members are, from left to right, (first row) Tom Ringos, Frank Bator, Julius Pallay, Julius Bodnar, ? Bazilla, unidentified, Jerry Semko, and Steve Hoffman; (second row) Tom Bobovnik, Mike Sefcik, John Klacik, ? Kana, Dick Ellis, Frank Magda, unidentified, Frank Slifka, ? Mikula, and Joe Hlinka; (third row) coach Heinie Martinko, Ed Valk, Martie Marshall, Albert Missik, Monsignor Kocis, head coach Eddie Vidis, Frank Belcik, Bob Hripko, Francis Bielik, and trainer John Bielik. (Courtesy of Frank Bator.)

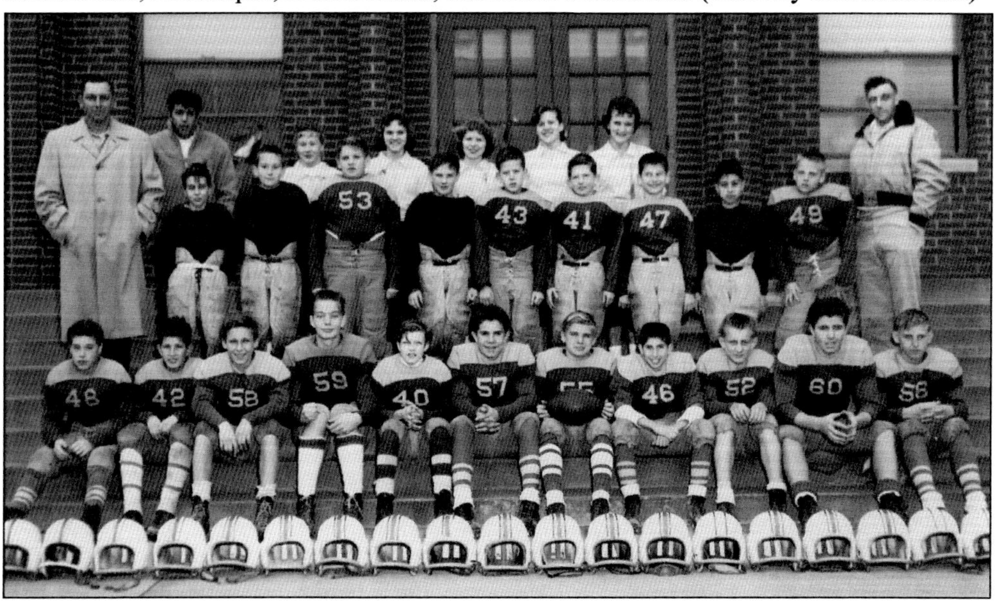

The 1958 St. Matthias School Warriors grade school football team lined up for a photograph with their coaches on the steps outside the school on Shady Run Road in Youngstown. (Courtesy of Michael R. Ekoniak Jr.)

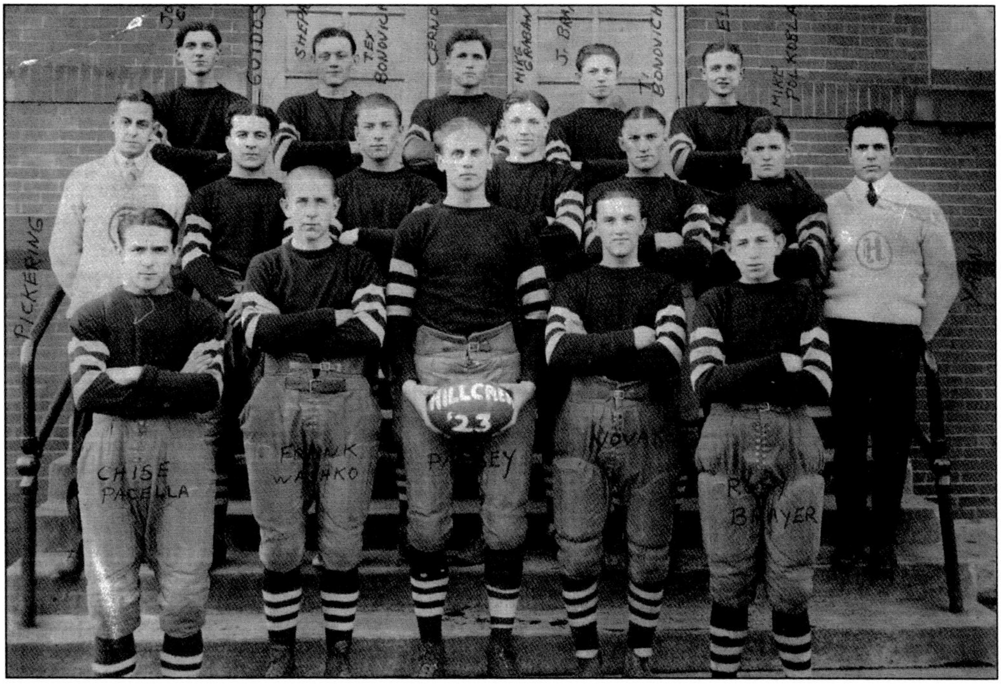

In 1923, the first Campbell football team sponsored by the Hillcrest Athletic Club included the following team members, from left to right, (first row) Dom "Chise" Pacella, Frank Washko, Tony Paulsey, John "Sheepy" Novak, and John "Rosy" Brayer; (second row) Ken Pickering, Mike "Jimmy" Guidos, Joe "Tex" Lubonovich, Mike Graban, Steve "Truck" Lubonovich, Mike Polkobla, and Ralph Yahn; (third row) Joe Check, Joe "Hank" Shepas, Tom "Teamus" Cernoch, Joe "Spider" Brayer, and John Elko. (Courtesy of the Campbell Historical Society, Florence Katula Galida.)

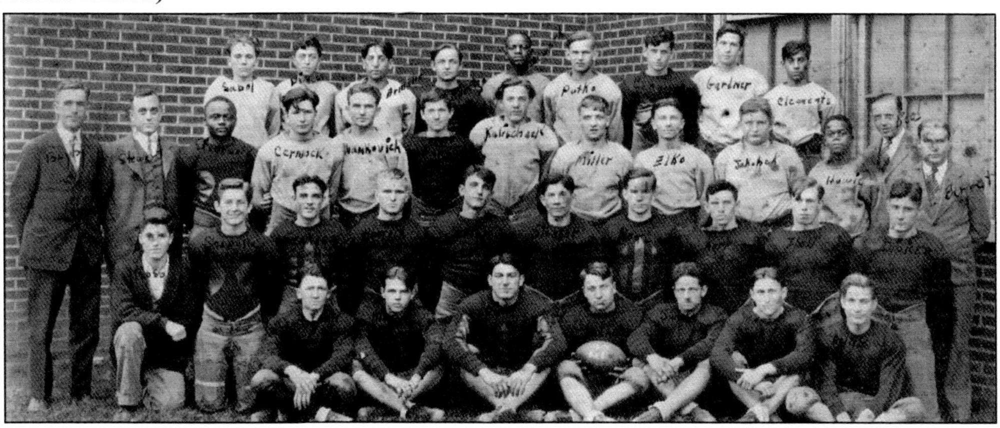

Shown is the 1927 Campbell Memorial football team. Pictured from left to right, with first names listed for those known, are (first row) Albert Centofante, Mose, Jim Rich, George Cebula, J. Switka, Mike Maro, and John Walters; (second row) Anthony Ross, Joe Shapella, George Szakas, Ollie Hamrock, Peter Solar, Frank Stanfor, Fred Moore, George Kopp, Paul Zbell, and Tony Dipiero; (third row) Milo Bugby, Stewart, Ed Stonework, Teamus Cernock, Wankovich, Matthew Wansack, Kalischak, Sam Miller, John Elko, John Jakobek, Howie, Bill Reed, and Birrey; (fourth row) Sabol, Limeet, Rocco Armeline, Mose Opretza, Al Stonework, Putko, Cunningham, Gardner, and Clement. (Courtesy of the Campbell Historical Society, Florence Katula Galida.)

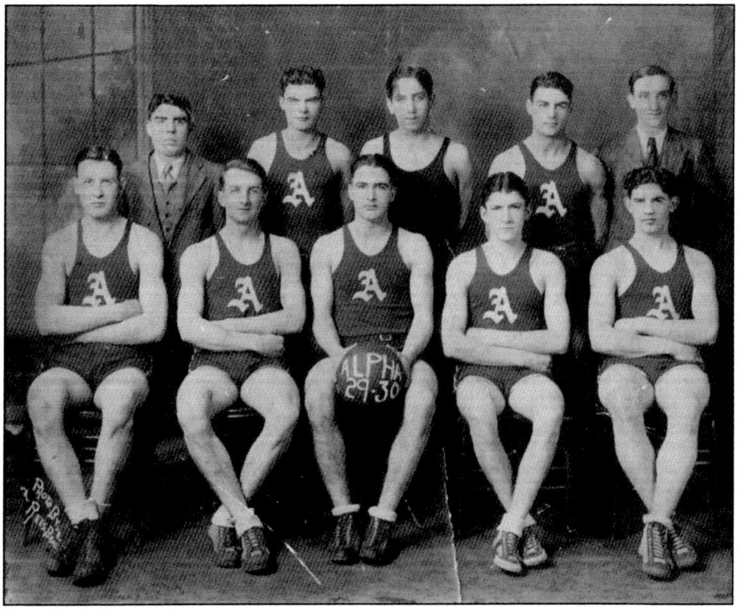

Shown is the Alpha Club 1929–1930 basketball team. Players are, from left to right, (first row) George Muretic, William Kondart, Matthew Yurak, Joseph Dravis, and Joseph Kopp; (second row) Anthony Dann, Theodore Katula, Rocco Armaline, Michael Katula, and Charles Testa. (Courtesy of the Campbell Historical Society, Florence Katula Galida.)

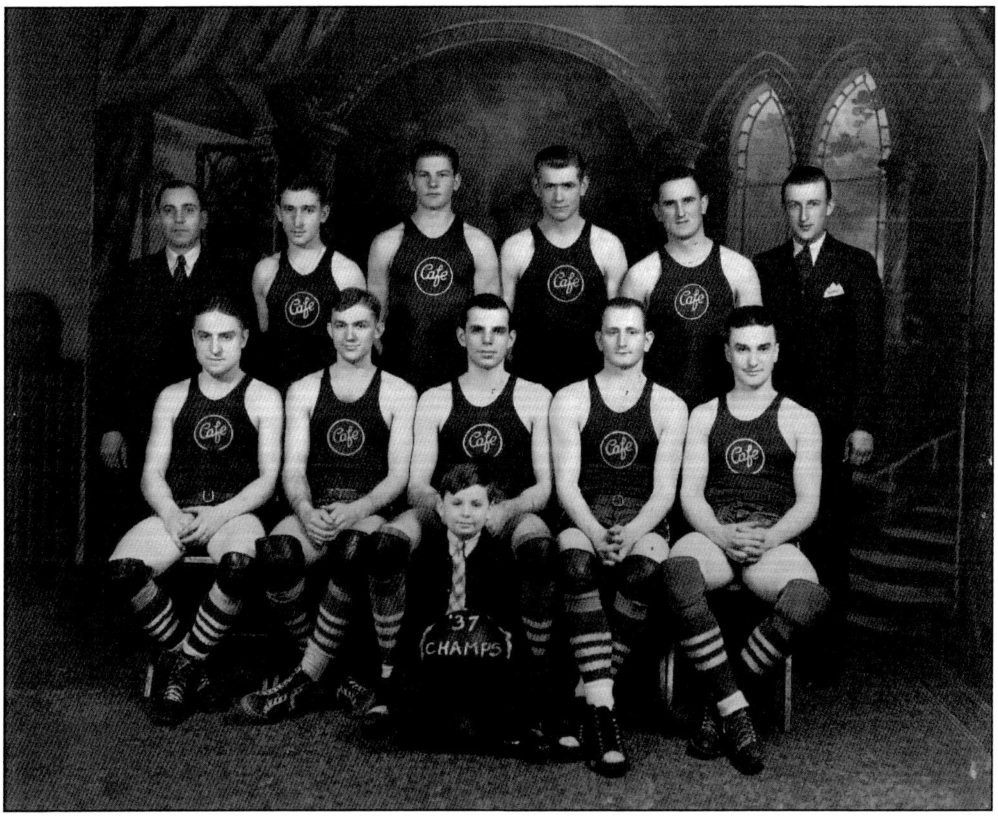

The 1937 champion basketball team from Edward Franko's Green Spot Café are, from left to right, (first row) Steve Olenik, unidentified, Joe Gonda, J. Krupa, and unidentified; (second row) unidentified, John Olenik, John Palatis, ? Olexa, ? Ferenchak, and unidentified. The boy holding the ball in front is a Franko. (Courtesy of Lucille Martinko Kramer.)

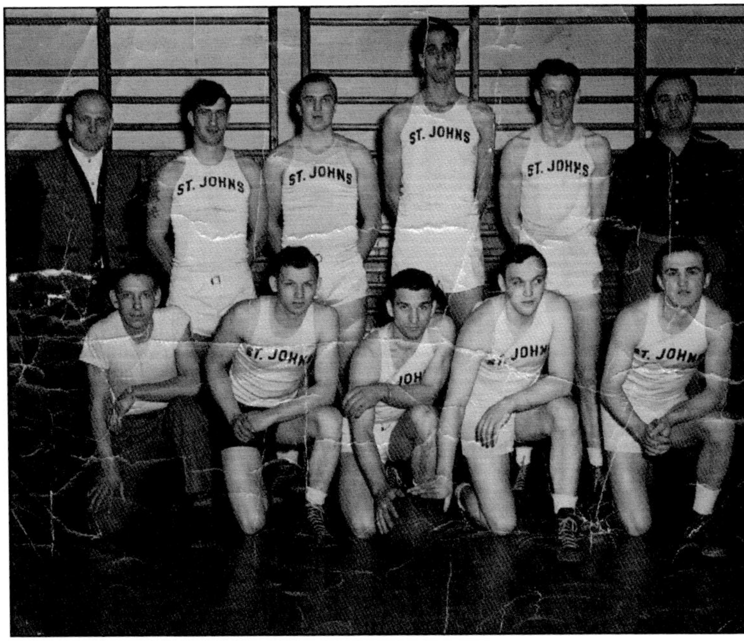

The St. John's basketball players are, from left to right, (first row) Frank Vargo, George Gresko, Sam Pezell, Mike Gresko, and John Matusky; (second row) Sloko Gill, Mike Durina, Joseph Mraz, John Roper, ? Zayac, and unidentified. (Courtesy of the Campbell Historical Society, Florence Katula Galida.)

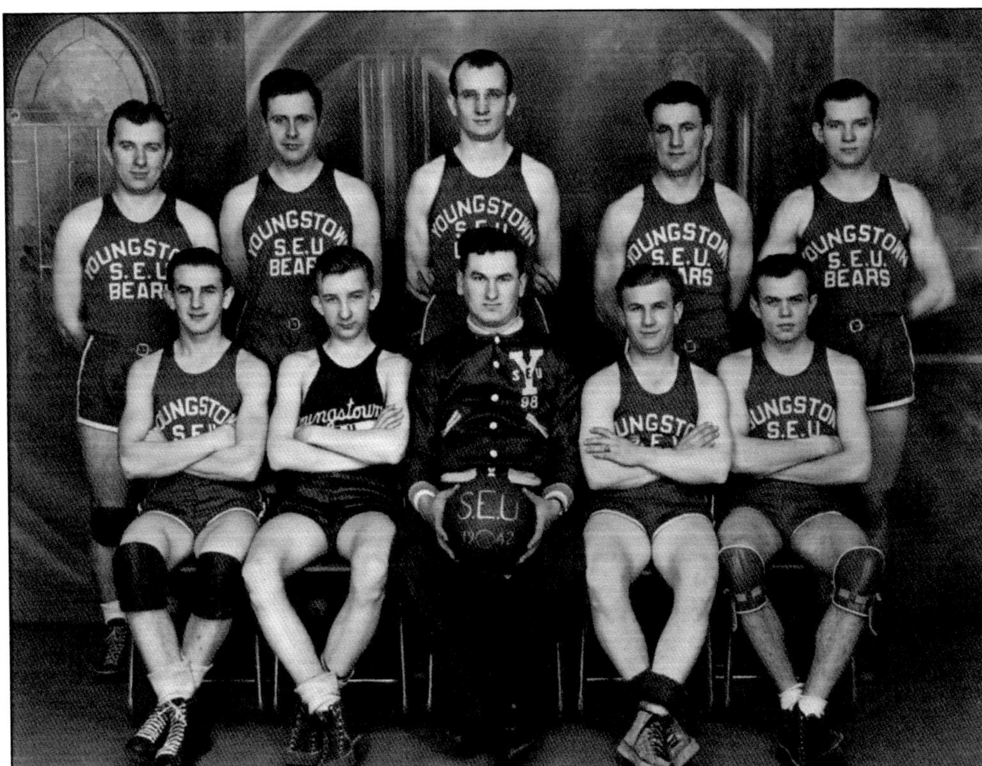

The 1942 SEU basketball team from John Hus Lutheran in Youngstown is shown from left to right as follows: (first row) J. Trnavsky, D. Travsky, P. Trnavsky, G. Barto, and P. Sherfel; (second row) P. Travsky, J. Gavalier, D. Jakubec, P. Lerch, and P. Jakubec. (Courtesy of Margaret Textoris Tomo.)

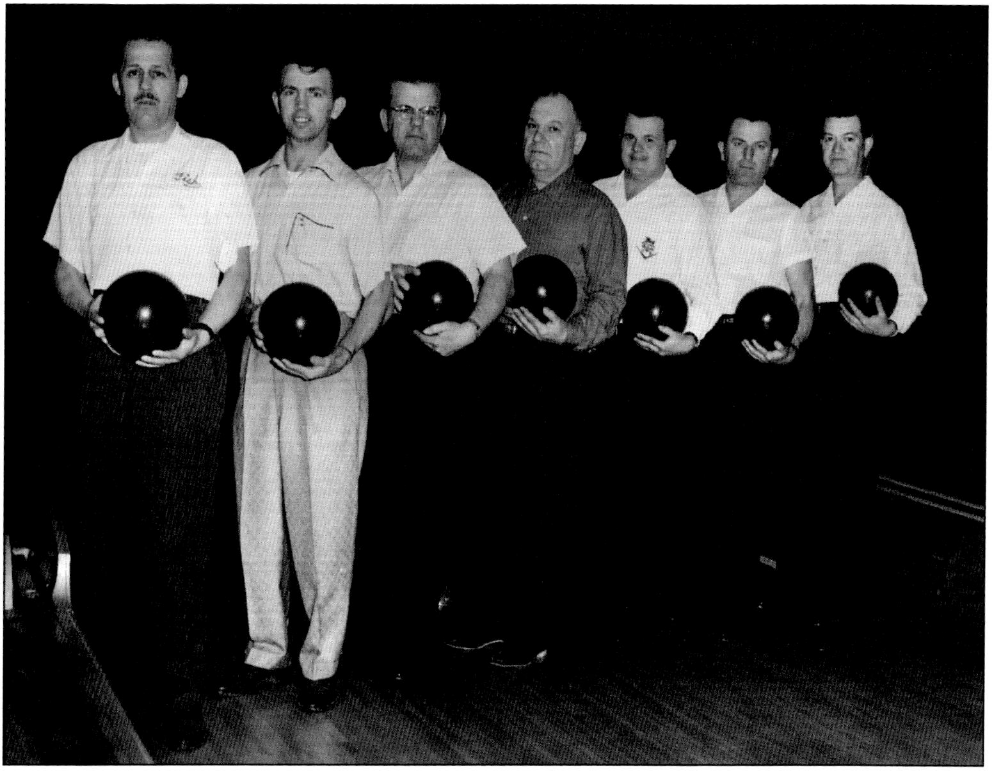

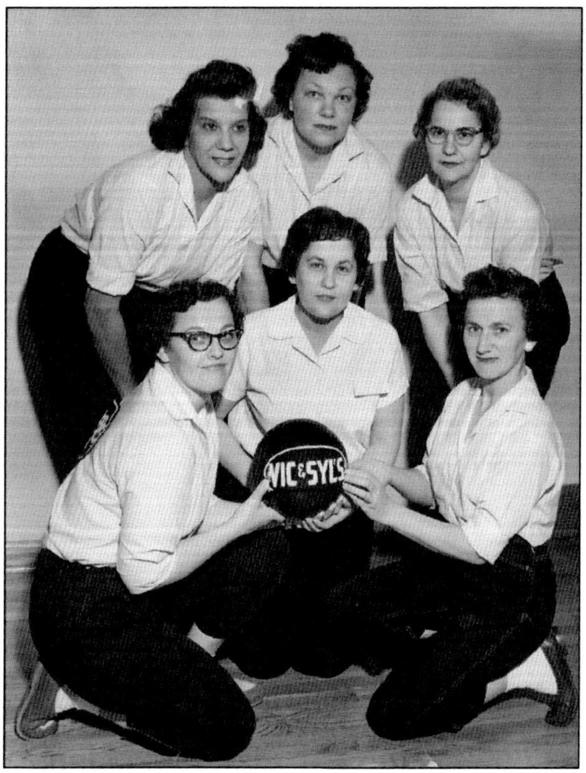

The Slovak Catholic Sokol men's bowling team is shown in the early 1960s. From left to right are Frank Harenčak, Frank Babik, three unidentified players, John Babik, and Paul Martinec. The Sokol sponsors national bowling tournaments, which are still held every year. (Courtesy of Gene Babik.)

Across the street from the Bernard Airport, located on the west corner of Jacobs and McCartney Roads, was the family restaurant Vic & Syl's. Bowling team members are (first row) Florence (Evanoff) Gozur, Helen (Hrehovcik) Seman, and Ann (Pacak) Sosnowchik; (second row) Mary (Simko) Cole, Eileen (Graban) Elash, and Esther (Sabula) Lesoganich. (Courtesy of Campbell Historic Society, Florence Katula Galida.)

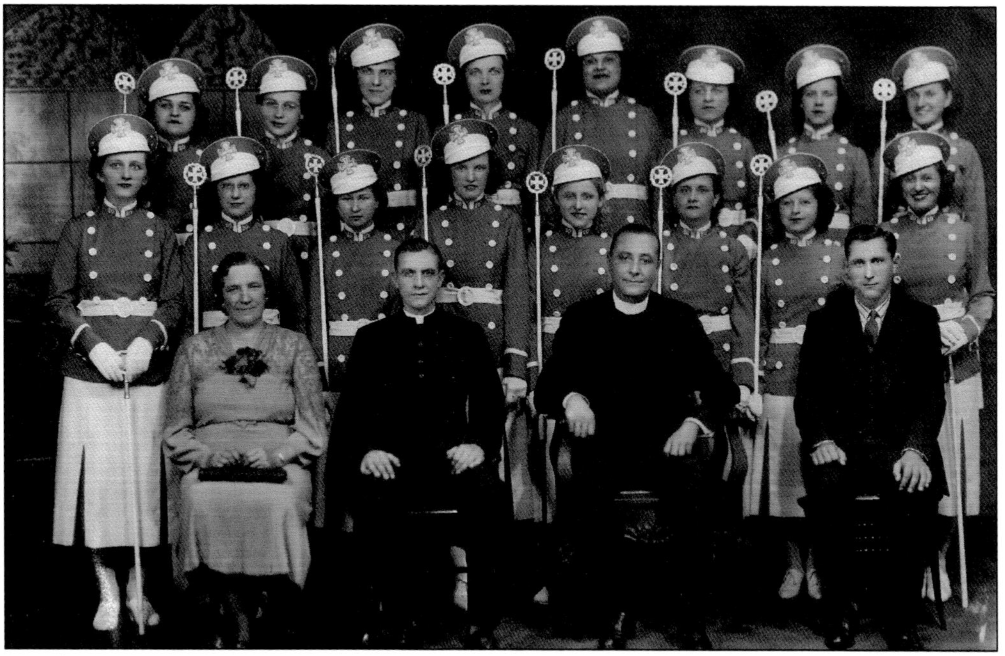

Members of the 1938 St. Therese drill team of the First Catholic Slovak Ladies Union Branch No. 105 are pictured from left to right as follows: (first row) organizer Susan Klučar, Rev. Albert Klein, pastor Reverend George Novak, and instructor Michael Maro; (second row) Mary Bednar, Julia Berchik, Ann Hovorsky, Dorothy Noga, Mary Elias, Catherine Kubyko, Helen Vodhaniel, and Julia Cvengros. In the third row, in no particular order, are Susan Ondulich, Ann Blasko, Dorothy Klucar, Cecelia Borisch, Frances Guidos, Catherine Hruby, Mary Hornak, and unidentified. Not pictured are Bernice Noga and Anna, Margaret, and Helen Martinko. (Courtesy of a Hruby granddaughter.)

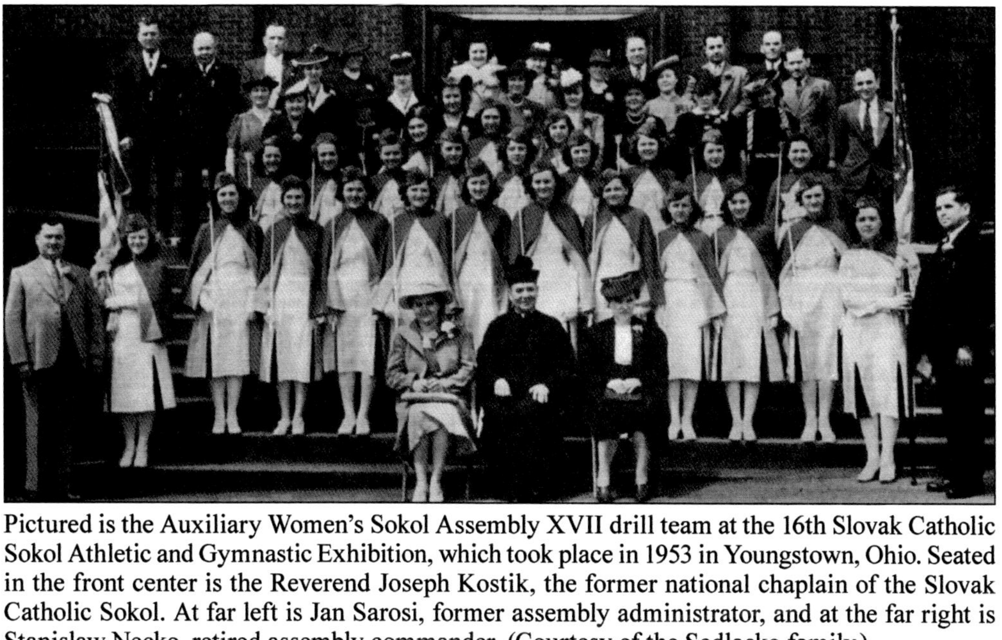

Pictured is the Auxiliary Women's Sokol Assembly XVII drill team at the 16th Slovak Catholic Sokol Athletic and Gymnastic Exhibition, which took place in 1953 in Youngstown, Ohio. Seated in the front center is the Reverend Joseph Kostik, the former national chaplain of the Slovak Catholic Sokol. At far left is Jan Sarosi, former assembly administrator, and at the far right is Stanislaw Necko, retired assembly commander. (Courtesy of the Sedlacko family.)

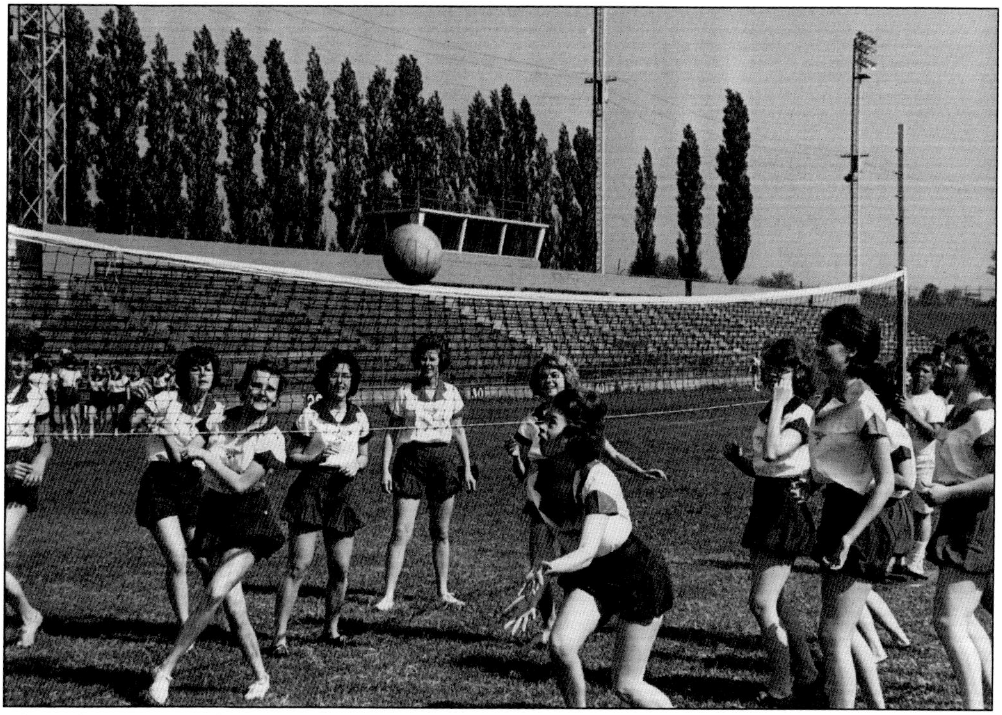

The Sokol Gymnastics and Field Day in the early 1960s had events for both men and women of all ages. Here is one of the girls' volleyball games held at Campbell Memorial High School stadium. (Courtesy of Gene Babik; photograph by Lloyd S. Jones.)

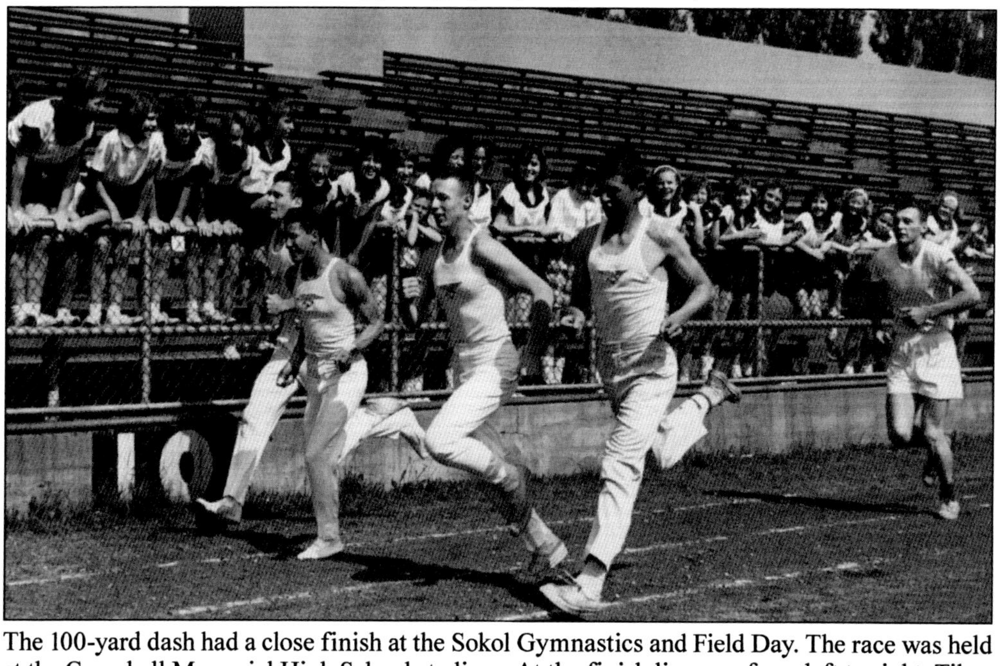

The 100-yard dash had a close finish at the Sokol Gymnastics and Field Day. The race was held at the Campbell Memorial High School stadium. At the finish line are, from left to right, Tibor Kovalovsky, Steve Kovach, Steve Uhrin, John Babik, and Pete Kovalovsky. (Courtesy of Gene Babik; photograph by Lloyd S. Jones, *Youngstown Vindicator.*)

Seven

Eat, Drink, and Be Merry

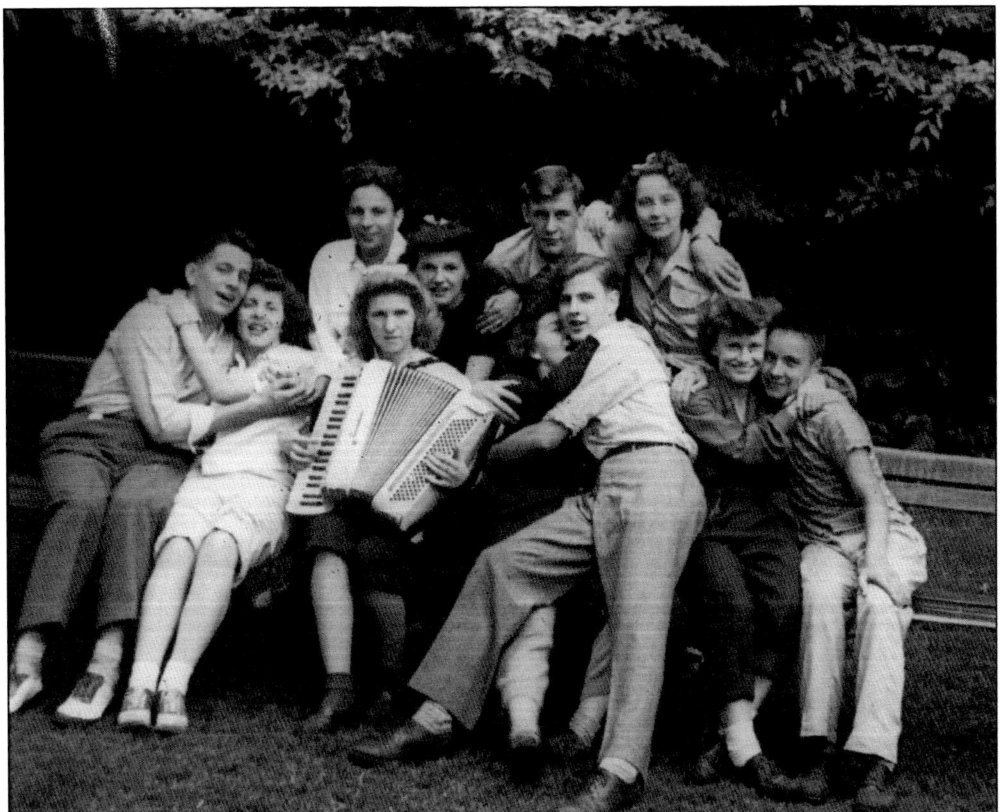

The lives of Slovak families centered on hard work. Reacting to a hard life, they made the most of every opportunity to celebrate. Whether a picnic or a wedding, a church play or holiday, there was always music, food, and camaraderie. Where there is a Slovak, there is a song! Pictured in 1944 is a Truscon Steel office picnic at Chestnut Hill Pavilion in Mill Creek Park. (Photograph by Eleanor Baker.)

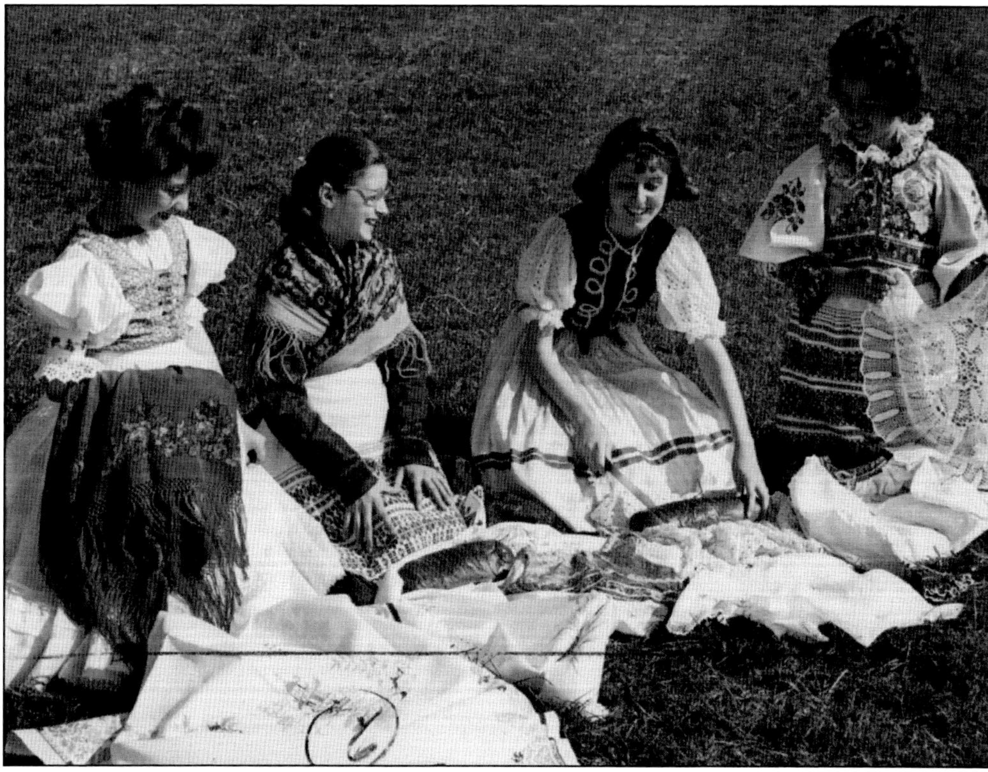

Young women at a Sokol event show off their native *kroj* (folk dress), needlework, and *kolače*. From left to right are Monica Bozick, Lorraine Armour, Arlene Evich, and Rosemary Hruska. (Courtesy of Bernadette Slanina Demechko; photograph by Lloyd S. Jones, *Youngstown Vindicator.*)

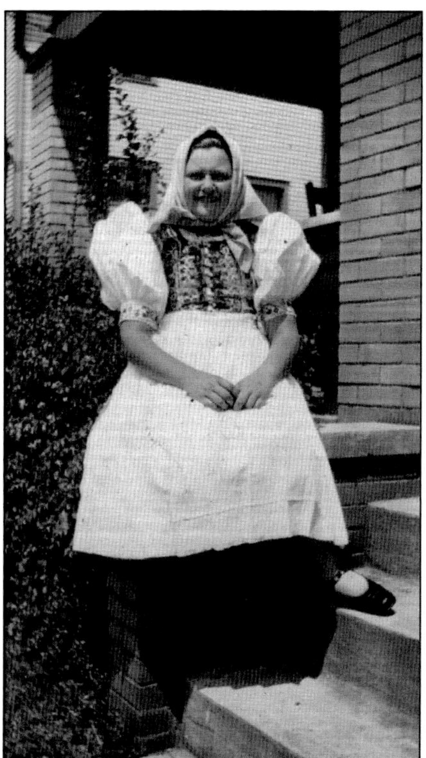

Helen Kollar, daughter of John Kollar and Mary Ondrejko Kollar, poses in the folk dress that was worn on special occasions in front of her parents' home in the Steelton area of Youngstown on Oakwood Avenue. (Courtesy of Mary Ellen Kurta Wilcox.)

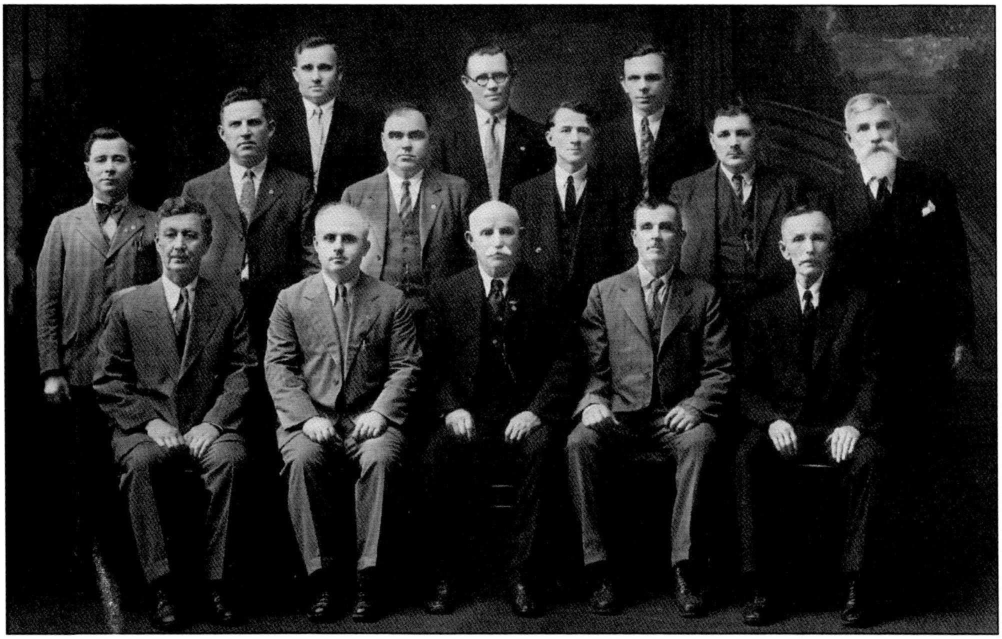

Fraternal organizations gave early immigrants a sense of belonging and offered many activities to enjoy. The National Slovak Society Branch No. 8 was organized in 1890 in Youngstown, Ohio. The officers and organizers are, from left to right, (first row) Joseph Martinko, Andrew Palenchar, Gaspar Kandrik, Miklos Lukach, and John Jurcho; (second row) Albert Smolko, George Puhalla, Frank Vidumansky, Andrew Cisar, George Pavel, and D. Kozicky; (third row) Joseph Fabry, John Wagner, and John Basista. (Courtesy of Janet Morris Repasky.)

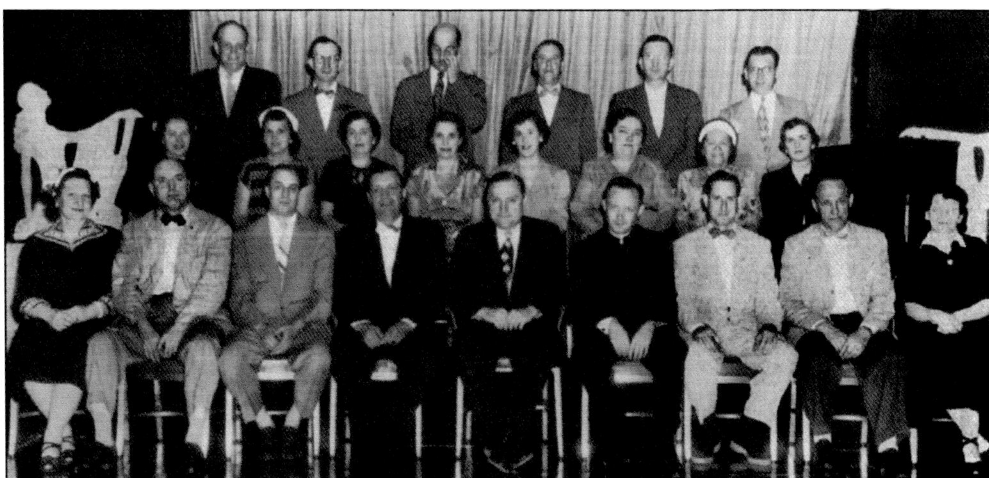

The 16th Slovak Catholic Sokol Athletic and Gymnastic Exhibition was held in Youngstown, Ohio, in 1953. The committee members are, from left to right, (first row) Helen Phillips, Stephan Ritz, Michael Maruskin, John Olejar, Stephen R. Olenik, Rev. George Franko, Chester Amedia, Andrew Hamrock, and Anna Roth; (second row) Mary Ruscak, Betty Ferenchak, Mary Zivčak, Anna Dolak, Mary Dzurey, Anna Weller, Anna Bires, and Anna Babnic; (third row) John Serenko, John Holecko, John Horvat, John Melikant, John Hnat, and John Pokrivnak. (Courtesy of the Sedlacko family.)

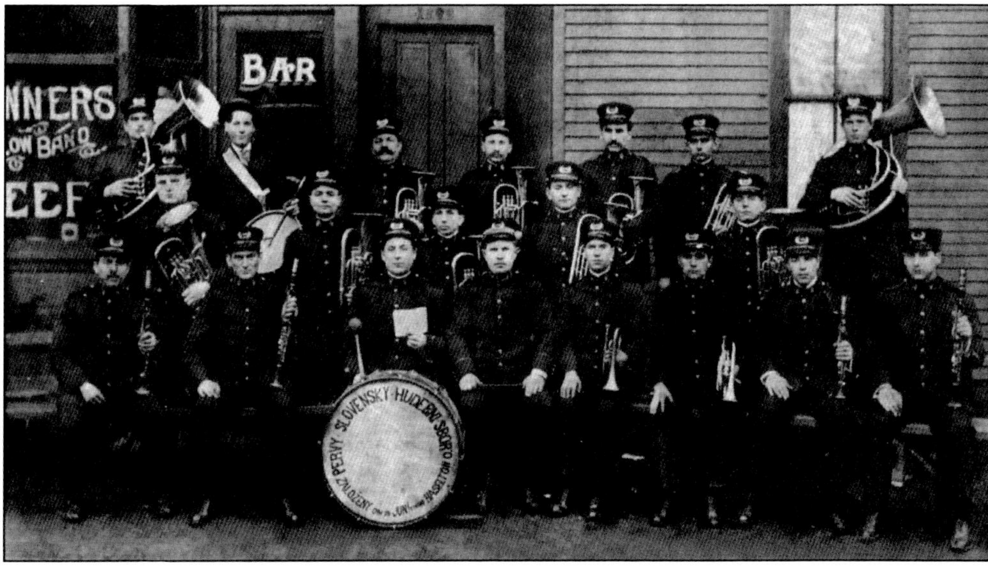

The Haselton Slovak Band, organized in 1908, is in front of Kupcik's Saloon on East Cherry Street. Mr. Kupcik was treasurer for the band, and Steve Dulin was director. Other members were Andrew Kolarik, Mike Volosin, George Novak, John Smorada, John Kotulick, John Novak, Louis Hamrock, John Ulichny, Andy Hlavaty, Joe Hasaj, John Babick, Mike Granchovsky, George Barach, Mike Kranack, Joseph Horvat on coronet, and Steven Horvat on alto tuba. (Courtesy of Joseph J. Rakocy Jr.)

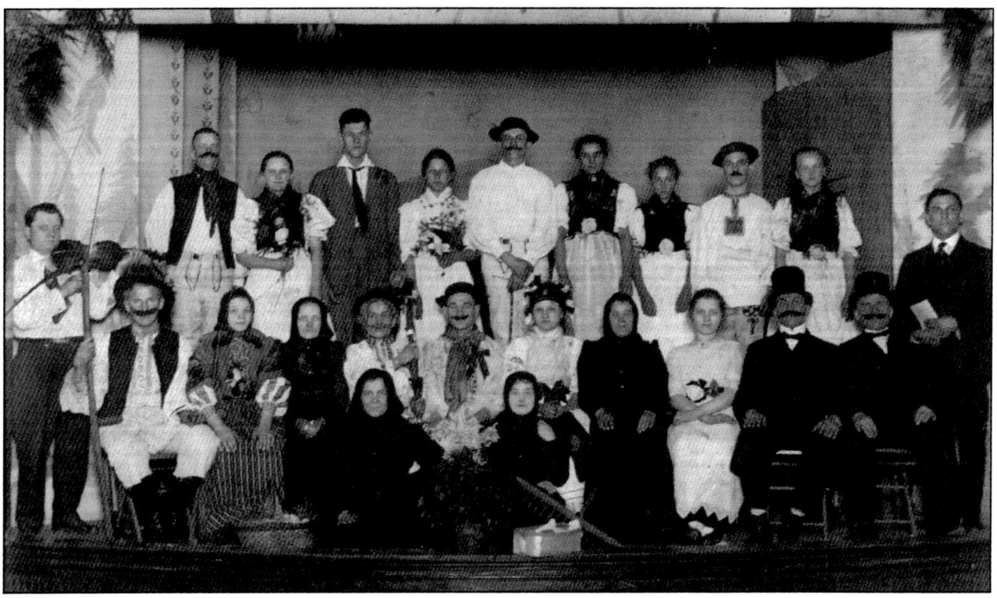

A Slovak play, *Rosemarin*, was performed in 1917 by parishioners of St. Matthias Church in the Sokol Hall on Homewood Avenue. From left to right are (first row) Mary Bivalec and Mary Pavuk; (second row) John Ulicni (violin), Stephen Bajtos, Betty Pavula, two unidentified performers, Joseph Javorsky, Mary Smotrilla, Franciska Mihlusko, Mary Franco, John Franko, John Olenick, and John Repasky; (third row) John Mrofcak, Anna Fabian, Andrew Hamrak, Anna Humanik, Valent Hlebovy, Helena Horvath, Anna Onderko, John Gordulich, and Mary Janci. (Courtesy of Bernadette Slanina Demechko.)

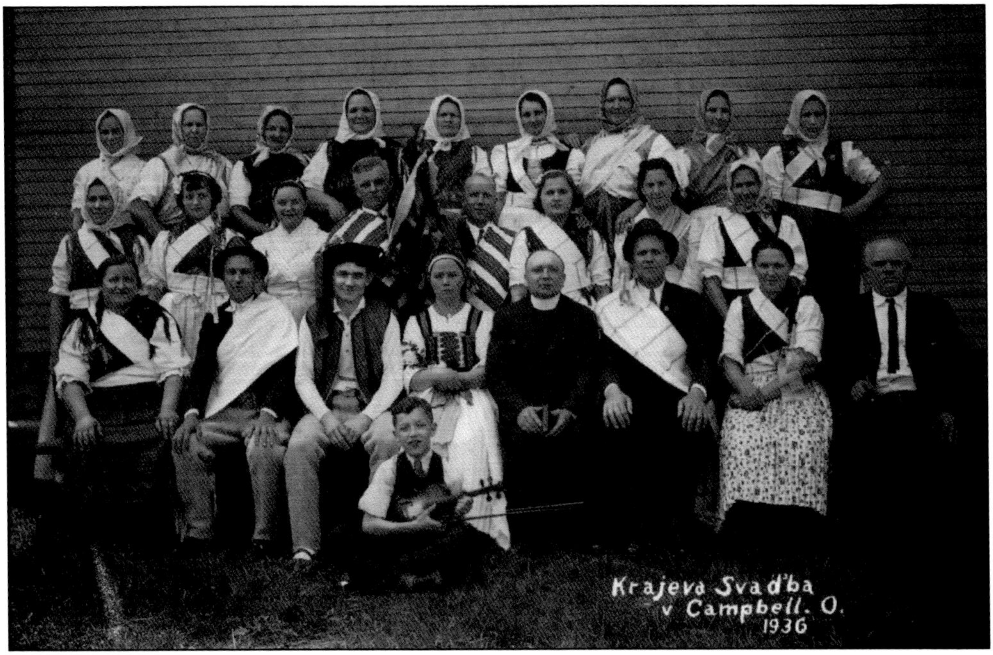

Reenactment of a folk wedding (*krajeva svadba*) was popular entertainment. Seated from left to right are (first row) Mary Shirilla, Mike Dubos, Joe Shirilla, Catherine Vrabel, Mike Volchko, John Vrabel, Mary Shirilla, and Mike Antos; (second row) Katherine Shirilla, Marge Bradich, Anna Vrabel, George Bradich, Peter Dubos, Helen Korchnak, Kay Sabula, and Verona Vrabel; (third row) Helen Macala, Helen Kirtos, Catherine Bakos, Anna Sabula, Mary Macala, Helen Sevachko, Mary Volchko, Katherine Geletka, and Sophie Dubos. Playing the violin in front is Steve Dubos. (Courtesy of the Campbell Historical Society, Florence Katula Galida.)

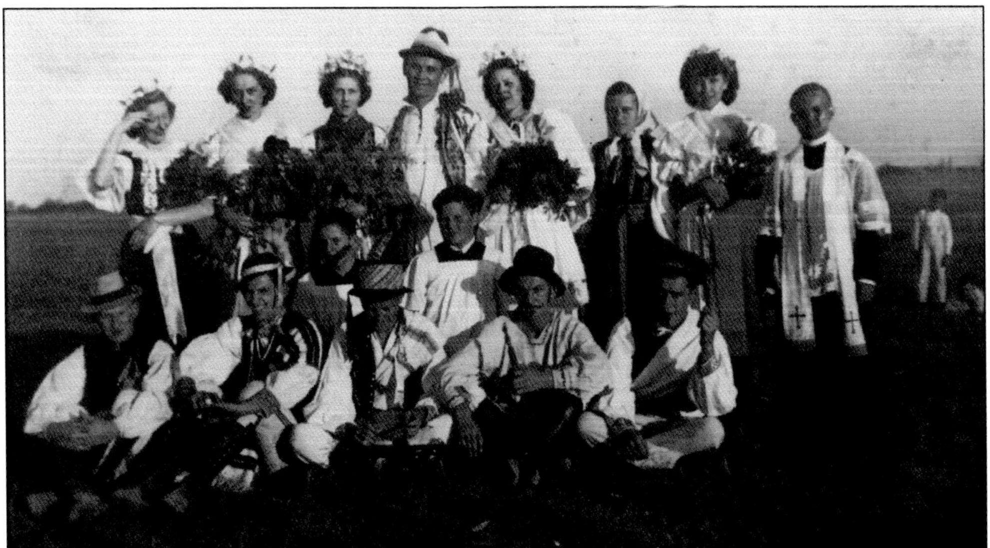

A Slovak folk wedding, such as this one reenacted at the Holy Trinity picnic grounds in Struthers, was a popular form of entertainment for Slovak emigrants. It let them relive fond memories of celebrations in their homeland. John Macalla and Margaret Zelinsky Macalla and their friend Peg Korechko Chasko participated in the fun. (Courtesy of Barbara Macalla Jennings.)

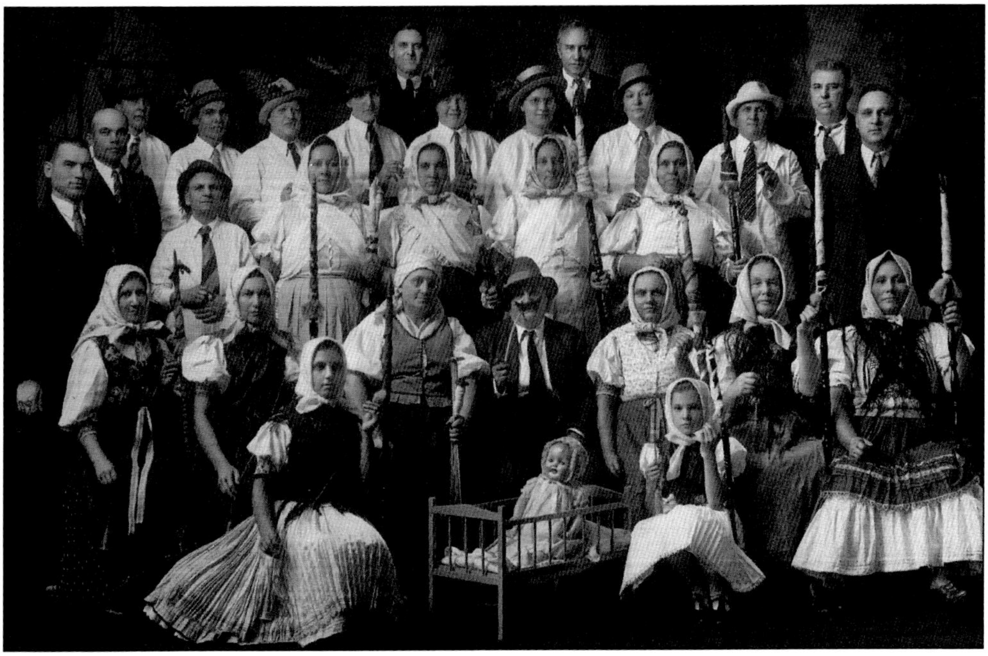

Prestav Lenta, a Slovak folk play put on at St. Nicholas Byzantine Church in the 1930s, includes the following players, from left to right: (first row) two unidentified girls; (second row, seated) unidentified, Mrs. Mike Tirpack, two unidentified people, Mrs. Koly, Mrs. Backus, and Mrs. Matichko Malek; (third row) Prof. John Horvath (wearing a suit), unidentified, Veronica Durshaw, unidentified, Veronica Koly, Mrs. Senda, and Mr. Koly; (fourth row) Mike Tirpack (wearing a suit), Mrs. Tirpack (wearing a dark hat), Anna Fabian, Mary Durshaw, Mrs. Dropp, three unidentified participants, Mary Geletka, and Mr. Garancovsky; (fifth row) two unidentified men. (Courtesy of St. Nicholas Byzantine Church.)

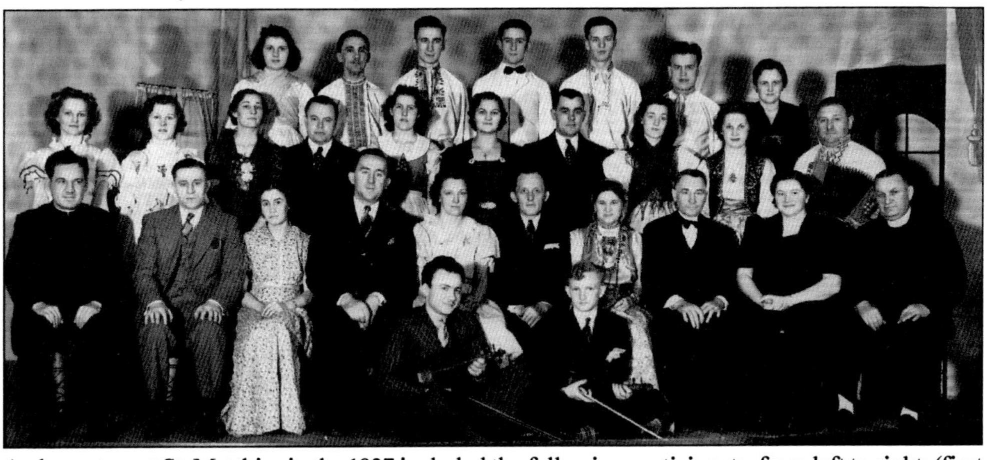

A play put on at St. Matthias in the 1937 included the following participants, from left to right: (first row, violinists) Joe Hudak and Paul Lilko; (second row) Rev. Andrew Hudak, Mike Gresko, Frances Smolko, Joseph Kana, Veronica (Janci) Mossynski, Sam Hladon, Veronicka Necko, John Martinko, Julia Krupa, and Rev. John G. Hamrak; (third row) Helen (Janci) Palatas, Catherine Kovach Yanek, Rose Tkach Halaparda, Steve Hamrack, Helen Belly, Peggy Tkach, Joseph Hudak, Jennie Novotny, Helen Olenick, and Phillip Kanka; (fourth row) Mary Kovach, Joe Bodnar, John Martinko, Andy Vagas, John Tkach, Mike Kacvinsky, and Ann Fabian. (Courtesy of Lucille Martinko Kramer.)

Picnics were always a great opportunity for getting together to enjoy good company, good food, and a little bit of music. John Babik (on violin) and Jack Popovich provide the entertainment at a country get-together at the Pitzo's farm. (Courtesy of Gene Babik.)

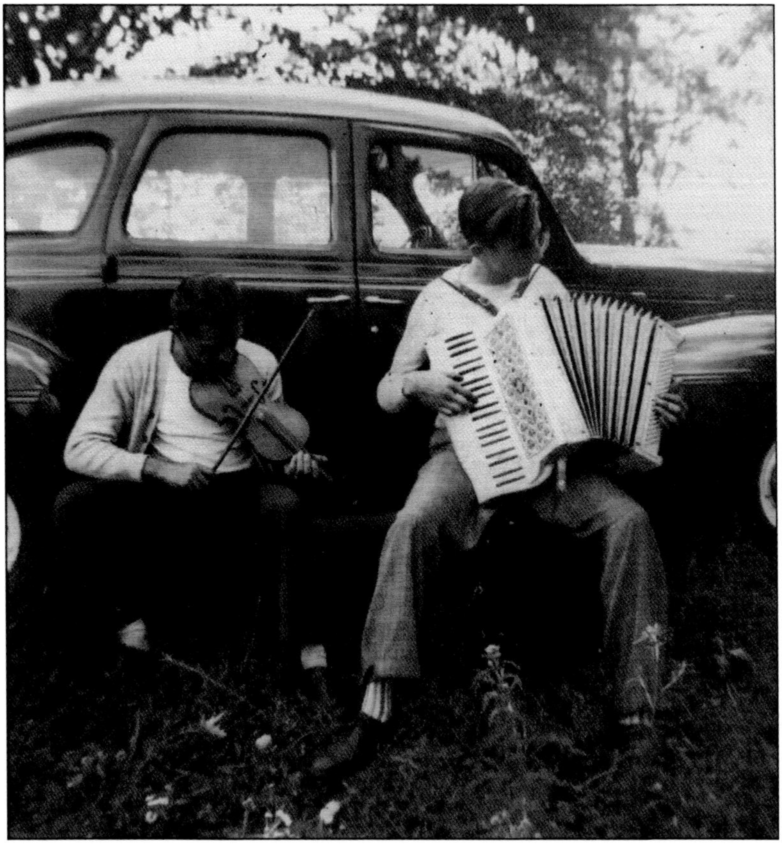

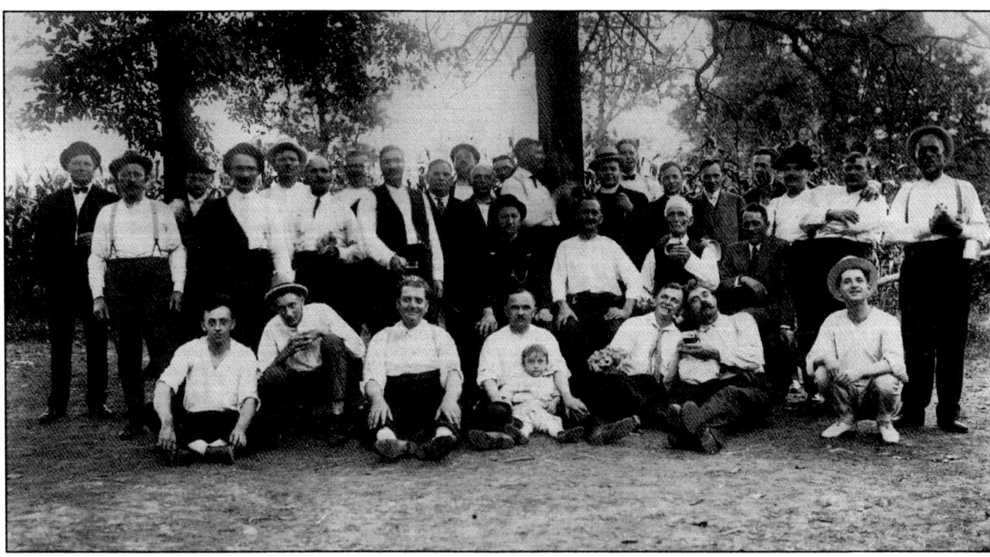

Sometimes the get-togethers were more organized—such as Slovak Day at Idora Park, which could attract thousands of area Slovaks—or they could be smaller and simpler. This photograph from 1923 shows one of the smaller events, Slovak Day at Southern Park (long before the construction of the Southern Park Mall). Interestingly, this seems to have been a men's-only event. (Courtesy of Kay Sakmar Bilka.)

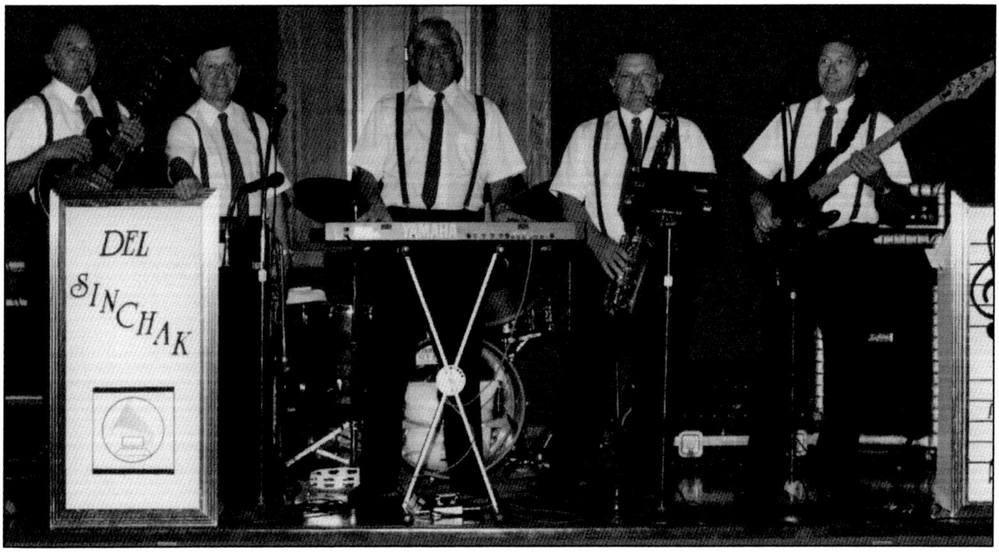

Polka bands have always been a popular form of entertainment at dances and weddings. Seen is the Del Sinchak Orchestra, which has been playing at Slovak events for over 60 years. Del and Bob have been playing in their own band since sixth grade at St. Matthias School. Band members are, from left to right, Paul Jacobson, Del Sinchak, Bob Smercansky, Joe Colapietro, and Dale Wilt. (Courtesy of Del Sinchak.)

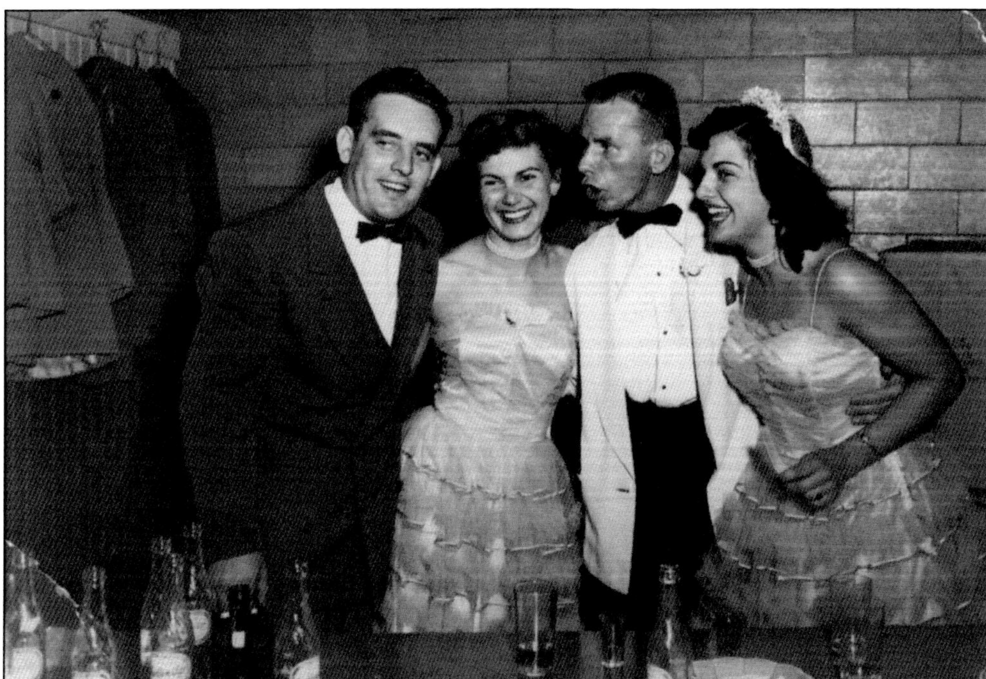

A celebration is always in order for a wedding. This Slovak wedding reception of Ann Evan and Frank (Fusta) Turocy in the early 1950s took place at Campbell's Croatian Hall. Pictured are, from left to right, Ace Lilak, Patty Komarc, Al Trill (who ran the Slovak Club in Campbell, Ohio), and Joyce Famor. (Courtesy of the Campbell Historical Society, Florence Katula Galida.)

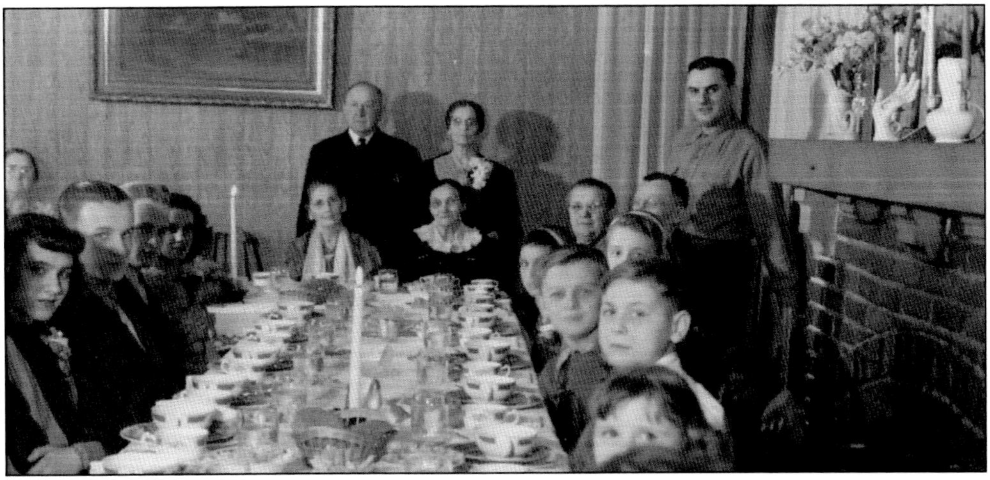

For many years, Slovak families celebrated major milestones—such as christenings, first communions, weddings, and anniversaries—at Horvath's Teahouse in Cornersburg. Pictured is the 47th wedding anniversary of John and Mary Novotny (seen standing in back). Friends, children, and grandchildren surround them. Seated in front of John and Mary are Veronika (Kalafut) Smolko and Catherine Slifka; (left side of table) Clara Slifka, John "Zooner" Novotny, Jerry Novotny, Delores "Dee" Slifka; (right side of table from front) Teresa Novotny, Eddie Baron, Leonard "Babe" Novotny, Eleanore Ekoniak, and Marie Ekoniak. Behind them are George and Anna Murdzak and Tony Slifka (standing by fireplace). (Courtesy of Michael R. Ekoniak Jr.)

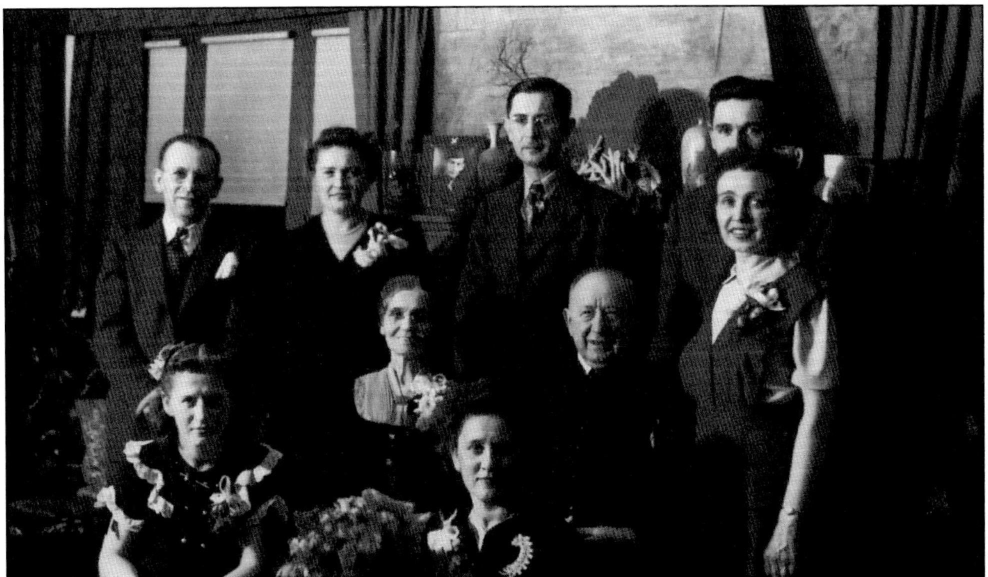

Pictured at Horvath's Tea Room, the Novotny family includes, from left to right, (first row) Mildred ("Millie"), mother Mary (Kalafut), Agnes, father John, and Justine ("Jay"); (second row) John Jr., Angeline ("Mary"), Joseph ("Jaso"), and Michael ("Chickie"). (Courtesy of Michael R. Ekoniak Jr.)

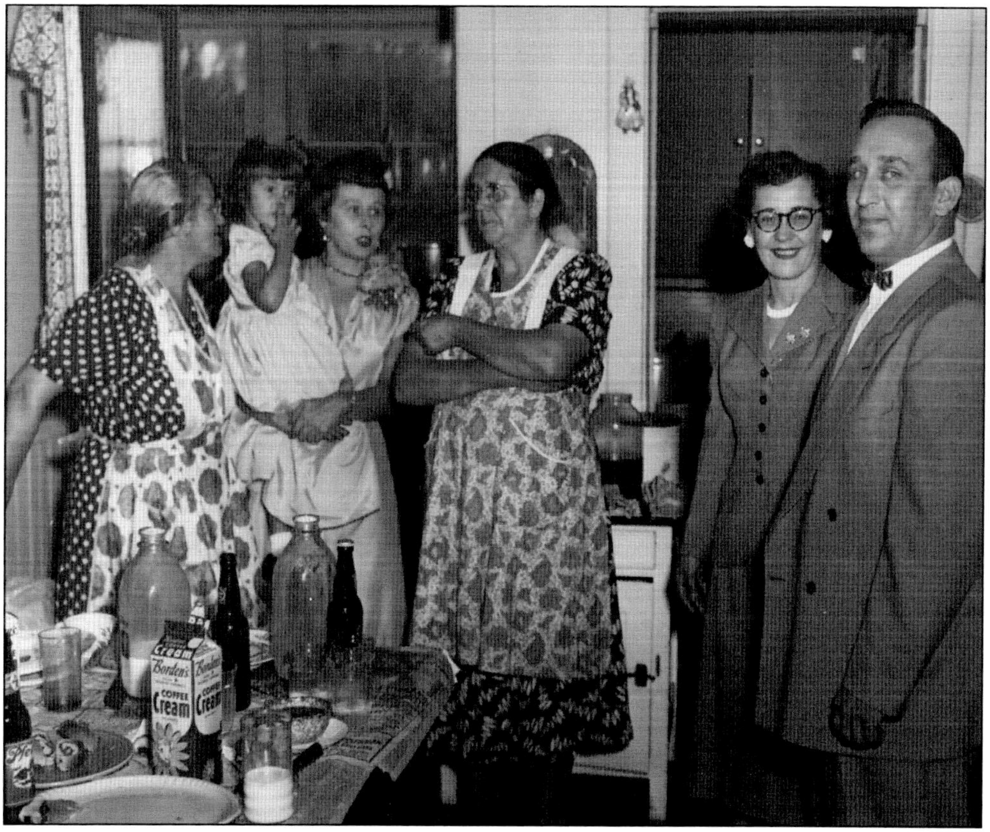

Often, the kitchen was the center of the social event. Gathered from left to right are Mary Pachuta, Betty Novotny holding Jackie Novotny, Elizabeth Schlosser, Agnes Diorio, and Albert Borzick. (Courtesy of Kathryn Novotny Franko.)

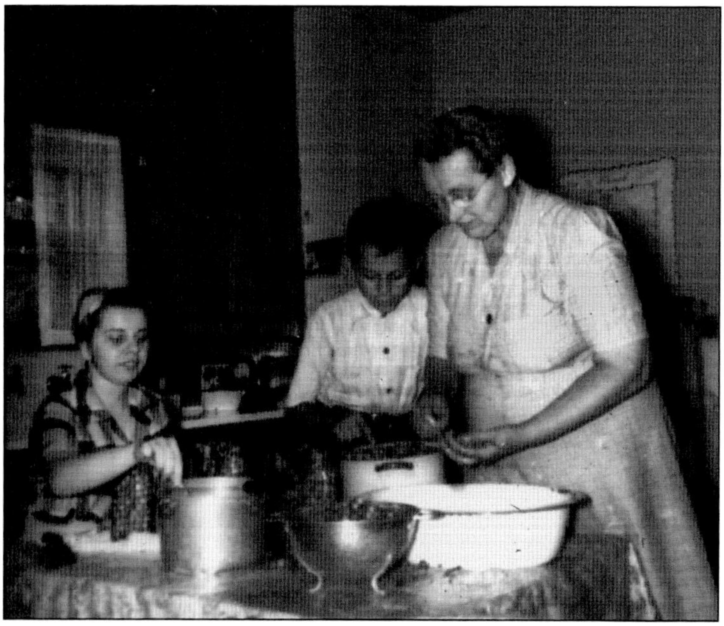

Mary Yalch shows grandchildren Eleanor and Robert Yalch the secrets of canning cherries. Spending time together is just as important as the process of canning. (Courtesy of Theodore Mrofchak.)

Holidays were major celebrations for the Slovak community. Everyone played a part. In this picture taken during the Christmas *Vilija*, or Štedrý Večer celebration, the Honorable Judge John J. Leskovansky plays the part of a *Jaslickár*, or Bethlehem caroler, while accompanied by Joseph Kana, known as "Polka Joe," on the accordion. (Courtesy of Bernadette Slanina Demechko.)

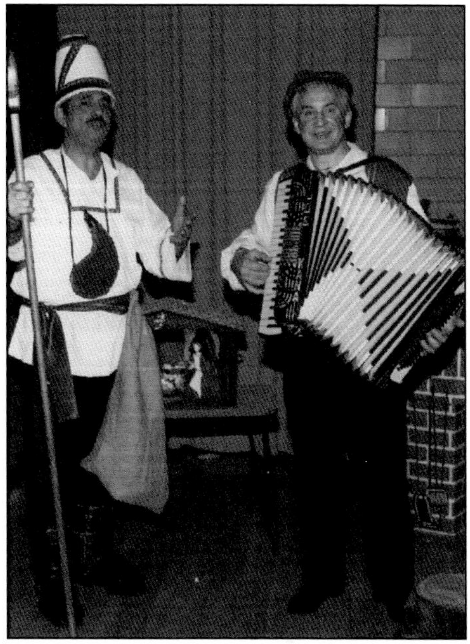

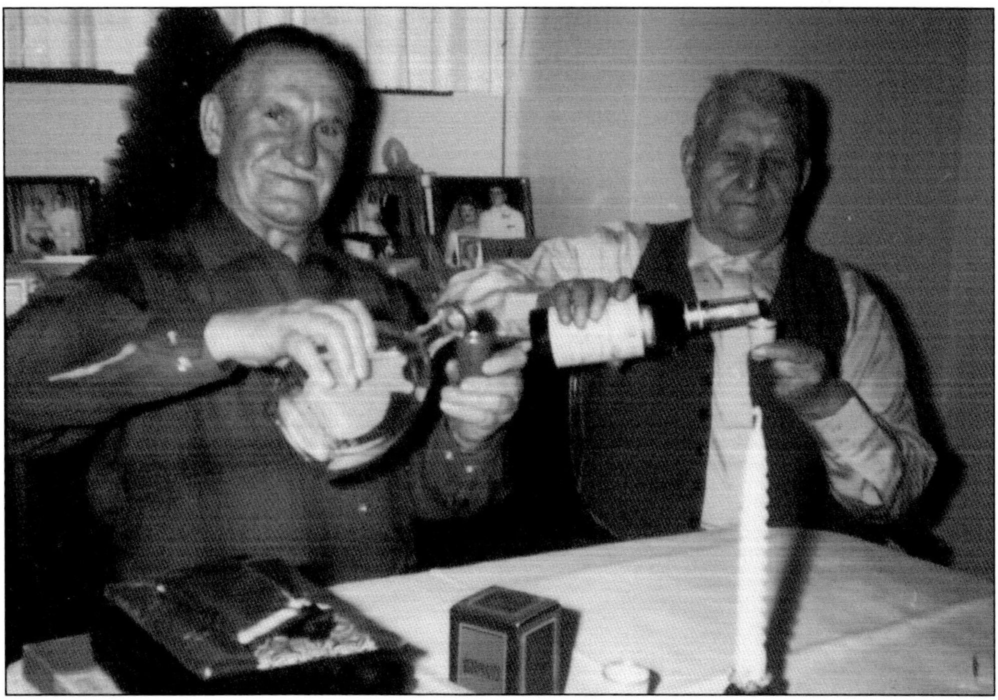

Nothing was more traditional for pledging a toast than *slivovica*, the fiery, clear Slovak brandy made from plums. Originally a home-distilled liquor made from fruit grown in the family garden, slivovica is still a popular libation for any celebration. Here, brothers Andrew (left) and Joseph Hirt enjoy a toast. And, thus, ends this celebration of Slovak heritage in the Greater Mahoning Valley. (Courtesy of Florence Tessari Hirt.)

Na zdravie! S Bohom!

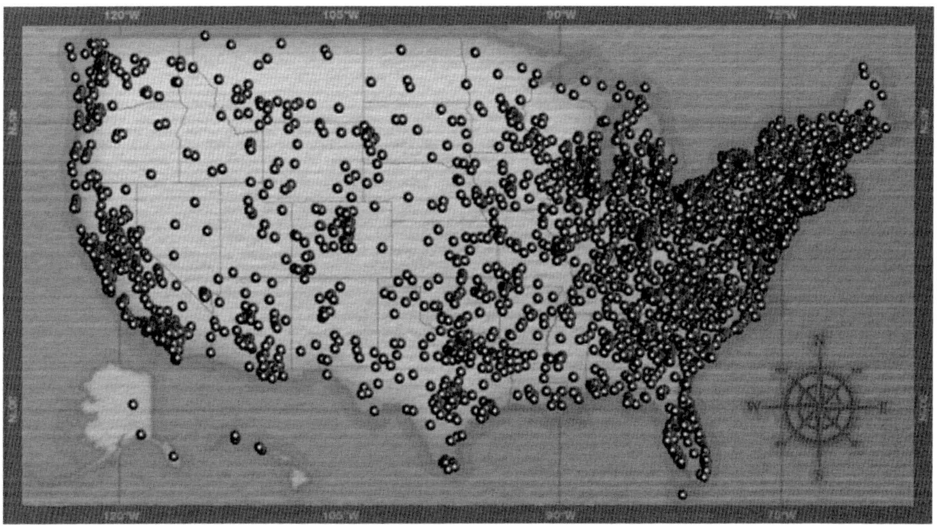